Blue Eyes on
African-American History

Blue Eyes on African-American History

A LEARNING ADVENTURE

Philip Reiss

ARCHWAY
PUBLISHING

Archway Publishing books may be ordered through booksellers or by contacting:

Archway Publishing
1663 Liberty Drive
Bloomington, IN 47403
www.archwaypublishing.com
1-(888)-242-5904

ISBN: 978-1-4808-0295-7 (sc)
ISBN: 978-1-4808-0296-4 (e)

Library of Congress Control Number: 2013916923

Printed in the United States of America

Archway Publishing rev. date: 10/3/2013

Preface

The plight of African-Americans never settled into my consciousness in any profound way until late in 1962. At that time I was in my mid twenties attending Temple University after a four year (1955-1959) Air Force enlistment. In early October I saw a notice posted in Mitten Hall indicating black activist Bayard Rustin was to speak at the meeting house of the Frankford Friends on a Sunday afternoon later in the month. Unfamiliar with Rustin, I knew nothing of his endeavors to promote equal rights for African-Americans. So, I decided to hear him speak. The Frankford Friends met less than a mile from where I attended high school in Philadelphia. His audience was roughly two dozen people. When he finished his presentation, I noted those in attendance seemed impressed with his message. I certainly was! During the question and answer session I thought all Americans should hear what Rustin has to say.

Until Rustin's lecture no other person had brought me so far toward gaining an understanding of what it was like for African-Americans living as second class citizens in this nation which, rather ironically, sponsors a pledge calling for "liberty and justice for all." He gave an impassioned speech pertaining to racial political and social injustices to the mostly white audience which included a married elderly black couple who were members of that congregation. Pivoting his presentation around various dimensions of racial prejudice, he never resorted to condemnations of all white people.

Eloquent, though he spoke with a slight lisp, he compelled the audience's rapt attention. At the time I was unaware of how well known Bayard Rustin was in black intellectual circles. Reading some of his thoughts at later times I came to understand just how intelligent and thoughtful a person he was.

As a consequence of Rustin's lecture I began to give attention to what was more frequently being reported in the news about racial tensions flaring up below the Mason and Dixon Line. I resolved to become better informed about the situations in which African-Americans living in the Jim Crow South found themselves. From colonial times to the mid 1960s most circumstances for African-Americans were predicated on not being able to present themselves in any sector of society on an equal footing with Americans of European ancestry.

From my perspective, a biased northern one, I originally thought racial inequities and injustices were something the South was solely responsible for. But, with my absorption of considerably more information, I came to understand the entire nation shared responsibility for the dilemma of deep seated injustices which African-Americans constantly faced. Until the time of Rustin's presentation, I hadn't given a thought to the racial implications of the northern white flight to the suburbs. It had dramatically begun in the 1950s, accelerated in the 1960s, and persisted as the 20th Century ended.

For a few years after Rustin's lecture, roughly the years 1963 to 1967, I also realized I was gaining imperfect knowledge of the racially charged issues as reported in what was essentially the white media. Getting past black anger, to delve into reasons for the anger, was not something the corporate sponsored mainstream media generally cared to do for the sake of educating the public. The media seemed to prefer focusing on episodes where the anger spilled over into lawless behavior. (This tendency enabled George Wallace and Richard Nixon to make "law and order" a major issue in their 1968 bids for the presidency.) I was unaware of how African-American publications, such as the popular magazines *Ebony* and *Jet*, were reporting the critical events and attendant issues associated with them.

On August 28th of 1963, Dr. Martin Luther King, Jr. gave his "I Have A Dream" speech at the gathering of 250,000 people, 80% black and 20% white, in Washington D.C. This occurred seven months after I received a bachelor's degree in January. While taking courses toward completing that degree, my Temple University American history professors never mentioned the significance of Frederick Douglass or Dr. W.E.B.DuBois. Basically the orientation of these courses was, simply put, white history. For example, there was no mention of black regiments being with Teddy Roosevelt in his well publicized charge up San Juan Hill in the Spanish American War. It was the same thing for the next three years as I pursued a graduate degree in history even though major civil rights legislation had been signed by President Lyndon Johnson during that time. My exposure to information presently understood as the African-American dimension to America's history was meager and that's a generous assessment. I had two degrees from Temple University, but that facet of American history had been omitted in my college educational experience.

If I were to learn anything of African-American history it would be of my own initiative coupled with the belief it was worthy of studying. So, by 1969, when I was designated to teach a course in African-American history at the community college where I had been hired two years earlier, I had become rather well versed in the subject and was prepared to accept the challenge of teaching the course. Specifics of how and why I came to take on the challenge are presented in my first chapter.

Ensuing chapters are presentations of historical events which I consider critical for understanding African-American history. Included too are some random assessments of certain issues often purposely bypassed by societal institutions in part because of corporate interest influence. Also, interspersed throughout the factual historical narrative are some of my experiences as a young boy, a young adult serving in the military, and those associated with teaching this course – some of which are rather humorous.

Something rather obvious was how pervasive the factor of hypocrisy meanders through America's history. This was evident in view of the experiences of people first brought to our shores in bondage and then had to endure when juxtaposed with principles stated in the Declaration of Independence. I rarely had to belabor this point to classes.

Inherent to this joint learning undertaking were many acknowledgments by students, down through the years, they had never previously been educated regarding African-American history in their earlier public school experiences. My early public school education mirrored theirs as well. So, in some respects, during my first year teaching the course my students' learning experience was in tandem not far behind mine.

Within my concluding chapter one will find my opinion regarding the issue of national budgetary priorities which I believe are presently tilted away from benefiting a great majority of Americans, especially African-Americans. The tilt actually favors a very small minority who profit greatly from their involvement with military industrial components of the Corporatocracy. As for the Military Industrial Complex (MIC), readers will readily discern my attention to concerns Dr. King expressed in his April 4, 1967 Riverside Church Address. At this time his views pertaining to systemic militarism are largely ignored by the media. It chooses to focus instead on his original message of challenging racism, but rarely goes beyond that to present his views on social injustice predicated on economic considerations. Today's corporate sponsored media isn't inclined to present Dr. King's post civil rights orientation which essentially addressed the taboo question: Who gets what and why?

Shortly before the last year of his life began, Dr. King decidedly focused on the economic implications to the concept of justice. As this became of great concern, it's no wonder he felt compelled to challenge unjust wars and examine what their economic implications were, especially for those struggling to exist as the working poor of which African-Americans are disproportionately over represented.

Though many years have flashed by since my retirement in 1999, I often look back and take satisfaction from what I believe was accomplished in my thirty-two year college teaching career. Presently, I'd like to believe students who took the African-American history course are still able and willing to factually and logically sort things out regarding society's inequities, especially those based on racial bigotry and economic disparities. Significant also, I hope former students, black and white alike, are as willing today as they once seemed to acknowledge the intrinsic value of what we shared in our mutual learning experience. Yes, no doubt, recollection of some historical events will fade as we age. But, an appreciation for the worth of others, something I always tried to instill, is what I hope will endure the test of time for those students I fortunately, though briefly, got to know.

On another personal note, I hope this book will be appreciated one day by my not yet teen age grandsons Andrew and Nathaniel Reiss. First of all, they'll learn about African-American history and then, hopefully, understand why I believed it was very important to know. Also, I'd like them, and others who may take interest, to know what I came to understand, and in some instances experienced, pertaining to certain events and issues occurring during my lifetime. Hopefully, readers will appreciate my endeavor to tell it like it was for me, this an extrapolation from the 1960s expression, "Tell it like it is."

This was never intended to be a popular version of American history, since that genre usually glosses over unpleasant events from our past, something I've rarely been inclined to do. Of course, I'd take satisfaction upon learning what I've presented is appreciated by those of all walks of life sincerely interested in the basics of African-American history to the turn of the 21st Century. A last thought is my belief this book would be of academic value to those teaching courses in African-American history or a survey course in American Cultural Studies.

Chapter 1

A fter receiving a bachelor's degree in 1963, my first full time teaching position was in the City of Burlington, New Jersey. It was there I first experienced teaching a significant number of African-American students. Accepted to pursue a master's degree at Temple University in 1964, I began taking evening courses while teaching full time during the day. It would likely take five years to earn a master's degree on that part time basis. So, I submitted a letter of resignation half way through my second year and began taking graduate courses full time in the Spring of 1965. Also, at this juncture, I had begun to visualize the possibility of obtaining a community college teaching position.

The decade of greatest expansion for establishing community colleges was 1965 to 1975. Approximately half of community colleges existing today opened in that ten year span. Thus, it came as no surprise when I learned the Oglala Lakota College had opened twenty years earlier in 1971 during a summer of 1991 visit to the Pine Ridge Reservation in South Dakota. Former tribal council member Bennett Sierra (his nickname was Tuffy) was enthusiastic about this college's mission and what it had accomplished in its first twenty years. To my surprise he offered me a teaching position. I was shown the fall semester's class schedule and saw the letters TBA next to the American history course listings. At the time I was appreciably higher on a salary schedule back at the community college in Middletown New York and had to turn down his offer.

Getting back to the 1960s, about the time I was awarded the bachelor's degree (1963) I learned a master of arts degree in a subject field was the entry level requirement for obtaining a community college faculty position. Therefore my desire to complete that degree as quickly as possible was steadfast, especially since my high school teaching experience hadn't been very rewarding. Married for two years, barely getting by on my first wife's paltry salary, approaching age thirty, and interested in starting a family, I wanted to wrap up a master's degree as quickly as possible and obtain a livable salary.

Six weeks prior to Temple conferring the master's degree (June 1966), I applied to four recently opened community colleges for a position. Rosilyn and I both had strong family ties in the Philadelphia area, so my inquiries remained within a one hundred mile radius of that city. I had one interview in Maryland shortly before commencement, but nothing came of it. The other inquiries brought responses indicating no history positions were available.

The keynote speaker at Temple's June 16, 1966, commencement was U.S. Vice President Hubert Humphrey. In his address he emphasized the expanded educational opportunities featured in President Lyndon Johnson's Great Society agenda. I was impressed by his message, but also came to understand why some of his political adversaries dubbed him "motormouth." Whew! With Hubert Humphrey there was rarely a second of hesitation. His delivery was rapid and to the point, unlike some I've heard in my lifetime. Humphrey wasn't as impressive as John Kennedy or Barack Obama, but his delivery was livelier than Dwight Eisenhower's, Jerry Ford's or Jimmy Carter's.

So, there I was with a master's degree but no community college position as I had hoped for. My wife Rosilyn and I had been thinking of starting a family once I had completed the degree, but minus a job that idea had to be reevaluated. The option still open was to apply to public school districts - maybe one would have an unexpected vacancy for a Social Studies teacher. Temple's job placement office informed me of such a vacancy in the Southern Lehigh District located in Pennsylvania's Lehigh Valley region. Economic necessity dictated I apply, but I wasn't happy about having to teach at the secondary level again.

A few days after July 4th, I was notified I had the job. My assignment was to teach five sections of tenth grade American history. Before my first day of class I suspected this district had very few or no minorities at all. I wasn't wrong. To be sure this school district was lily white! I didn't have a single African- American or Hispanic student. It would be quite a contrast from my Burlington New Jersey teaching experience where one in five students were African-American. Presently the Southern Lehigh school district still has a miniscule minority population as compared with Allentown's schools. One could presently view a zone of approximately twenty square miles in the Lehigh Valley region and readily discern a recognizable pattern of de facto segregation.

My morale was boosted when Penn State offered me an evening class to teach in their Lehigh Valley extension program. Being hired by Penn State acknowledged the hard work and sacrifices my wife and I had made to obtain the master's degree. It was soon to facilitate achieving my stated goal. My first Penn State evening class was held at the Hamburg State Hospital located about thirty miles west of Allentown. Once, in early December, I drove to class just as it began snowing. After class concluded, three hours later, I was lucky to make it home to our apartment because of hazardous driving conditions on old route 22.

After paying a first month's rent and deposit on the apartment we moved into, two miles west of Allentown, the amount remaining in our savings account was about forty dollars. The first Southern Lehigh paycheck was wonderful and then slightly more than a month later the Penn State paycheck made us believe we could again think of starting a family. (We didn't know Rosilyn was already pregnant since the Labor Day weekend.) By late October we learned our son Andrew was due in early June of 1967. Things became upbeat for us again as we quickly realized how readily a few steady paychecks will chase the blues.

I applied for a position at Orange County Community College in Middletown, New York in February of 1967. This was a school I hadn't applied to the year before because it was beyond the 100 mile radius limitation I had self imposed. During Spring recess, Rosilyn and I drove to Middletown for interviews. (We were surprised to see how much snow was evident on campus the first week in April.) My first meeting was with Robert Greenman, the Academic Dean at the time. Next, I met with Harold Jonas who was chairperson of the Social Sciences Division. Both interviews went very well. On June 4th, 1967, my son Andrew was born and about a week later I was notified I had the community college job. I took the job despite the fact I wouldn't be teaching American history.

My initial assignment was to teach a two semester course known as the "History of Western Civilization." Today most progressive historians would view this course as basically a history of Europe's development - white folks history. Anyway, this course would be a challenge, but I was up for it. Sooner or later I believed circumstances in the department would likely change and I would have an opportunity to teach American history. My teaching load was less than what it had been at the secondary level and my base salary had appreciably increased, plus I had the option to earn extra money teaching evening courses and/or in a summer session. The master's degree was now beginning to pay off!

Rosilyn, baby Andrew, and I arrived at our apartment on a road in a rural setting seven miles west of Middletown on July 1st, 1967. My classes didn't begin until after Labor Day. (These days most college classes start the week before Labor Day.) This meant I had two full months to immerse myself in the historical literature pertaining to the history of western civilization. I was highly motivated and enjoyed the task at hand. The effort to put myself well beyond being just one page ahead of students paid off as things went smoothly in my first semester.

One of my better students that first semester happened to be African-American. Louis Stewart, he preferred Lou, was from the city of Newburgh which had the largest African-American population in Orange County. Since we hit it off, my wife and I had Lou and his girlfriend Betty visit us at home. Some of my colleagues wouldn't approve, not necessarily because of racial bigotry but because of the appearance of becoming too friendly with a student. I learned this was frowned upon - familiarity or fraternizing with students was considered unprofessional.

By the second semester (Spring of 1968), Lou frequently visited during office hours and we discussed various historical and current political issues. One topic was the ghetto riots in various northern cities the previous three summers. Lou was profoundly troubled by them because he greatly admired Dr. King's philosophy of non-violence. I appreciated his concern about the effect of the riots. We both understood there would be many whites ready to use inner city violence for making blanket condemnations of all African-Americans. The corporate media had begun to use the term "black militant." Lou wondered if any black person, such as himself, who saw injustice would be so designated. One didn't have to be a genius to realize how the term was being applied. It had a negative connotation.

We shared the same observation regarding the racial makeup of our troops then serving in Vietnam. African-Americans were decidedly over-represented there in terms of the American population as a whole. To us this was blatantly an injustice. Lou pointed to the fact many young black men didn't go to college because of economic hardship and consequently were more likely to be drafted and sent to Vietnam. Alabama's governor, George C. Wallace, running for president in 1968, wouldn't remind supporters African-Americans were over represented in the military then fighting in Vietnam. He focused instead on ghetto riots and made his big issue one of "law and order."

How I failed to learn of Martin Luther King Jr.'s assassination long before I actually did still baffles me. It wasn't until just before noon on the day after it happened that I was first told about it. Apparently I was busy with class work during the evening of the day it happened and didn't have the radio or television on. My wife wasn't aware of the tragedy either. She told me she was busy with our baby son and other chores and also heard no media information that day. The day after he was shot I didn't have my car radio on as I drove into town to meet my ten o'clock class.

After parking and walking across campus toward my classroom, I didn't encounter any colleagues who might have informed me of Dr. King's tragic death. The ten o'clock class was followed by my eleven o'clock class held in the same room. Between classes I didn't go into the hallway to chat with any nearby faculty members either. Looking back on that morning I've come to realize how peculiar it was that none of my students in either class talked about his assassination. A buzz about that event would have been something I would have noticed and responded to with an inquiry. Out of class, just before noon, and walking toward the cafeteria for some lunch brought me face to face with Lou. He said, "Oh, Mr. Reiss, I can't believe what happened - can you?" I was still clueless. However, I observed how distraught he appeared. I immediately thought he had a personal problem and responded by asking, "What's upsetting you Lou? Did something happen to you?"

"No, no, nothing happened to me. Didn't you hear? Dr King was assassinated!"

I responded, "Lou, are you sure? When did it happen?"

"Yesterday, in the late afternoon, in Memphis, Tennessee," he replied.

This encounter with Lou was extremely awkward for me. I felt very stupid and must have seemed rather out of it to him. I informed him of my circumstances which hopefully explained why I hadn't heard the dreadful news sooner. Lou shook his head in disbelief when I informed him no students in either of my recent classes raised the issue and brought it to my attention. He was taken aback by that information. At this point he seemed on the verge of tears and I understood why. I've often thought of the irony of this encounter. Here was a very sensitive and intelligent African-American young man, who I had befriended, being the first to tell me of the hideous death of the man he idolized.

To be sure, I'll never forget that encounter with Lou when reminiscing with others about the death of this very inspirational human being. Martin Luther King Jr.'s death was indeed a tragedy and the grief Lou exhibited was most certainly spontaneously shared by millions more. Regarding that infamous date of April 4, 1968, I highly recommend the book by Michael Eric Dyson. He reviewed events associated with Dr. King's murder with ideas and information more profoundly than what had previously been presented in popular literature on the topic. His book is a must read!

During the academic year 1967–1968, one question raised by some colleagues had to do with ascertaining the percentage of black students on campus as full time day students. One dozen was the number offered by a consensus of opinion by this small group - less than 1%. Ten years later (1977-1978) my estimate was about forty out of a total full time enrollment of about eighteen hundred - that's roughly 2.5% were black. This indicated more than a doubling of blacks on campus in ten years. But, in terms of total numbers, really nothing to boast about. However, by the time of my retirement, in 1999, I estimated black enrollment at two hundred, give or take a dozen, out of a total enrollment of twenty-two hundred. That figure is within 1% of being 10%. Enrollment of blacks students appreciably increased in the first five years of the 21st Century in part because of the creation of the Newburgh satellite campus.

In the early 1970s a Black Student Union was organized. About ten students showed up on a regular basis for weekly meetings. By 1990, the group had changed its name to the Cultural Awareness Club and Hispanic students were welcomed. This resulted in attendance at weekly meetings rising to twenty plus on a consistent basis. I was the faculty adviser in the late 1980s and into the mid 1990s.

The college had four vans – ten seats in each. They were used to transport the school's athletic teams to away games. However, they were available for the Cultural Awareness Club's use during evenings to visit neighboring colleges such as S.U.N.Y. at New Paltz and Ramapo College in New Jersey, especially for Black History Month events. School policy, I suppose for insurance purposes, prohibited students from driving the vans. So I was the only one authorized to drive to events off campus.

One student mentioned going to an event in a van was how it was done in many black churches. He was from the Bronx and said the first time he went to the Bronx Zoo was in his church's van. Most white folks aren't likely to give transportation issues for inner city black families much thought. Are they aware not every black family can afford an automobile – despite Ronald Reagan's references about "welfare queens" driving Cadillacs? A family outing by those without autos is often undertaken as a church sponsored event whereby the church's van is used.

In the Fall of 1968, a black student named Bill Green arrived on campus. Not eighteen or nineteen, as most students were, he was twenty-three and had served in the Air Force. I overheard some English department faculty referring to him apprehensively. They described him as "cool and cynical." One said, "He has a big chip on his shoulder." Another said, "I wouldn't be surprised if he's a Black Panther." All this talk about him aroused my curiosity and I determined I wanted to meet him. I forget where I first encountered him, but I approached him and said, "You're Bill Green – right?" He seemed pleased I knew who he was. Because he had been in the Air Force, as I had, I thought that might be a basis for relating to him more readily. I soon learned he was very aware of the harsh treatment Air Force veteran James Meredith encountered after he was finally enrolled at the University of Mississippi in 1962.

I responded, "That's not going to happen to you here Bill. Mississippi's a different world. There's a big difference between New York's S.U.N.Y. system and the University of Mississippi."

His response was, "the difference isn't as great as you might think it is professor. Because you're not black, you wouldn't be able to understand."

When I responded, "So, how do you feel about whites who try to understand?" He said nothing but just smiled.

Our conversation resumed and he expressed his belief not enough was being done on campus to "promote Black pride," which he believed was necessary to enable African-Americans to better cope with racism. I said S.U.N.Y. colleges would be more likely to do that than colleges in Mississippi. He said, "that may be so and that's what I'd like to find out." I realized Bill Green was more intelligent than anyone in the English Department would be inclined or bother to learn about him.

Changing the subject, I asked him what he thought of the Democratic Party's convention held in Chicago the previous month. He laughed rather cynically and said, "Those white students for McCarthy got a taste of how cops treat black folks. But when they beat on us nobody's taking pictures like they did in Chicago." We parted after that observation. Yes, it would be unfortunate if my faculty colleagues underestimated his intelligence because of a stereotype perception that he was simply just another angry black man.

During the Fall semester (1968) Bill Green and a handful of other black students drew up a petition to promote incorporating certain Black Studies courses into the liberal arts curriculum. This committee's petition proposed the adoption of certain courses, such as African-American history and literature, into the Liberal Arts curriculum. Robert Greenman, the Academic Dean, received the petition in a respectful manner in December shortly before the holiday recess began. Within a few days Greenman responded to Bill Green with the information he was sending the petition to our division to be evaluated immediately after the Spring semester began. Before my division chairman told me, Bill informed me he was to be allowed to participate in evaluation discussions of the course proposals by our division's select committee.

Bill Green went the non-violent route. He had a special courage enabling him, in effect, to challenge the status quo evident at the college. His *modus operandi* can be summed up by the admonition "Question Authority" - seen on a political button in the late 1960s. I often told classes questioning authority was a very significant difference between the 1950s and the 1960s. Few dared question authority in the 1950s, during the Eisenhower era, for fear of being called a communist sympathizer. This was a general fear permeating society at that time.

Things changed rather dramatically in the 1960s as a result of two groundswell movements. First there was the plethora of protests directed at Jim Crow rule in the South, then in its immediate aftermath the second wave of massive protests challenged America's misguided foreign policy in Southeast Asia. People, especially young men eligible to be drafted, began questioning why the United States was waging a war in Vietnam - against a people with no capability or intent to do Americans in the U.S. any harm. Protesting students knew the U.S. was the aggressor and the people of Vietnam its victims.

As things turned out Dean Greenman must have viewed the black students' proposals as reasonable. This was indicated by the direction in which my new division chairperson, Dr. Emil Domac, steered the select committee's deliberations. Ideas favoring the acceptance of the proposals, many of which I helped to draft, were embraced by Domac - sometimes to my surprise. However, I knew my suggestions weren't the bottom line. As I saw it Domac's demeanor indicated Dean Greenman had given his prior approval. This was not lost on the committee judging by how things moved amicably along toward final approval. At the first meeting of the Curriculum Committee in the Spring (1969) our division's recommendations in support of Black Studies courses were placed on their agenda for review. Our division's committee members were invited to speak to the Curriculum Committee regarding the desirability of offering the proposed courses.

At the time this Black Studies business seemed like a big deal, but was it really? From today's perspective it really wasn't. After all, Bill Green's committee only wanted three courses: an African-American history, Black Literature, and a course in economics designated as Urban Poverty. Bill Green wasn't an unreasonable person. He laughed at one committee member's observation there was no such thing as black mathematics. And another committee member wondered about student enrollment - would white students be allowed to enroll in these courses? Bill wisely replied in the affirmative. As our last meeting concluded I looked at Bill and said something to the effect that the approved courses should move attitudes toward promoting Black pride. He quickly responded, "It's a start, but there's still a long way to go professor." In agreement, I had no response to that observation.

It seemed the Curriculum Committee was very impressed with the presentation we made urging approval of the three specified Black Studies courses. Many times requests for new courses would require two or three meetings worth of deliberations before a vote was taken. Our Black Studies course proposals were deliberated and approved at a first meeting. This was beyond our expectation. I had told Bill Green there was likely to be some resistance, but was surprised and pleased there weren't any serious objections. So, these courses were approved and soon to be listed in the college catalog for the academic year 1969 – 1970. I had no idea if the Academic Dean, behind the scenes, had urged the Curriculum Committee chairperson to look favorably upon these course proposals and that he, in turn, conveyed this to his committee members. Perhaps the committee members actually acted independently of any pressures because they sensed the time had come to do the right thing for the benefit of all concerned.

My division chairperson, Emil Domac, was now faced with the task of finding someone qualified to teach, as he said, "Black History." Many times in the following months, while the search was ongoing, I had to remind Domac we were looking for someone to teach African-American history, not Black history. Black history could readily be understood to mean the history of sub-Sahara Africa and the black diaspora to various places around the world. That wasn't what this course was to be about I had to remind him. He finally got it that this course was American history with a special emphasis.

Actually the number of potential students for the course was not promising. You couldn't insist every one of the roughly twenty or so black students on campus, the first year it was offered, had to take it. The student enrollment potential for the first two or three years was perhaps ten to twelve black students and maybe five or six white students. Because of this it was well understood there would only be one section of the course offered. And initially that one section would only be offered in just one of the two semesters in a given academic year.

Of note here is the fact I taught African-American history for seven years prior to the hiring of the first full time African-American classroom faculty member to get tenure. I'm referring to Mary Sands, a very talented teacher. She was hired in 1977 to teach occupational therapy. Prior to my retirement (1999), she won the S.U.N.Y. Chancellor's Award for Excellence in Teaching in 1993.

Location, location, location, means a lot in the real estate business. And we soon learned the axiom had profound meaning as well in our search to find a qualified person to teach the one section course in African-American history. The dean didn't fudge about race on this question. His preference to hire a qualified African-American was perfectly understandable to me. But where would he find such a person in a county where maybe only five or six African-Americans held a master's degree in 1969? And their master's degrees were likely in education not a Master of Arts in History. Perhaps such persons drove thirty miles (toward New York City) for full time employment in a Rockland County school district where they had competitive salaries and good fringe benefits. Advertisements for the position were placed in *The Chronicle of Higher Education*, The *New York Times*, and our local paper the Middletown *Times-Herald Record*.

It was basically assumed someone living in New York City, or its metro area, would have the qualifications we were looking for. After all some colleges in the city had been offering courses in African-American Studies since 1963. Now it was 1969, and there should have been some persons who had earned at least a master's degree in African-American history available. Indeed, such persons existed, but they were quickly filling full time position openings to teach undergraduates in east coast four year colleges. African-American history had, almost overnight, become a hot area for employment for someone having a graduate degree in that specialization. With the demand for qualified persons growing rapidly, it had become quite competitive regarding hiring such persons. Orange County Community College was at a distinct disadvantage in the competition.

Our college was trying to find someone to teach just one class section of the African-American history course we wanted to offer. This meant a small part time salary and no fringe benefits. Realistically there was no way a qualified person living in or near New York City would consider commuting 60 miles (120 miles round trip) or relocating to Middletown, New York to teach just one course. By late August of 1969, it had become apparent our search had come to naught. It was then decided we couldn't offer the course that fall but would do our best to offer it in the Spring semester of 1970.

Toward the end of September Emil Domac called me to his office to discuss an "important issue." I didn't know for certain what he had in mind, but I suspected it had something to do with the African-American history course. My suspicion was correct. He informed me the administration, to that point, had not found anyone willing to accept the position to teach the course in question. Did I have any suggestions, he inquired. I indicated my belief the search had been carried out in good faith, but that I was at a loss as to where we could go forward at that point.

Without hesitation, and to my surprise, he then posed the question, "How about you Phil, do you think you could teach the course?" In my mind, I replied, it wasn't a question as to whether I could do it, but rather the question: "How would the black students feel about a white instructor, namely myself, teaching the course?" Domac, sly fox that he was, acknowledged it was also the critical question he faced, but that he had already spoken to Bill Green about it. And, according to him, Bill Green said he wouldn't have a problem if the white instructor was me. I entertained a doubt this exchange with Bill Green had actually taken place. Was this Domac's attempt to hustle my ego? Maybe he read my thoughts because I was then told to talk to Bill Green about the matter. The next day I located Bill Green. He confirmed he had spoken with Emil Domac and had told him he wouldn't have a problem with me teaching the course.

At our October, 1969, division meeting Domac announced I was willing to teach the course in African-American history. My colleagues didn't see this as a plum to further professional advancement. If anything some saw it as giving students a big opportunity to hassle me. They had a tendency, thanks to what was being reported in the media, to see black students as angry and resentful. Perhaps they likened most black male students to Stokely Carmichael, the militant activist, who denounced Dr. Martin Luther King Jr's philosophy of non-violence. One question posed to me was, "What if your black students, because of reverse racism hostility, bad mouthed you? That certainly wouldn't help you get promoted." The difference here was most of my colleagues usually wanted to play it safe. But, I wanted this challenge. I had challenged myself to teach the western civilization course and this would be another one. An additional motive was my desire to teach one less course of the History of Western Civilization. This would get me involved in teaching American history again. For me African-American history was, for the most part, an almost systematically overlooked part of American history.

During the first few years, until the mid 1970s, there were times when my coping skills were challenged by the negativity some colleagues had expected I would encounter. Reverse racism attitudes did occasionally surface in some classroom exchanges. In dealing with these episodes I managed to keep things in perspective by trying to better understand my students' views, especially the reasons for why they held them. When the terms "whitey" or "honky" were tossed around I never took offense. Criticism of the so- called white race didn't easily offend me. Historically there were many reasons why the white race deserved harsh criticism.

One initial objection, voiced with some resentment, regarding my teaching African-American history was based on the convenient assumption only a black person should teach the course. I had many responses to that notion. "Would you prohibit a psychiatrist or psychologist from specializing in child behavior because he or she didn't have children?" Also, "should an African-American person with a Ph.D. in child psychology be barred from helping white children having psychological problems?" As for the English language, I would ask, "who should teach the works of Shakespeare since he was white? What if a black or white American mastered the Japanese language, should they be prohibited from teaching it because they weren't Japanese?" Overall my classes got the point I was making that racism shouldn't have a place in the academic pursuit of knowledge.

In 1971, the college's counseling center hired an African-American woman to fill a full time position. This was Betty Johnson, who I'd say was about 47 or 48 at the time. She and her husband lived in a rural part of Sussex County New Jersey. Her daily commute to the college was approximately thirty miles. She was very supportive of my teaching African-American history. I extended invitations to her to sit in on my classes which she did on several occasions. After a visit she would send a memo telling me what she had found interesting in the class. It wasn't too long before I realized Betty Johnson was recommending my class to black students she counseled. Thank you Betty wherever you are!

By the mid 1980s, the word being passed on was "the dude teaching African-American history is white, but he really knows the deal." Jeff Starr, an army veteran, indicated he passed that observation on to "the brothas and sistahs." Consequently, when students walked into my classroom for the first time they weren't surprised to see me sitting at the front of the room. It was gratifying to know the initial objection to my teaching the course was no longer an issue.

Betty Johnson and I saw the administration of Ronald Reagan go about the business of cutting various types of funding to America's public school systems. Inner city schools, without the same monetary resources as the affluent suburban schools, weren't given the same priority as they once had been given fifteen years earlier in the Great Society programs of the Lyndon Johnson administration.

Lack of financial resources had negative consequences for black students going to those inner city schools. For example textbooks purchased in the mid-1960s were still in use twenty years later in too many of those overcrowded schools. Affluent suburban schools were more likely to have reading teachers, speech therapists, special needs teachers, science labs, and swimming pools, while inner city schools were lucky to have a librarian. Betty and I agreed black students from inner city schools were usually playing "catch-up" when they came to college.

Chapter 2

U pon my arriving in Orange County New York in 1967, there were no discernible racial tensions in the county. But, the racial animosity fallout resulting from the riots in major urban centers, such as Cleveland, Detroit, Newark, New York City, Philadelphia, and Rochester, in the three previous summers probably hadn't as yet fully impacted attitudes there as yet. However, at bottom those riots prompted many living in the New York City metro area to relocate to villages and towns in Orange County where the minority populations were less than one percent in a majority of those communities. Riots in the aforementioned cities had resulted in hundreds of millions of dollars worth of property damage and scores of deaths and injuries. Most sociologists would agree those events prompted an acceleration of the white flight to the suburbs. Indeed sociologists observed many whites running scared and wanting out of the cities in the late 1960s. Initially, the white flight to suburbia had been spawned by the post WW II Levittown boom.

Many moving to Orange County in the late 1960s and the 1970s were New York City firemen and police officers with their families. They were willing to drive long distances commuting because housing became more reasonably priced as the distance away from the city became greater. Others holding jobs in New York and the metro area were also willing to drive forty to sixty-five miles to work from their homes in Orange County. A prime motive for doing this was the perceived safety and stability of the county's various small town public school systems which appeared free of racial unrest.

Recent highway construction of the early 1960s went to regions lying beyond the early defined suburbs of the 1950s. For example Route 17, where it had close proximity to the Harriman interchange of the New York Thruway, then became a four lane artery through Orange County passing by Monroe and Middletown toward the Catskills to ultimately arrive in Binghamton. By 1975 this highway had enabled Monroe, New York, roughly forty miles from New York City, to have an observable suburban ambiance with approximately a quarter of its adult population having employment in New York City or its adjacent metropolitan areas. That the Monroe-Woodbury school district had a minority population of less than one percent at the time was a factor in the region's observable growth spurt.

In the mid to late 1960s, there were various voices articulating the grievances of black America. But, be mindful, not all were advocating the violence that erupted in an urban setting somewhere every summer in the middle of the decade. It seemed many of the whites fleeing to the suburbs only heard those advocating "burn baby, burn!" So, frightened whites were not likely to make distinctions with regard to what various black advocacy groups were saying. To be sure members of the National Association for the Advancement of Colored People (NAACP) were opposed to the new message of Black Power put forth by newer (with younger members) organizations.

The NAACP tended to see Black Power advocates as irresponsibly causing disruption of the measured and timely progress on the civil rights front that it, and other similar groups, had brought about without panicking otherwise reasonable whites. The NAACP and the Urban League didn't resort to inflammatory rhetoric condemning whites as "blue eyed devils" or advocate the tactic "burn baby, burn." The riots of the mid-1960s were unfortunate and regrettable to most African-Americans, especially those belonging to the NAACP. At the time probably most African-Americans were of the opinion meaningful progress was being achieved by President Lyndon Johnson's civil rights initiatives.

Orange County's commuters believed their children would be in "good" schools. Real estate salespersons said the word "good" with a voice inflection which amounted to it being a buzz word. I had telephone conversations

with some realtors and I believe how they said the word "good" was implied
to mean the school system in question had no, or very few, minorities. Such
Orange County communities as Chester, Cornwall, Florida, Goshen, Harriman, Maybrook, Montgomery, Monroe, New Windsor, Otisville, Pine
Bush, Pine Island, Port Jervis, Walden, Warwick, and Washingtonville had
public schools where black students numbered less than one percent in the
1970s. Because Middletown had a black population of three or four percent and Newburgh's was slightly higher, white commuters preferred not to
live in either city even though houses in both places cost less. At this time
Middletown has an Hispanic population which has more than doubled
since 1975.

Belief their children were going to "good" schools was reassuring to
those white folks wanting to avoid racial tensions and other issues associated with New York City's public schools. Being in a district where the
minority population was less than one percent was somehow viewed as a
guarantee the schools would be trouble free. But, predictably, few of this
white flight would admit their reasons for moving were based on racial attitudes. Some parents eventually learned, to their surprise, realtors never
mentioned how many students in these "good" schools had been designated drug possession offenders.

From the mid 1960s and into the 1970s racist attitudes toward African-Americans were slow to subside in various regions of the north – especially in blue collar and white ethnic communities. At this time certain
politicians like George Wallace of Alabama and, to a slightly lesser degree,
Frank Rizzo of Philadelphia engaged in tactics based on racial fears. However the winds of change, not blowing at hurricane force as yet but waft-
ing gently in some parts of the South, motivated Georgia's Jimmy Carter,
unlike Alabama's Wallace, to base his electioneering for governor on the
premise a "new South" had to move on and put race based politics aside.

Many whites hadn't bothered to make distinctions between the messages of H. Rap Brown and Dr. Martin Luther King, Jr. In his 1968
presidential quest George Wallace wasn't about to educate white voters to
understand the difference between Brown and Dr. King. However, many
Americans remembered Wallace's well publicized statement "segregation
now and segregation forever." He played a racial fear card in Democratic
presidential primaries and in some northern states attracted alarming support. Based on "Wallace for President" bumper stickers I saw in the student

parking lot, it was apparent George Wallace had supporters in Orange County, New York in 1968.

The first semester I taught the African-American course, which came two years after the assassination of Martin Luther King, Jr., I told my class about a personal experience that occurred a few days after it happened. On the first Saturday after his tragic death, I had gone to a barber shop that morning. Located in the Washington Heights neighborhood at the edge of Middletown, it was my first time there. The barber was white as were his customers. Shortly after I sat in the barber's chair, three men ambled in within a few minutes of each other. After sitting down they didn't talk to each other much, but did exchange some quick comments indicating they knew each other. I'm sure they saw me as an outsider and that's how I felt.

The assassination of Dr. King came up when a fourth entered the shop. He was greeted with the comment, "Hey, glad to see you made it back from Tennessee. When can I get my rifle back?" Following this remark another chimed in by saying, "He didn't use your rifle. I loaned him mine. It has a scope." These two remarks prompted laughter all around as I sat in silent anger. When I got home and told my wife Rosilyn of the incident, she responded, "Oh my God, that's so disgusting!" I told her I regretted not having the courage to voice an objection to the exchange. She said, "That would have been foolish honey, you were outnumbered." One black male student, always quick with a cynical quip, responded to my story by saying, "if you said something they would only beat you, but I'd be lynched!"

My story seemed to make some white students in the class a bit uneasy. Perhaps they realized they had a relative or knew someone who might have laughed or made such obnoxious comments. A response from another student was, "Professor, you were in a bad situation. It wouldn't have made sense to say something." Well here we are in the 21st Century and most of the times it would be safe to articulate a challenge to a racist remark, but still most folks don't speak up. Challenges to racism are still needed if a climate of subtle, and not too subtle, racism is to become truly a thing of the past.

In a first or second class I asked students if they remembered a first encounter with someone racially different from themselves. Down through the years the most frequent answer I got from black students was this first occurred in kindergarten or first grade because their teachers were white. A few, in the 1970s, said they remembered going shopping with their parents, before going to school, and saw only white sales clerks and customers. Generally the white students indicated first encounters with a black person came at an older age and in circumstances that were more varied. One said he visited where his father worked, when he was nine or ten, and his father introduced him to the black janitor.

Many said they never interacted with black students until junior high school because their neighborhood elementary schools were all white. When asked how many blacks were in their junior high some said four or five and others said nine or ten. White students from Newburgh indicated the number of black students in their junior high was probably one hundred or so in the mid 1970s. At this time I would estimate the African-American population in Newburgh has easily more than doubled since that time.

The discussion about a first encounter with another racially unlike oneself always came around to me. Usually the first question was, "how old were you when you saw your first black person?" I indicated my northeast Philadelphia neighborhood (in the vicinity of Castor Avenue and Magee Street) was lily white to be sure. My elementary school had no black students. So, a black man who had a shoe shine stand outside a neighborhood tavern was someone I vividly recall seeing at age eight or nine on more than one occasion. That was in either 1945 or 1946. His customers referred to him as "the Admiral" because he wore an old naval officer's hat and jacket which looked like something from Gilbert and Sullivan's *H.M.S. Pinafore*. Part of his shtick (to use a Yiddish term) was to appear comical. He certainly knew better than to appear threatening to his often inebriated white customers. Essentially he adopted the role of a clown which probably facilitated gaining more business.

My father learned the Admiral's name was actually Joe. Well, maybe that really wasn't his name, but that's what I remember hearing him say it was. Also, I recall one day observing the shoe shine stand was no longer there on the corner. I'd say that was in 1947, when I was ten years old. It certainly wasn't there in 1950 when the Korean War started. Did people in the neighborhood notice the Admiral and his shoe shine stand's disappearance? I've often wondered how many others did. Life has taught me things often change in ways people don't immediately notice.

In the summer of 1948, when I was eleven, my father took us (two younger brothers and my older sister) to see the Phillies play the Brooklyn

Dodgers. We had heard of the exploits of the very talented Jackie Robinson who was then in his second year with the Dodgers. But, it was a Phillies' rookie, Richie Ashburn, (named National League "Rookie of the Year" in 1948) who we were anxious to see. As for Jackie Robinson, he was and is more widely better known than Ashburn because he was the first African-American to break the color barrier of baseball's major leagues in 1947 when he was "Rookie of the Year."

What I didn't understand at age eleven was why so many fans applauded when Jackie Robinson made a hit or stole a base – after all he was a Dodger not a Phillie! I had no comprehension of the racial dynamic occurring at the time. My father explained the fans cheering for Jackie Robinson were black and came to see the Dodgers because they had Robinson, while the Phillies didn't have a black player. Robinson's talents impressed my father. He was exciting to watch! He beat out a bunt and then stole second base.

Basically black Philadelphians didn't go see the Phillies play in the late 1940s and into the 1960s. But, when the Dodgers came to town attendance figures nearly doubled because of the black fan base the Dodgers had - thanks to their star player Jackie Robinson and then, two years later, all star catcher Roy Campanella. It wasn't peculiar to Philadelphia. In every National League city when the Dodgers played, because of Jackie Robinson, a large black fan base attended that wasn't rooting for the home team. Blacks in Chicago didn't go see the Cubs play other National League teams, but showed up in droves at Wrigley Field when the Cubs played Brooklyn.

Now as for the name Robinson, Alvin Robinson was the only black student at Woodrow Wilson Junior High School when I arrived there in 1948. What I remember most was he always seemed to have a frightened demeanor. Of course it wasn't until I reached adulthood that I came to understood why he constantly appeared apprehensive. Many junior high age kids can be thoughtless to others respecting their feelings. Given this was 1948, I believe we can safely assume Alvin heard the 'N' word more than once during the week. He was likely insulted in other ways as well because of racial bigotry. On the other hand, I also remember a few kids trying to be nice to him by saying, "Hi Alvin." But those students didn't go beyond that simple greeting by engaging him in any ongoing friendly conversation.

Alvin Robinson always walked by himself in the halls between classes. I never saw anyone walking and talking with him. It's not unreasonable to conclude Alvin Robinson was unhappy about attending Wilson Junior

High School at the time. When I knew of him I was in seventh grade and he was in ninth. The next year I suppose he moved on to tenth grade at a high school somewhere. For the next two years (1950 & '51), while I was in eighth and ninth grades, no black students attended Wilson Junior High on Cottman Avenue in northeast Philadelphia.

In January of 1952, I began high school as a sophomore at Frankford High School. To the best of my memory there were, perhaps, eight or nine black students attending at that time. In tenth grade home room, where attendance was taken before going to classes, I sat in front of a black student named Norman Richardson. He must have dropped out or moved away because I never saw him again after the beginning of the following school year. When I graduated in January of 1955, there were only three black students in our graduating class. And, as I recall, none of them went to the senior prom.

In the Spring of 1952, my first semester, Frankford High School played in the city's public league baseball championship game. The team had no African-American or Hispanic-American players. Sixty years later, in 2012, Frankford won the public league's championship with a team comprised of all Latino players. As Philadelphia's public league football champs in the Fall of 1954, Frankford's team had no black players and there were none on the 1954-1955 basketball team either.

A particular high school sports story of interest to some was my account of Frankford's basketball team playing Wilt Chamberlain's high school. My school's team held Wilt Chamberlain (a former NBA All Star who holds records to this day) to less than twenty points. It was the only time it ever happened in his three years of playing for Overbrook High School in Philadelphia. Upon graduating, Chamberlain went to the University of Kansas at Lawrence. At the time I was stationed at the air base near Topeka, only 30 miles west of Lawrence, I induced a buddy who had a car to drive us to K U's campus so we could see Wilt Chamberlain play for the Jayhawks.

Students learned that up to and including my graduation from high school, the extent of my interaction with black people was very minimal. I brought their attention to the fact there were no black families living in my neighborhood, or others within four or five miles. There were many neighborhoods with identifying names, like mine had, in the Northeast section of Philadelphia. But, unlike those in South or West Philadelphia, the neighborhoods in the Northeast were easily 96% white in the 1940s and 1950s. Also, no black youths ever played in the local recreation center (named Max Myers) where a swimming pool had opened in 1958. Some observed my situation wasn't so unique at that time. They were right. The circumstances I grew up in were known as de facto segregation and was the reality applicable to most Northeast Philadelphia neighborhoods until the early 1980s. De facto segregation is still prevalent in desirable suburban areas adjacent to Philadelphia and the suburban areas of other northern big cities as well.

A question frequently asked was: When did I have daily interaction with African-Americans after graduating from high school? I indicated it occurred after I enlisted in the Air Force in July of 1955. There was a draft at the time and I thought the Air Force would offer me useful training applicable to a civilian job. Classes had a good laugh when I revealed my training as a "munitions handling and loading specialist" wasn't a skill corporate America had a dire need for. I took basic training at Sampson Air Force Base in upstate New York beginning on July 26 of 1955.

During basic training tables with four chairs typified the seating arrangement in the mess hall. The black fellows tended to sit together during meals. But in orientation classes everyone sat wherever there was an empty seat regardless of who sat next to them. I noticed white guys from the north would readily borrow something, like a razor blade, boot polish, or a bar of soap, from a black airman. But, of the white recruits from the South, I can't recall any of them asking to borrow something from a black airmen during basic training. Keep in mind at this time, the summer of 1955, it was only seven years after President Harry Truman gave his order to end segregation in the military. Also, the number of African-Americans enrolled in the military academies, Annapolis and West Point, didn't have a combined total of a dozen attending at that time. Two years later in the Fall of 1957, when I was stationed at Goose Air Base in Labrador, President Eisenhower ordered troops to Little Rock to enforce a federal court order ending the segregation in public schools there.

On Thursday, December 1, 1955, I was in an Air Force training class at Lowry AFB in Denver Colorado unaware Rosa Parks had refused to give up her seat to a white person on a segregated bus in Montgomery, Alabama that day. This incident sparked the subsequent Montgomery bus boycott. This boycott action, lasting approximately thirteen months, was the first phase of a southern civil rights movement which soon spread like a prairie grass fire across the South. However, the Montgomery bus boycott was unbeknownst to me and probably tens of thousands of others serving in the military at the time.

After completing the munitions handling and loading training in March of 1956, I received orders to report to Forbes Air Force Base. It was a Strategic Air Command (SAC) base located about six miles south of Topeka, Kansas. On a daily basis at this duty station I interacted with other enlisted airmen who happened to be African-Americans. Nineteen, at the time, if I hadn't been in the Air Force it might have been many years before I would interact, if ever, with African-Americans as frequently as I did at that time and continued to do for the rest of my enlistment.

The loading crew I was assigned to had a white crew chief, Warren Pancoast, from New Jersey. Our assistant crew chief, Lee Williams, was African-American. Like Pancoast he was also an airman first class, but Pancoast was in grade longer which explains why he was crew chief. Williams, back from Korea about a year, was pleased to be stationed at Forbes, located approximately sixty miles west of his hometown of Kansas City Missouri. The non commissioned officer in charge (NCOIC) of our duty section was a master sergeant from North Carolina. Sergeant Garrett always seemed respectful toward Lee Williams who didn't mind being called Willie by him. Also, Lee Williams didn't mind the rest of us on the crew calling him Willie. In April of 1956, Pancoast was promoted to staff sergeant as an inducement for him to reenlist. It didn't happen. By the end of the month he took his discharge and headed back to New Jersey.

After Warren Pancoast's discharge, Lee Williams became our crew chief. This was fine by us because Willie was very competent and, more importantly, easy going just as his predecessor had been. Compared with "gung-ho" crew chiefs I would later have, Pancoast and Williams rarely "sweat the small stuff." They didn't let the authority of extra stripes go to their heads. However, Lee Williams was crew chief for little over a month. He went back to being assistant crew chief because a recently arrived staff sergeant named Hall, whose first name eludes me, was designated as crew chief. One of my students, always quick to see a racist motive in things, quickly exclaimed, "was the sergeant who replaced Willie white?" I informed him Sergeant Hall was black.

When I raised the question was there such a thing as reverse racism, our class discussions got very lively. Generally black students couldn't envision a situation where that might occur. The white students agreed there were blacks who strongly disliked whites and acknowledged it was therefore possible. I would then ask if anyone had ever encountered reverse racism. Usually the white students couldn't recall an incident they experienced or knew of a person who had experienced it. Then, to get their reactions, I would present a personal experience which I believe had reverse racism implications.

In May of 1956 I was a lowly airman third class hoping to get promoted to airman second class. I had no doubt, if Sergeant Hall hadn't showed up, Willie would have secured a second stripe for me. Performing my duties the way I had for Pancoast and Williams suddenly wasn't good enough for Sergeant Hall. He was much harder to please than his predecessors. Hall was on the path to do twenty years and get a pension. Like many making the military a career, he did things by the book. Thus, he did sweat the small stuff.

Sergeant Hall was less than a month from finishing his second enlistment and he intended to reenlist for a third. He was about to use accumulated leave before reenlisting and, in so doing, would be gone at the time recommendations for promotions were submitted. Before going on leave, Hall told Williams he wasn't recommending anyone for promotion. Willie knew I was looking forward to being promoted and I sensed it was difficult for him to tell me Hall wasn't going to recommended me. I was deserving, he said, and if it were up to him I would get promoted.

"Sure, I know that," I said. "But why won't Hall recommend me?"

Now Williams seemed even more uncomfortable. He said, "it doesn't seem to have anything to do with job performance."

I persisted, "Well, what's his problem?"

"What can I say Reiss? It's a color thing."

"Because I'm white?" I asked in disbelief.

"Basically that's it," Willie responded.

"Not much I can do about that," I said.

"Know about that – been there," Willie replied.

"I'm sure you have Willie, but this is a first for me."

Shaking my head in disbelief, I started to laugh because the irony of the situation came to me. Willie knew I wasn't angry with him, so he joined in laughing with me. When we stopped laughing, he said he was going to see "Sergeant Garrett about it," and that I should "keep that quiet."

Willie was going to bat for me. He responded, "No problem," after I thanked him. Standing in the chow line behind Willie that evening, he turned to me and said, "Hey man, I spoke with Sergeant Garrett and he said when Hall's on leave I'm the crew chief and that means I can recommend whoever I want." That bit of news made my day.

After relating this, I would pause waiting for a reaction. Classes always seemed to sense this and after a minute or two usually a student would say something like "I suppose reverse racism is possible, but most of the time we experience race prejudice – not white people." I would agree with this observation and most white students did also. Frequently, after another pause, I was then asked, "So what happened professor? Did you get promoted?" Most were pleased to learn African-American Lee Williams had done the right thing and enabled me to become an airman second class. Students had a good laugh when I indicated the promotion amounted to eight dollars more in my monthly paycheck.

Chapter 3

By the second or third class meeting after discussions about our first encounters with someone racially different from ourselves, I asked the question, "What did you learn about slavery in school?" A frequent response from black students was a groan followed by the question, "Do we have to talk about that nasty business?" My response was yes we did. Indeed it was a nasty business, but was important because of its long term psychological and socio-economic implications. A student once responded, "Yeah, I suppose it's important. Look what slavery did to mess up our heads."

One approach toward facilitating understanding the totality of the African-American experience is to know the enduring consequences of slavery and to what extent those consequences have lingered. Some have recently been acknowledged, but many others go unacknowledged. For the most part the racism African-Americans became subjected to was spawned in the 17th Century emergence of colonial Virginia's tobacco plantation economy.

A convincing case can be made that because of slavery racial attitudes became embedded in the American psyche. Race and slavery went hand in hand. Before the 17th century ended American slavery had taken root based on certain quickly accepted premises regarding what race should or shouldn't mean. Slavery is gone but some of the racial attitudes based on those premises to justify it lingered for decades and persist to this day in many layers of society. In conjunction with this, I always made it known my Philadelphia public school education (1943 to 1955) up to age eighteen was just like theirs in that I was never taught anything about slavery and its historical implications.

Students always informed me they never learned the Portuguese explored the tropical west coast of Africa. Those explorations resulted in interaction with African peoples which other Europeans hadn't as yet begun to experience. Thanks to activities of the Portuguese some tribes converted to Roman Catholicism. Within a dozen years of Columbus' first voyage to the "New World" (1492), the Catholic Church had already elevated an African to archbishop thanks to the influence of the Portuguese. But how meaningful were Portuguese endeavors to convert Africans to Christianity, if they were the first Europeans to remove Africans against their will to other locations? Did Christianity's Golden Rule mean anything to them?

The Portuguese had established a small scale plantation type of economy in the Azores and the Canary Islands before Columbus made his first voyage. Africans were taken to those islands to work on these plantations. Removing Africans was greatly accelerated when Portugal laid claim to Brazil. In Brazil vast sugar plantations were soon being carved out of the jungle. At roughly the same time the Brazilian sugar boom began, the Spanish realized they could duplicate the sugar plantation system in their Caribbean Islands. Cuba became most notable in this regard. By 1550 both countries had begun to reap the rewards of importing "white gold" into Europe. Within a century (1650) the importation of sugar had increased almost two hundred fold. Portugal and Spain were profiting greatly by the addiction to processed cane sugar by the populations in other European countries. To facilitate sugar production the demand for slave labor soared. Satisfying that demand became a booming enterprise in itself. The slave trade became enormously profitable. It wasn't long before the Dutch, French, and finally the English wanted a piece of the action. People of African origin were soon a commodity known as "Black Gold."

The question of the status of Africans when first taken on board Portuguese and Spanish ships in early instances is not known with certainty. However, it seems unlikely Africans voluntarily boarded ships at the behest of people not speaking their language, were racially different, and likely promising things which no African person could verify from a personal experience. It quickly became convenient, and certainly profitable, for the Portuguese and Spaniards to impose the status of slave upon those they removed from Africa. So, most likely within two decades of Columbus' last voyage, it became widely understood one's condition as a slave was determined by one's race and place of origin. Africa conveniently supported the specifics of that determination. Once in the New World the status of slave was passed on to the offspring of females held in bondage.

In the late 1960s and into the 1970s, some students, especially those enthralled with black power ideology, didn't want to acknowledge many African chiefs were as culpable as were their white trading partners in helping to establish the trans-Atlantic slave trade as a major economic feature of the 16th, 17th, 18th, and early 19th centuries. With their ship at anchor a white crew was in circumstances of being vulnerable - greatly outnumbered by Africans. The small number of whites, making up the ship's crew, wouldn't think of penetrating the jungle to capture slaves, unless certain local chiefs had given them assurances they wouldn't be attacked. Also, the natives weren't stupid. Once they learned of the purpose of such incursions by the Europeans, they would logically alert each other as to why the whites were coming among them and initiate measures of resistance, unless they were inclined to cooperate with them.

Convincing some students that people destined for the Middle Passage journey were often brought to the whites by opportunistic African chiefs wasn't easy. Black folks greedy? Oh no, not black folks! This was an assertion black power devotees sometimes made in the early 1970s. But that notion was sometimes challenged by a statement such as "Hey man, tell me the brother pushing dope to twelve year olds in the 'hood isn't greedy." Basically common sense prevailed as most students realized if none of the African chiefs wanted to trade with the Europeans then people they had captured, from rival tribes, wouldn't have been transferred to whites for some sort of recompense.

After presenting the very plausible historical scenario regarding chiefs selling fellow Africans, I cautioned students to keep in mind no race or ethnic group has a monopoly on virtue. Often greed goes beyond all societal condemnation boundaries when engaged in by persons acting in collusion. In instances where the participants are found out, one party is likely to point a finger at the other and charge them with a greater degree of culpability. But as the saying goes: "it takes two to tango."

The voyage from Africa to Caribbean Islands and/or Virginia was called the Middle Passage. Many students never heard the term before. Depending on the winds it could take as few as thirteen days or upwards of near four weeks to complete the voyage. A lengthy trip meant food and water rations had to be cut. This frequently resulted in weakness and susceptibility to sickness. Disease often spread rampantly below the main deck. Frequently the dead were left below in their chains for two or three days before being removed to be thrown overboard.

Taking too many captured Africans up to the top deck to stretch out and breath fresh air posed risks. Some might jump overboard at first opportunity as they came to understand the horrors awaiting them given the conditions on board their ship. Ship's log entries, by captains, recorded significant losses of persons due to sickness and suicide. A slave ship owner was also aware the crew might be overpowered by a concerted uprising enabling captives to take control of the ship. So, not to suffer that possible loss or one imposed by a disastrous storm at sea, they bought insurance.

One account reported sharks followed slave ships from the coast of Africa right into the Caribbean. They had come to expect the bodies of the dead, thrown overboard, as a reliable food source. Another account claimed a slave ship's rough proximity, though not in view, became known because its stench was noticeable at a downwind distance of up to ten miles. Men willing to crew slave ships were the social dregs of waterfront seaports. After the second or third voyage ships were so foul it became difficult to enlist a crew. It seems even cutthroats had certain standards. After a third voyage ships were usually pulled apart for fire wood or just burned down to the water line at a safe distance from the nearest dock.

Space between slave ship decks was usually four to four and a half feet. Captives couldn't stand erect. They were chained to each other and to the deck itself. Imagine being chained to someone who's been dead for three days! When captive Africans were finally brought ashore, I asked classes to think about their condition. It was agreed it was very difficult to fathom their exhaustion, mental and physical, with any certainty. By the mid 1990s, when asked for my opinion of such deplorable circumstances, I said many were probably suffering, by varying degrees, something akin to what today is called post traumatic stress disorder - PTSD.

For the most part people generally associate PTSD symptoms with military experiences. However, many negative non-military experiences can also result in post traumatic stress disorder. The horrendous conditions aboard a slave ship I can readily envision triggering post traumatic stress syndrome. A young woman said PTSD could result from being kidnapped and raped. I agreed. Another student said he couldn't sit in the front seat of a car as a passenger because of a head-on auto accident he experienced. Certainly, I'd say it's not unreasonable to attribute his fear to a dimension of PTSD. As a person who likes to think in humanitarian terms, I often wonder how many of those detained by the U.S. at Guantanamo Prison will be suffering from PTSD for the rest of their lives?

After presenting the Middle Passage experience, I asked students for their reactions. They were in agreement greed usually does facilitate "nasty business." Once a student said, "the nasty business of slavery still wasn't as bad as the nasty business of war." She observed slave ship owners really wanted the slaves to live, if they didn't survive their profit would be less. War materials manufacturers, on the other hand, have no bottom line interests in how many survive a battle or war. They make money no matter what. Some, she asserted, probably want body counts to mount up, "that way they'll know if the products they've made are doing what they're supposed to do - kill people!" I sensed the others in the class appreciated the point she made, I certainly did.

Englishmen who first settled at Jamestown had some knowledge of how things were done regarding strenuous physical labor in the non-English regions of the Americas. Granted extra shares by the London Company if they went to Virginia, these men didn't expect to engage in rigorous labor to survive. After all share owners in an enterprise usually don't believe they, themselves, will have to do physical labor. Implicit in this attitude was the expectation they would get natives to labor for them as the Spanish had done in their colonies. As things turned out they couldn't get the natives to work for them as the Spaniards had in Mexico and Peru. Indeed, simply put, Powhattan's people didn't allow the English to gain mastery over them. Left to their own devices many of these sons of aristocrats fared poorly, not being accustomed to physical labor. The first six years or so of their struggle to survive became known as the "starving time."

Something to keep in mind is the alarming numbers of natives who died from the diseases, of which they had no immunity, the English and Spanish brought to their respective regions. With native populations declining rapidly, the Portuguese, Spanish, and lastly the English became even more dependent on Africans to meet their labor requirements. For almost one hundred years before the English settled at Jamestown, the African slave trade was part of the economic dynamic existing between Iberia and the Americas.

As in the Spanish colonies the Jamestown settlers saw the local native population drastically decline because of the diseases they introduced to them. A dozen years later, the English settlers of the Massachusetts Bay colony saw the natives there, who taught them to plant corn, begin to die off in great unexpected numbers as well. Not easily subjugated and dying in large numbers after contact with the English, it became apparent the native population was not a reliable labor source.

In the Spanish colonies, the European men soon began to intermarry with native women. As racial differences began to disappear in Mexico the drastic decline in the population slowed down considerably. The English male settlers in Virginia showed little inclination to intermarry with the native women. One can make a case there is a subtle racist dimension inherent in that fact. A people rigidly maintaining their differences from others, yet living in close proximately, will likely foster an attitude of "it's us versus them." Naturally that attitude won't readily foster cooperation, but rather suspicion of the others. (To some degree we can see the Israeli - Palestinian conflict in this light.) Greater cooperation amongst peoples is more likely when differences are kept in check thanks to a recognition of commonalities. Also, very noticeable in Mexico, racial intermarriage blurred the us and them distinctions evident when the Spanish first arrived. Racial intermarriage tends to take things in the direction of minimizing differences and, thus, more likely to promote cooperation for mutually recognized desired goals.

But that which was happening in Mexico, a mixing of the European with the native, was not to become the social norm in Virginia or other English colonies founded later. That fact had societal ramifications for white Virginians as well as for the people brought in from Africa for economic exploitation. In all English colonies the natives realized the English were staying apart, viewing them as savages and treating them with contempt based on notions of racial superiority. The English, later Americans, persisted in relating to native peoples with behavior intended to defeat and then dominate them whenever possible.

One known record indicates 1619 as the date when Africans first arrived in Jamestown. Were they regarded immediately as slaves or as indentured servants is the question as yet unresolved for lack of conclusive

evidence. By that date whites were also being brought into the colony as indentured servants. This meant they were required to serve whoever bought
the right to their indenture obligation – most often a seven year requirement. Indentures were set by courts with authority to do so in addressing
petty criminal offenses or as an alternative to a local debtor prison sentence.
They were basically a legally sanctioned punishment. After the obligatory
number of years were served, the person in question became free. In many
instances, for a number of years, Virginia gave those recently freed from
indenture status a parcel of land to own.

From the 1620s through the mid 1640s there are few records clarify-
ing the question of slave versus indentured servant regarding the status of
blacks. One record of interest, however, indicated some blacks owned land
free and clear in the 1650s, this at the very time when laws relegating blacks
to slavery started to appear in the colony's legal statutes.

Indeed 1619 was a watershed year in terms of the caste Virginia's society would take because of the economic implications inherent in the tobacco production boom. John Rolfe sent tobacco back to England that
year. The English had learned natives smoked this plant's leaves and those
who took up smoking claimed a certain pleasure from so doing. It was also
claimed smoking tobacco had a medicinal value. (That claim persisted into
the 1940s.) When first introduced to England the king himself referred
to tobacco as the "noxious weed." It quickly became less noxious when
the King realized it would provide him with revenue thanks to an import
tax. Initially wealthy aristocrats, indulging themselves, were the first to use
tobacco.

I often informed classes personal acquired habits become dimensions
to social behavior when a sizable portion of a population engages in the
habit in question. Social psychologists study this phenomenon. Many have
done studies indicating most people are status insecure. When such persons
perceive their social betters engaging in a particular behavior they often
become imitative of that behavior, hence to feel part of the envied group.
The advertising business knows this only too well. The psychology of advertising makes three basic assumptions about human nature: first, people are
insecure about their social status, secondly, we are suggestive, and thirdly
people are imitative. On this last point more than once a student would
blurt out, "Monkey see, monkey do." So, if the lord of a rural manor takes
up smoking, because he learned people at court in London had, it wouldn't

take long before the local common folk, his tenant farmers included, would be imitating his behavior. Ah yes, where would consumer capitalism be if it weren't for people striving to keep up with the mythical Jones family.

Within twenty years of tobacco first arriving in England, it was likely half of the adult males had taken to its use. Hence, planters back in Virginia wanted to put as much acreage into tobacco production as possible to satisfy the dramatically rising demand for it. Can there be any dispute tobacco production was ultimately responsible for enslaving people of African origin in Virginia? Growing tobacco on large plantations in Virginia had much in common with growing sugar in Brazil and Cuba. Both enterprises sanctioned slavery to satisfy perceived extensive labor requirements to facilitate the success of these incredible profit making enterprises.

When indentured servants finished their terms, the tobacco planter had to pay again to get replacements for them. If he didn't he wouldn't be able to plant and harvest the same size crop the following year. That, of course, meant a decline in profit. No, he would never consider planting less. His constant goal, an obsession, would be to get even more acres into production. (Greed accelerates) So, naturally, he would have to get more indentured servants than previously, if he wanted to increase the size of his crop for the lucrative export enterprise in which he and others eagerly participated.

Soon, however, the planters realized it made more economic sense if their source of labor went uninterrupted - became predictably steady through a one time purchase of a person for a lifetime of service. Another requirement viewed as necessary, under those circumstances, was having the right to physically punish such persons at their discretion. Laws allowing for this were enacted by the planter class for the purpose of serving their own interest. In effect persons purchased for a lifetime of service were soon defined by law as chattel property.

Legally defined as property, slaves could be bought and sold to facilitate the economic interests of the emerging planter class. A planter confronted with an economic necessity question possessed the legal option to sell anyone to satisfy a debt. Thus, a planter was permitted to sell a twelve year old girl away from her family, without any legal constraints, if he chose to do so. From today's perspective that reality can readily be judged perverse. Recently Annette Gordon-Reed articulated a question not likely heard in the South of the antebellum era. She asked, "In what universe could the

humanity, family integrity, and honor of slave owners count for more than
the humanity, family integrity, and honor of the slaves?"

Looming as a most offensive external threat to the integrity of a slave
family was the possibility of a female member being raped. Having no
legal standing, slave women could not charge a man with rape. A white
man could, for all practical purposes, rape with legal immunity a black
woman who belonged to him. Slave women had no legal recourse. Their
testimony wasn't admissible in a court of law - a court where the judges
were obligated to enforce slave laws enacted by the slave owners themselves. Slave mothers did their best to shield teen age daughters from
attracting the attention of plantation owners, their young adult sons,
brothers, cousins, uncles, and for that matter the overseers as well. Obviously they were frequently less than successful in their endeavors to protect their young daughters.

After 1660 legislative measures were routinely and systematically initiated to sanction a pervasive slave code. The code gave the planter class its
needed permanent source of labor. Black people, held as slaves, were then
defined as chattel property which made them valuable assets. This is quite
different from the status of indentured servants who were never regarded as
a planter's personal property to do with as he saw fit. The new laws defining
one of African ancestry as a slave allowed white indentured servants to understand they were, essentially, exempt from the social disadvantages black
people had recently been burdened with. As Annette Gordon-Reed noted,
indentured servants were "encouraged to identify with their white masters while distancing themselves from the blacks with whom they worked."
Practical considerations, as well as legal ones, meant poor whites would
take "refuge in their whiteness and the dream that one day they, too, could
become slave owners." Implicit in whiteness was the freedom to acquire
property. The flip side was the societal understanding whites were never to
be regarded as property.

Students picked up on my statement indentured servants frequently
evaded their indenture obligations by running away. They understood
slaves didn't have the same chance of succeeding at evading their legally
sanctioned circumstance by running away. When white indentured servants fled to a distant new location, most likely a frontier region, these fugitives were not immediately seen as runaways but rather as just new persons
in the locale. If they seemed self sufficient, worked on some community

improvement undertakings, plus helped to fend off Indian raids, few were likely asked, "Are you a runaway indentured servant?"

As for escaping slavery by running away, the circumstances for blacks became quite different once slavery became institutionalized. Slavery based on race prompted an immediate suspicion every black person arriving in a new location was a fugitive slave. A challenge to a black person would occur immediately because it had become socially understood most blacks were owned by someone somewhere. This recently evolved societal understanding was convenient to whites in general and particularly to plantation owners. Virginia's colonial society, dominated by prospering white plantation owners, had set in place the burden of race.

Continuing on the topic of running away, I related the experience of John Punch. He was black and had run away in the company of two white indentured servants. A Virginia court record of 1639 specifically referred to John as "a negro." Another indication John was understood to be a slave, as opposed to being an indentured servant, is based on the punishment he received as compared with the two whites. The judge added an additional year to the service obligation the whites owed to their master. In John Punch's case there is no mention of an additional year being added to his term of service. This strongly suggests the court understood his legal obligation to be lifetime service to his master, as opposed to an indenture obligation of a specified number of years. Telling also, respecting punishment, the record indicates John was whipped whereas the two whites were apparently spared any physical punishment.

A rather cynical remark made by a white student, whose motive for taking the course I always wondered about, was "the white guys made a mistake by running away with John Punch - the black guy." However, his remark did help me to make the point a distinction based on race was observable at that early date, just twenty years after John Rolfe had first sent tobacco to England.

Approximately one hundred and twenty years later, after the French and Indian War ended (1763), slavery was more extensively rooted in the South than in the North. Agriculture in the North tended to be based on relatively smaller farmsteads growing a variety of crops as opposed to southern plantations growing a single exportable cash crop. At harvest time northern farmers were more likely to use hired hands, on a seasonal basis, not slaves. Then, shortly after independence during Washington's second term, Eli Whitney's invention of the cotton gin ensured the plantation system would become a permanent feature in sustaining the southern agricultural economy.

By the time Andrew Jackson left office in March of 1837, southerners were beginning to use the term "King Cotton." Later, when Lincoln was sworn into the presidency (1861), cotton's value was greater than all other American commodity exports combined. It accounted for the biggest flow of credits coming back into the United States. But, three decades before Jackson became president and Whitney's cotton gin was impacting the South's economy, many northern states had abolished slavery. So, from the time of the Missouri Compromise (1820) until Lincoln's election (1860), slavery loomed as the most controversial issue to be avoided because of its ominous potential to become calamitously divisive – a threat to national unity as expressed by the concept of a Union.

In the halls of Congress, during that forty year span, slavery was the proverbial elephant in the room most tried to ignore. For the sake of national unity there was a politically motivated understanding its presence was not to be acknowledged. Slavery was unquestionably the issue to be assiduously avoided at every political turn. To raise the issue was usually acknowledged by a majority to have the greatest potential for promulgating irreconcilable differences. However, readily observable were abolitionists, such as Frederick Douglass, doing their utmost to dramatically exhibit the elephant to the general public.

Every semester someone would eventually ask, "Why didn't Congress abolish slavery?" This question indicated their unfamiliarity with provisions in the Constitution. The wording and the spirit of the Declaration of Independence which held "all men are created equal" was soon constrained, glossed over if you will, by superseding principles placed in the Constitution of 1787. Ratification of the Constitution essentially placed property rights ahead of the noble but often elusive ideas associated with human rights as delineated in the Declaration of Independence.

Southern states asserted the principle of states' rights was of utmost importance within the context of a new government intending to promote a political identity known as the Union. Creating and sustaining a Union of the states expressed in terms of a national government capable of making laws for all states in that Union became the objective of those attending the Constitutional Convention of 1787. They placed a greater priority on working out governmental form and function details than allowing for philosophical discussions to bring into focus what might be required to enhance and sustain earlier major premises found in the Declaration of Independence - premises such as "all men are created equal."

After ratification of the Constitution of 1787, the common lot of people living north of the Mason and Dixon line didn't look closely at its provisions acknowledging "such persons" as property who belonged to others living mostly in the South. To secure ratification of the Constitution by southern states, the convention's northern delegates agreed to the inclusion of the dubious three-fifths clause as a provision, thus allowing southern states to count three-fifths of their slaves for representation purposes in the U.S. House of Representatives. This was astonishing! It allowed the South to maintain an advantage enabling it to ride high as the political fulcrum on all issues coming before Congress until 1850. Other measures placed in the Constitution, giving the South a pass on slavery, were accepted by northern delegates under threat by southern representatives to withdraw from further participation in the constitutional convention.

As for the students' question why didn't Congress abolish slavery? We must keep in mind the Constitution sanctioned slavery, albeit without mention of the word per se. So, after its ratification any resolution introduced to Congress calling for slavery's abolition would essentially be viewed as a radical challenge to the legitimacy of the Constitution, as well as to its greater purpose to sustain the viability of the Union. One compelling facet in defining patriotism was, for three generations, one's commitment to supporting the Union. Lincoln utilized this understanding of patriotism when he called for volunteers to redefine their *support* of the Union to then mean *defend* the Union. At the same time northern newspaper editors implied defending the Union was equivalent to sustaining the sanctity of the Constitution.

In America's second generation the dedicated abolitionist William Lloyd Garrison condemned what had transpired with the ratification of the Constitution. He called it a "compact with the devil" and once went so far as to publicly burn a copy of it. Garrison and Frederick Douglass claimed ratification of the Constitution was too great a price paid for national unity as expressed in the concept of a Union with slave holding southern states. For them it served only the interests of the few in that region while denying for many others, held in bondage, that which was postulated as their birth-right in the Declaration of Independence.

Down through the years, right into the late 1990s, when asking students if they ever heard of Frederick Douglass or William Lloyd Garrison usually only one or two out of thirty said they had heard of Garrison, none had ever learned about Douglass. As for my high school experience, many years earlier, it was similar to theirs because I never learned about those prominent abolitionists of the 19th Century either. Given that fact also reminds me slavery per se had never been addressed in any of my high school history classes at Frankford High School in Philadelphia during the 1950s.

During my thirty-two year teaching career (1967-1999) at S.U.N.Y.-Orange in Middletown, New York, it was readily apparent the only historical African-Americans my students ever learned about were Booker T. Washington and George Washington Carver. A few admitted to writing book reports about Booker T. Washington's *Up From Slavery*. Once, when one student mentioned Carver, she got a reaction from another who said, "Oh yeh, wasn't he the peanut guy?"

Washington's *Up From Slavery* is fluff compared with *The Souls of Black Folk* written by W.E.B.DuBois. But, of course, my students hadn't learned about DuBois, the towering African-American intellectual for over fifty years. But, not to be a hypocrite, I readily admit I had only become acquainted with DuBois, and his long career, shortly before I began teaching the African-American history course. It happened as a result of my delving into the origin and history of the National Association for the Advancement of Colored People (NAACP).

Though students didn't know about DuBois, or Marian Anderson either, by the mid 1990s they certainly knew of Denzel Washington. Black and white audiences alike enjoyed performances by this rising Hollywood star. As for me, I especially enjoyed the parts he played in *Glory* and *Malcolm X*. In 1990, Denzel Washington was nominated for an Oscar in the best supporting actor category for his role in *Glory*. This movie brought attention to the heroic all black 54th Infantry Regiment sponsored by Massachusetts during the Civil War.

In high school I do recall learning about genius inventors such as Thomas Edison and Alexander Graham Bell, as well as the Captains of Industry like Andrew Carnegie, John D. Rockefeller, and Henry Ford. But, I wasn't taught about black or white social reformers including those fighting for the rights of labor such as Eugene Debs or African-American A. Philip Randolph. There was never mention about courageous workers challenging Captains of Industry in struggles to unionize so they could make demands for living wages from the likes of anti-union Andrew Carnegie.

It wasn't until college that I first learned about Eugene Debs as a union organizer, presidential candidate in 1912, and opponent to America's entry into World War I. Enthused about Debs, I asked my mother if she ever heard of him. She excitedly told me about her father (my maternal grand-father) voting for him. Debs was the Socialist Party candidate in 1912. I guess it's genetic why I've voted for third party candidates for president in my lifetime.

Though he wouldn't indicate his position regarding support for So-cialist Party candidates too openly, certainly not as editor of the NAACP's publication *The Crisis*, none the less Dr. W.E.B. DuBois was very favor-ably disposed to the candidacy of the Socialist Party candidate Norman Thomas, who ran against Franklin Roosevelt in the 1930s. Later, in 1948, along with Paul Robeson, DuBois favored the Progressive Party candi-dacy of Henry Wallace who opposed the Democrat Harry Truman and Thomas Dewey the Republican. Presently the uninhibited African-Amer-ican intellectual Cornel West is very open about his democratic socialist inclinations.

Back to African-American labor leader A. Philip Randolph. He was re-sponsible for organizing the railroad porters' union. It was finally formally recognized after an eight year job action on October 1, 1935. This union represented men who wore red caps and helped with passengers' luggage, turned beds out in the Pullman sleeping cars, and were otherwise helpful in assisting travelers on long train trips. Less than six years later Randolph was very instrumental in getting President Franklin Roosevelt to create a Fair Employment Practice Commission (FEPC). This federal agency would challenge corporate discriminatory hiring practices in the 1940s.

Some students had learned of Helen Keller and how she had overcome her disabilities (she was blind and deaf), but none knew she was a social-ist. Neither did I until I was approaching my thirtieth birthday. Since they knew little about Helen Keller, I safely assumed they knew nothing about Ida B. Wells Barnett. Her mother was a slave, hence she was too. Born on a Mississippi plantation just months before Lincoln issued his Emancipation Proclamation, as she grew into adulthood she constantly challenged herself to obtain as much education as was available to her. Consequently, Ida Wells Barnett gained superb speaking and writing skills.

By the 1890s, Ida Wells Barnett was talking the talk and walking the walk in her opposition to Jim Crow laws and the practice of lynching which was occurring with alarming regularity across the South. Various newspapers began presenting her thoughts in the 1890s and she stayed engaged in writing on issues pertinent to African-Americans until her death in 1931. She excelled at being a journalist and social activists. As for an African-American woman currently vigorously engaging in activities to promote social justice, as was Ida Wells Barnett, I encourage readers to become acquainted with Alice Walker. She first gained national literary recognition with the publication of *The Color Purple* in 1982.

Many teaching college level history share my opinion high schools do a poor job teaching about people who challenged injustices sustained by the *status quo* in previous times. Figures from the past who played prominent roles in reform movements are often marginalized or deleted entirely from popular history. Popular history is essentially taught at the secondary level and tends to be oriented toward offending no one and frequently passes on the spin everything was fine with no one having any complaints in those bygone eras. So, those having complaints and who dared to question authority back then are often negatively viewed or receive minimal historical recognition. If recognized such persons are often labeled radical, subversive, or un-American.

Today the corporate media presents most critics of corporate sponsored national policies in an unfavorable light. This then sets in motion a process which popular history follows which is to ignore or defame the figure the media originally condemned as a radical. In this regard a person who immediately comes to mind is present day African-American intellectual Dr. Cornel West. He's been critical of the capitalist paradigm maintaining the status quo which allows for serious social ills to persist.

Will criticism Cornel West offered be relegated to obscurity because of popular history's orientation to eliminate beliefs and ideas considered negative in the past? Time will tell, but I suspect by the year 2050 students will learn very little about West. After all I was in high school just thirty years after Eugene Debs died and I never learned anything about him and what he courageously stood for. Cornel West will most likely share the same fate as Eugene Debs thanks to the status quo orientation of popular history. On the other hand, to my chagrin, George W. Bush's election to a second term, in 2004, will see popular history convey the notion he must have been a great leader, as popular history will ignore the dozens of books which factually presented information pertinent to closely examining his administration's lack of integrity because he condoned duplicity by his cabinet members.

Dr. Martin Luther King, Jr. is presently better known than Dr. Du-Bois. Yet, I wonder what will be known of King, of his entire message, in fifty years? Presently a process of neutralizing his message is underway. Those paying homage to him at public ceremonies now focus mostly on the civil rights issues of his time, but not those he began to address eighteen months prior to his assassination. In effect his written observations and those he spoke of regarding societal ills, systemic to capitalism, are already being glossed over and not likely referred to in future ceremonies celebrating his life. I seriously doubt his statement, "A nation that continues to spend more money on military defense than on programs of social uplift is approaching spiritual death," will resonate throughout the land each January in speeches commemorating his birthday.

Ask high school seniors today, in either suburban or inner city schools, what Dr. King or Muhammad Ali thought of the Vietnam War. They wont have a clue. And I wouldn't be surprised if what is taught in African-American history courses, at the historic black colleges, avoids or skims over the fact Frederick Douglass opposed the Mexican-American War. Courageous acts don't always involve wearing a uniform and carrying a weapon. Heavyweight boxing champion Muhammad Ali refused to put on a uniform to fight in Vietnam. He, like a few million other Americans, didn't believe the Vietnamese were interested or motivated to do harm to Americans. They had no capability to attack or invade American soil anywhere, such as Hawaii, but the United States invaded their country.

I've seen classified advertisements in bold print indicating a football coach position was available. However, regrettably near the bottom of the ad in much smaller print was the requirement the applicant should also be certified to teach social studies or history. Such advertisements accurately indicate what is considered more important as a value in American culture. Persons hired to coach football, and then incidentally to teach history, aren't likely to present historical figures involved in issues which at their core challenged the status quo of their time.

Many in my classes readily acknowledged learning something about Andrew Jackson. Most recalled he was the hero of the Battle of New Orleans, yet knew little else about him. Ah yes, we give much attention to military heroes, but scant attention is paid to social reformers. Jackson certainly wasn't a social reformer. Students didn't know he bought and sold slaves. Also, they were unaware he epitomized the frontier attitude of his time which held "the only good Indian is a dead Indian." Do today's students know Jackson imposed a forced exit of the Cherokee people out of their eastern ancestral homeland to the unwelcoming geography of Oklahoma in the 1830s?

Classes were usually surprised, perhaps I startled some, when I said, "Andrew Jackson doesn't deserve to be on the U.S. twenty dollar bill. A more deserving person whose likeness should appear on the bill is Frederick Douglass." More might agree with me if they became informed of his considerable achievements in view of the obstacles presented by slavery he had to overcome. Douglass made important contributions to America's social history in the area of analyzing its long history of racial attitudes and beliefs. Douglass was an intellectual giant compared with the intellectual pygmy Andrew Jackson.

One aspect of American culture is anti-intellectualism. Thus both Frederick Douglass and W.E.B.DuBois were for the most part ignored by an overwhelming majority of Americans in their respective times. Certainly a twofold handicap played a part in this. In addition to being intellectual they were African-Americans. In their particular eras it wasn't expected black men, and certainly not black women, should engage in rigorous social analysis.

Prior to the Civil War when an African-American such as present day Michael Dyson managed to get a book published, people with influence and authority wouldn't pay attention to it. Well, OK, some might give it a cursory read but not allow themselves to be impressed by ideas presented because black folks, after all, weren't believed to posses critical thinking skills. Most libraries, certainly southern ones, wouldn't buy books written by black authors. For the most part black authors had to depend on attracting attention to their works by word of mouth recommendations.

With respect to Douglass, DuBois and intellectuals in general, one thing rings true in American culture, the more you know the less you're listened to if it has little to do with selling something or making a profit.

Then too, of course, you're certain to be ignored if you're overly critical of how some do reap profits. This means Ida Tarbell's history of how John D. Rockefeller made his billions isn't likely to be required reading by students majoring in business administration. These days I wonder if history and journalism students become familiar with Tarbell's seminal work? Let's hope some of them do.

Looking back on our history, it seems various societal institutions are indifferent about the general public's historical amnesia of certain events – such as slavery and its ramifications. But, when popular historical narratives offer patriotic feel good versions of history, various societal institutions acknowledge and help to imbed those versions of history in the public's consciousness. When it comes to historical controversy our corporate sponsored media and other institutions generally go into the avoidance mode. They would rather the record of those who reaped enormous profits from buying and selling slaves or in this time accruing profits resembling plunder by those getting Pentagon contracts to go unexamined.

Actually the fact most students hadn't learned about Douglass or DuBois came as no surprise. Overall high school social studies generally presents a veneer of feel good facts for indoctrination purposes; basically it's popular history that's being taught. This means the United States is always presented as just, noble, and righteous. Those so believing are likely to have a bumper sticker on their SUV calling for God to "bless America" and chant "USA, USA, USA" at Olympic events with nearly the same fervor heard at late 1930s Nazi rallies.

If Dr. King were alive today I think he would ask God to help America – help America overcome its hypocrisy. The hypocrisy evident in a system giving billionaires incredible tax relief while dismissing proposals calling for raising the minimum wage, extending unemployment benefits, or providing non profit based universal health care.

Back in the 1840s, did American workers intent on shouting down Douglass and Garrison, for trying to expose the reality of slavery, understand to what extent cotton production interests controlled the government? No they didn't, and similarly today the average American has no clue regarding the influence and power the Corporatocracy has in determining public policy under the guise of democracy. Obviously slavery wasn't in place to promote the greatest good for the greatest numbers. Neither is our virtually unquestioned present economic system which rigorously promotes the needs of corporate enterprises ahead of any considerations regarding the human needs of the majority.

A question frequently posed in class was "who did the whipping" when slaves didn't do what was expected of them? To be sure there were many commands and rules to be obeyed on the plantation. (A most serious offense was to be absent from the plantation without the owner's permission.) I replied it depended on many factors one of which was the size of the plantation itself. A man who owned about one hundred and fifty acres wasn't likely to own more than three or four slaves. Such a small unit, typically the size of a northern farmstead, meant the owner often worked in the fields along side his slaves - especially when the cotton was ready to be picked. In such circumstances the master wasn't wealthy enough to employ an overseer. This meant he would have to punish a slave himself - usually in the form of a whipping.

What was an overseer? I expected this question every time I taught the course. Students were unfamiliar with the term. I explained he was sort of like a modern day foreman at a job site. If the size of the plantation was approximately two thousand acres, the owner probably needed twenty-five slaves to work his fields. This prompted an owner to hire an overseer because by himself he couldn't keep that number under a watchful eye. Overseers were usually unmarried men, sometimes from the North, but regardless of where they were from often had drinking problems.

Overseers were hired to supervise tasks assigned to the slaves and make sure they were completed. Physical punishment, usually a whipping, was imposed on slaves for not completing assigned tasks and for engaging in activity violating plantation rules. Hiring an overseer meant the plantation owner was relieved of the task of physically punishing his slaves. Physical punishment was bad enough, but think how horrendous it would be if the overseer had a sadistic streak to his personality.

On very large plantations a common practice was to divide the slave labor force into gangs having six to eight members per gang. (These gangs included women who labored in the fields side by side with men.) Close supervision of a gang was the responsibility of a slave known as a driver. Drivers were selected by the overseer and answered to him about getting various tasks done satisfactorily. Physical punishment of fellow slaves was also done by drivers. If a driver wasn't willing to comply with this requirement, he would be dismissed from the position.

Slaves serving as drivers on large plantations were themselves under the close supervision of a white overseer. The driver was expected to impose a strict work regimen on the slaves making up the gang he supervised. For complying with the overseer's orders, drivers were usually given some token privileges. Also, in many instances they could look forward to receiving a more frequent ration of what the others received only infrequently, such as eggs, a slab of bacon, cured tobacco, and sometimes coffee and sugar. I suspect some slaves reminded drivers, probably in indirect ways, that their small recompense was symbolically equivalent to the thirty pieces of silver paid to Judas for his having sold his soul also.

Plantations having roughly three to five thousand acres acres would likely be considered large. In the cotton belt there were many counties having two dozen or more plantations in the five thousand acres category. According to historian Annette Gordon-Reed, George Washington's will provided for the manumission of his 316 slaves. Such a number of slaves is indicative he also owned vast land holdings. Those with economic circumstances similar to Washington's would be held in high esteem by their neighbors and, hence, have great political influence at the county and state levels.

Keep in mind large plantation owners were, in any given southern county, the power structure. They were the movers and shakers who determined the direction political and social affairs took. They set the political agenda adhered to by the men they sent to state legislatures and the U.S. Congress to represent their interests - not those of poor whites and certainly not slaves. Such men in South Carolina were responsible for sending John C. Calhoun to Washington on a regular basis. Local public opinion on various issues was shaped by the views the plantation aristocracy held. So, naturally views that questioned the existing social order were never considered by those following the lead of the planter class.

One reason public education lagged behind in the South was because plantation owners didn't want their land holdings taxed to support public education. After all, they were wealthy enough to hire private tutors for their children. This was indicative of an unwillingness to do much for the benefit of poor whites. A student made the observation it's still that way today. She claimed the rich send their kids to private schools while asking public school boards to reduce taxes (their taxes) by cutting certain programs beneficial to poor minorities. "You know Congress takes care of banks and corporations before doing anything for us," another student added.

Having noted large plantation owners were the local power structure in the South of that bygone era, I would then ask, "What present groups are key in local power structures of this time?" Knowing about and understanding how local power structures functioned was a mystery to most students. It was something they never dealt with in high school social studies. One astute older student inquired, "You mean who has the most influence regarding positions city councils and mayors take – right?" Bingo! She had some understanding about how things really worked in local governance.

Some groups had more influence than others, I explained. At the top of the local power structure would likely be the Chamber of Commerce, local owners of small manufacturing enterprises, retail shop owners, restaurant owners, auto dealership owners, and apartment complex owners, to name a few. Many in the previous groups were also members of the local Rotary Club, the Lions Club, Kiwanis, and conservative veterans organizations. Most of these groups have access to elected public officials and are usually courteously well received. Religious leaders, such as Catholic Bishops and others with large congregations, get the attention of public officials as well.

These varied organizations, representing certain interests, play a role in what goes on an agenda for local officials to consider for determining public policy. After this mini civics lesson I would ask, "How many African-Americans participate in such influence groups?" One student's response was, "Well, very few or none are in the ones you mentioned, but sometimes local NAACP chapter officers participate." I replied, "Right, sometimes, usually to avert a crisis, but not likely on a regular basis."

As for poor whites in the antebellum South, they were predictably anxious about losing their white privilege. That deep seated fear motivated them to help sustain slavery and then the Jim Crow system after the Civil War. Until Roosevelt's New Deal of the 1930s, they never got government sponsored economic perks, but took satisfaction from being able to say, "I'm free, white, and twenty-one." I first heard that saying in the 1940s, but it was beyond my comprehension then. Basically it was a racial smugness comment implying superiority to black people. Now almost forgotten, I can't recall hearing it but once or twice after 1950 when I entered my teen years. However, I suspect that saying lingered into the 1960s among certain white southerners resisting the momentous changes occurring in that watershed decade.

Chapter 4

As indicated earlier, sentiments expressed in the Declaration of Independence regarding "inalienable" rights were drastically compromised with the ratification of the Constitution of 1787. The South's peculiar institution was acknowledged by wording in the new Constitution which sanctioned the legitimacy of slavery. This was accomplished by utilizing words and phrases carefully selected to avoid the necessity of specifically using the word slave or slavery to legitimize the practice. Thus slavery was sanctioned within the text of the Constitution and accepted as the law of the land with its ratification by the states.

Northern delegates to the constitutional convention had caved in to southern demands to accept their institutionalization of slavery, though many others in the North's population were not pleased with slavery's legitimization in the newly established republic. Opponents of slavery would frequently hark back to wording in the Declaration of Independence which was basically antithetical to slavery's existence.

One very early northern expression of opposition to slavery was in 1688. That year a resolution condemning slavery was passed by members of the Germantown Friends Meeting. (No longer at a distance from old Philadelphia, Germantown is now one of many neighborhoods within present city limits.) Also, an anti-slavery society had been founded in Pennsylvania by Benjamin Franklin and Dr. Benjamin Rush a year before the Declaration of Independence was signed. Upon arriving in Philadelphia from England, Thomas Paine's first widely recognized essay for the *Pennsylvania Magazine* was a condemnation of slavery.

Though Franklin opposed slavery Founding Fathers from the South, such as Thomas Jefferson and George Washington, owned considerable numbers of slaves and neither ever called for Congress to abolish slavery. This fact is usually glossed over or never mentioned at all in most junior and senior high social studies classes. After all, our Founding Fathers are supposed to be men of great unblemished virtue.

By the mid 1990s, information regarding the relationship Thomas Jefferson had with Sally Hemings, his slave, was becoming visible through the frayed curtain of the long maintained historical coverup. Their relationship epitomized one of many unsavory facets inherent to the reality of American slavery. Thomas Jefferson wasn't the only owner of a female slave of whom he could require sexual relations. However, for most white males in other circumstances demand would be a more accurate word than require.

Occasionally students, usually female, indicated awareness of Sally Hemings' circumstances. Some were familiar with Fawn Brodie's book first published in 1974. Brodie didn't get as detailed and specific regarding the Hemings and Jefferson relationship as did the later and more scholarly work by Annette Gordon-Reed. In 2008 she brought out a fascinating account of that relationship titled *The Hemingses of Monticello: An American Family*.

In addition to Pennsylvania, John Jay, diplomat and jurist, was president of the New York Society for Promoting the Manumission of Slaves. In 1786 he drew up a bill to prohibit the sale and removal from New York of people born as slaves in that state. As Governor of New York, he signed into law provisions for the gradual emancipation of slaves. As a Founding Father John Jay's writings suggest he was ahead of his times on the issue of slavery and racial equality. It seems he actually envisioned a biracial society based on complete equality. Not as strident on the issue of racial equality, Alexander Hamilton was also an early member of the same New York abolitionist group.

Abigail Adams expressed an anti-slavery opinion likely shared by many others in Massachusetts. In a letter to her husband John regarding slavery, when he was a delegate to the First Continental Congress, she said, "It allways (sic) appeared a most iniquitous Scheme to me – fight ourselfs (sic) for what we are daily robbing and plundering from those who have as good a right to freedom as we have." (The direct quotation indicates her misspellings of the words always and ourselves.) Elsewhere in New England, as the first state admitted to the Union by act of Congress, Vermont's state constitution prohibited slavery.

Generally students revealed little knowledge of the abolitionist movement. This came as no surprise. After all I didn't know of the Germantown Friends Meeting calling for the abolition of slavery, so I couldn't expect students to have learned about New Jersey's John Woolman either. In the mid eighteenth century he published a pamphlet condemning slavery which was first circulated in Burlington County. We can safely assume among the first to read his tract were members of the Moorestown, Mt. Holly, and Mt. Laurel Friends meetings since Woolman himself was a Quaker.

Since an overwhelming majority of students, as well as myself, had never heard of Fredrick Douglass in our respective early education experiences, then certainly we had never heard of David Walker. He was another early outspoken African-American critical of slavery. He authored a pamphlet calling for the immediate abolition of slavery. He may as well have been a relief pitcher for Kansas City for all my students knew of him. But my obligation, since I learned of him first, was to bring his stirring written *Appeal* to their attention. He published it at his own expense.

Like William Lloyd Garrison, David Walker lived in Boston and his hard hitting *Appeal* came out almost two years before Garrison brought out his first edition of the *Liberator*. There's reason to believe Garrison read Walker's tract calling for immediate emancipation. It's interesting to note Garrison then came out for immediate emancipation also in his first edition of the *Liberator*. Prior to its publication, Garrison was known to favor gradual emancipation, viewed as more tolerable to more prominent citizens having reservations regarding slavery. Did David Walker's *Appeal* move Garrison to embrace immediate emancipation? Ah, yes, history is replete with such questions pertaining to causation and who was influenced by whom, etc., etc.

One provision in the Constitution allowed southern states a grace period of twenty years whereby Congress couldn't prohibit the importation of slaves. The Constitution specified the year 1808 as when Congress would be permitted to legislate a prohibition of the practice. At the time of the Constitutional Convention, James Madison had wanted the practice of importing slaves abolished immediately. He viewed the constitutional provision allowing for a twenty year grace period as "dishonorable to the American character."

How many tenth generation wealthy southerners today would readily admit their ancestors owned slaves? How many southerners today would admit their grandparents used the "N" word back in the 1940s and '50s on a routine daily basis? More recently, I'll assume the "N" word was brazenly used on June 7, 1998, near Jasper, Texas by three white supremacists using a pickup truck to drag James Byrd Jr. to his death. So, is Madison's term "dishonorable to the American character" an appropriate assessment regarding the instances just mentioned? Keep in mind James Madison himself owned slaves to labor on his huge plantation.

By act of Congress in late 1807, a bill was passed and signed into law by President Thomas Jefferson which prohibited the further importation of persons for the purpose of slavery as of January 1, 1808. It's well known the law was usually flaunted over the next fifty years. That fact was acknowledged early on by James Madison during his presidency (1809-1817). Also, regarding the illegal importation of slaves after 1808, I turn to historian John Hope Franklin. (His *From Slavery To Freedom* was my required textbook for many years.) Franklin observed, "from the beginning, the law went unenforced. The long unprotected coast, the certain markets, and the prospects of huge profits were too much for the American merchants and they yielded to the temptation...." One student responded to Franklin's observation with one of his own. He said violating an unenforceable law for impressive monetary gain "was as American as apple pie." He reminded the class of how mobsters made money hand over fist during the prohibition era of the 1920s.

There were economic ramifications inherent in the prohibition against importing slaves after 1808. Some students wondered if it would impact in any way those already held in bondage? My answer was "yes it would." Cutting off the steady supply, by prohibiting further importation, brought the dynamics of supply and demand to an acute awareness on the part of the slave holding class. It quickly became understood any decline in the slave population would make those living more valuable as property. To make up for the possible loss of "such persons," a greater emphasis on domestic increase became the order of the day. Thus, young women, especially those in their late teens, became greatly prized. A woman's potential to bear many children became a high priority consideration for those contemplating the purchase of a female. This was a tacitly acknowledged solution to keep the supply of slaves equal to the growing demand.

The non-importation law came at roughly the same time Whitney's cotton gin was making a dramatic impact on the economy across the South. Would the new law in any way curtail the insistent geographical spread of the cotton culture? The decade following the importation ban saw a westward movement known as 'Bama fever. (It had nothing to do with college football.) Back then 'Bama fever had to do with the westward movement surge to establish new plantations for cotton production purposes. This phenomenon was being played out in the region to the west of Georgia.

Native American claims to this region (Alabama and parts of Mississippi) had to be ignored. Andrew Jackson played a major role in defeating Choctaw, Chickasaw, and Creek warriors trying to defend their lands against white settler encroachments. At the Battle of Horseshoe Bend, Jackson didn't halt the slaughter of many non-combatant natives, including those trying to surrender. In many respects the mentality of Andrew Jackson and his men was evident again in 1890 when American troops slaughtered Lakota native peoples at Wounded Knee near Pine Ridge in South Dakota.

I'll always remember a very bright student's response to what Jackson permitted. He said, "Can you believe? Native peoples ruthlessly killed so enslaved people could be brought in to work their lands and help make privileged whites filthy rich. And no one, then or now, really gives it a second thought." I couldn't resist facetiously responding, "but God is on our side, so the popular assumption would naturally be she approves of events like this." Some in the class snickered and guffawed briefly because I referred to God as she.

As for those participating in the Alabama land rush, not only did they believe in race based slavery but also held the generally widespread belief "the only good Indian is a dead Indian." That, of course, is another racist belief. It doesn't stop there. In the first decade of the 21st Century a similar attitude, worded slightly differently, was evident in most U. S. military operations in Iraq. Many violations of Iraqi human dignity were perpetrated by American troops again acting on racist assumptions, such as "the only good hajji (Muslim) is a dead hajji." When young men and women sign up for the military are they aware part of their training (indoctrination) is to dehumanize the enemy and it's often compatible with racist thinking? So, big surprise? It seems present circumstances, activities and beliefs, are in many ways linked to what transpired in our past. It's difficult to escape the past. I just wish certain bygone beliefs, mythical and otherwise, were more critically examined as a matter of course in public endeavors to educate many uninformed Americans.

With significantly more cotton plantations being established in Alabama and Mississippi the need for slaves there was outpacing numbers available in those locations. At roughly the same time Maryland and Virginia were in a cycle of having a surplus of slaves. By 1830, both states became places from which slaves could be supplied to the newer regions in the southwest. The phrase "I've been sold down the river," refers to what happened to many slaves born in Virginia at a time when their labor was no longer in demand there. Sold by their owners, right off the very plantations where they were born and had family, the traders took them to Parkersburg on the Ohio River. There they were herded onto paddle wheel steamboats ultimately destined for New Orleans.

The trip south on the Mississippi River was usually punctuated with stops at St.Louis, Memphis, and Vicksburg, where endeavors to sell them were successful. Across the river from Memphis lay Arkansas where new plantations were being chopped out of resistant underbrush. Conditions on the newer plantations in Arkansas and Louisiana were much harsher than what had previously been experienced in the long ago settled areas of Virginia. For many such forcibly transplanted persons there was a strong nostalgic yearning - expressed in the lyrics "Carry Me Back To Old Virginia."

Students basically understood the concept of supply and demand. If the slave population didn't keep pace with the demand for plantation labor, then the value of those in that population was certain to rise. During the thirty years prior to the Civil War, the believed need for slave labor was greater than the numbers available to meet the demand. Hence, the price for slaves continued upward. Healthy young men, between the ages of eighteen and thirty, to work as field hands were at a premium in Arkansas, Louisiana, and Texas. But it was also likely a pregnant eighteen year old would sell for more than such men.

Slave traders engaged in a wretched business. The large plantation owners actually thought of themselves as a better class compared with those engaging in the business of buying and selling slaves. Slave traders were looked down upon by the large plantation aristocracy. Socially they didn't interact with plantation society. A plantation owner's wife wouldn't think of inviting the wife of a slave trader to tea at her columned mansion. Which way do you slice hypocrisy?

Hearing a rumor one might be sold was often likely to prompt a slave to run away. Those living in Georgia, not far from Florida, might choose to go south as opposed to those living in Kentucky or Virginia who would head north to Ohio or Pennsylvania. However, Florida was not a safe haven for runaway slaves once it became a part of the United States in 1819. While Florida was under Spanish authority the Seminoles were living their traditional lifestyle in peace, since the very small population of Spanish subjects had not been encroaching on their lands. That relative peace was shattered once Florida became part of the United States and white American settlers started pouring in.

Since Seminoles had never been effectively subjugated by Spanish authority, they were not inclined to allow it to happen under American authority either. What irritated American authorities most, however, was the Seminole acceptance of runaway slaves into their communities as equals. The South wanted to prevent Florida from becoming a safe refuge for runaway slaves. The stage was set for major confrontations which played out as the sporadic Seminole Wars of the 1830s and into the 1840s.

Runaway slaves fought side by side with resisting Seminoles in their refusal to be captured and returned to slavery. At the same time Seminoles were refusing treaty terms, it was evident the South was prepared to support military activity there for however long it took to ensure control of the institution of slavery. The South was determined Florida wouldn't continue as a safe haven for runaway slaves. Thus, the Seminoles had to be subjugated and forced to agree to return runaway slaves. Spanish authorities in Florida probably heard of the cruelties of American slavery from some runaways. However, there's little written record of their stories being officially documented. And, slave stories weren't likely passed on to the small Spanish population living there.

Chapter 5

As for the experience of fleeing to the North, it was replete with obstacles. Some known in advance, but many others were unanticipated encounters along the way. Upon reaching a free state, runaways might luckily come upon abolitionists who aided them with food and clothing and listened attentively to their personal stories. Assisting runaways at the Underground station in Philadelphia was African-American William Still – a major figure in Philadelphia's abolitionist circles.

The runaway who gained prominence in the North was Frederick Douglass. Upon safe arrival in New Bedford, Massachusetts, in the fall of 1838, he obtained a job working in a ship yard. This job was his first experience where he didn't have to turn his wages over to a white person. In roughly a year's time Douglass teamed with militant abolitionist William Lloyd Garrison who saw in Douglass a legitimate source to relate first hand the evils of slavery. Thus Garrison took Douglass on speaking tours that were, for the most part, well received. Garrison acted as a mentor of sorts to Douglass for roughly seven years.

Douglass was impressive on stage and fearlessly inveighed against slavery. His oratory skills developed rapidly and in many instances were soon superior to others then on the abolitionist lecture circuit. After three years or so his command of English and his demeanor of complete confidence led some to doubt the authenticity of his life's story. In his biography of

Douglass, Philip Foner quoted a white abolitionist colleague advising him to "have a little of the plantation speech than not; it is not best that you seem too learned." That just wasn't going to happen. Frederick Douglass wasn't about to alter his influential demeanor for the sake of supposed authenticity. Probably troubling to certain white abolitionists also was the fact Douglass would not hold back and suffer fools gladly.

In May of 1845, *The Narrative of the Life of Frederick Douglass* came off the press. As his biographer Foner noted it was a "small volume of 125 pages selling for fifty cents, with an introduction by Garrison and [Wendell] Phillips." By January, 1848, "eleven thousand copies had been published in this country" and it "was translated into French and German." One New England reviewer praised it as "the most thrilling work which the American press ever issued – and the most important. If it does not open the eyes of this people, they must be petrified into eternal sleep." By today's publishing standards Douglass' autobiography would command literary prize recognition. I don't suppose the few public libraries in the South contributed to its impressive sales success. Douglass traveled to England and then to Ireland and Scotland on an extended speaking tour. In these places he was incredibly well received.

Shortly after his return from abroad, Douglass joined with Garrison on an extended speaking tour to Ohio where he was enthusiastically received in many towns. However, by tour's end, he and Garrison had a misunderstanding which became an obstacle to continuing a cooperative relationship. Douglass then moved to Rochester, New York and began publishing his own abolitionist newspaper which he named *The North Star*. His first edition was published on December 3, 1847.

Frequently I asked students if they knew the significance of Douglass' title for his paper – why *The North Star*? Once in a while a response indicated an understanding of how the North Star served as a celestial compass for keeping slaves on a proper course north to freedom. Knowledge of this was expressed by a female student familiar with the legendary song *Follow The Drinking Gourd*. As for myself, I had never heard of that song and its veiled meaning until I saw a televised Black History Month program on a PBS station in the early 1970s.

Speaking of PBS television, and television in general, whatever happened to those televised Black History month programs presented with predictable regularity every February in the 1970s and into the '80s? By the

mid 1990s, the networks seemed to have slacked off from previous commitments to show those kinds of programs. Back in the 1970s, Bill Cosby
narrated a very informative series pertinent to African-American history.
However, a majority of professional media reviewers would probably agree
the most compelling Black History program in the 1970s was the adapta-
tion for television of Alex Haley's book titled *Roots*. It ran four nights with
multiple hour segments. A valuable program, it served as a springboard
sparking interest among black and white Americans in various aspects of
African-American history. I certainly recall hearing white folks talking to
each other about this program. The tremendous audience viewing rating
went well beyond what the sponsoring network expected. Haley's book was
also on the *New York Times* best seller list for a considerable length of time.

Back to the North Star, it significantly assisted runaways. When one
fled, hoping to arrive at some point in the North, basic geographical details
regarding an appropriate route were not usually clearly or precisely known.
Slave lore merges with reality regarding the usefulness of the North Star.
Following it kept one heading in a northerly direction. Fleeing from a Kentucky, Tennessee, or Virginia plantation was a challenge not to be taken
lightly. There were serious obstacles encountered along the often randomly
taken routes. One major difficulty encountered by a runaway was the un-
predictability of the weather. Implicit in this problem was how would a
runaway get a location fix from the North Star on a rainy or very cloudy
night? It certainly wouldn't be of much use under such conditions.

Those fleeing the plantation knew the first twenty-four hours were
most critical for a successful escape. Timing, when to leave, was of utmost
importance in planning to flee from the plantation. Why? I would ask my
classes. Most understood the longer your absence went undiscovered the
better your chance to put some significant distance between yourself and
the overseer supervised posse. For one thing a person's scent is strongest in
the first twenty-four hours. After that lapse of time, it became difficult for
bloodhounds to detect the scent for staying in meaningful pursuit. Wading
in a creek for a half mile or so was a tactic that made it difficult for bloodhounds to stay on your scent and follow it.

Pertaining to the question who was likely to run away, the plantation owners had definite ideas. Their thinking was similar to what became
known as racial profiling in the 1990s. African-Americans, living in the late
20th Century, knew of the racial profiling syndrome called driving while

black - DWB. (That syndrome, fully understood by African-Americans, enabled black comedians to perform some hilarious routines, to mixed audiences, based on DWB experiences.) Regarding slaves running away, there was an assumed basic profile defining who was most likely to flee the plantation. It was generally acknowledged young men, without romantic attachments, in their late teens or twenties were likely prospects to flee - especially after a punishment believed uncalled for or severely harsh had occurred.

Often plantation owners wanted to pair off young females and males to deter the male from running away. It was supposed a young man was less likely to abandon a young woman with whom he had recently "jumped the broomstick." Many owners believed a married man was less likely to desert his wife, yet they could at their own convenience sell a man or woman away from their respective spouse. Does hypocrisy immediately come to mind in this regard?

Sometimes slaves living in the quarters knew of their owner's gambling debts. This circumstance could spell disaster for familial relationships. He could sell off anyone he chose to satisfy his debts. In some instances a creditor could go to court and get an order requiring the sale of a person to satisfy an outstanding debt. Though slaves were recognized as married by those in the quarters with them, such a relationship was never considered legal where slavery was sanctioned by the white man's law.

What other circumstances played a part in whether one would or wouldn't reach a northern safe haven? This question usually initiated a lively classroom discussion which rolled into another question: why would a slave take such risks to run away? In the midst of addressing the two questions, there was often someone, not necessarily participating in the discussions, who would ask, "Is this running away business going to be on the next exam?" My answer was usually vague but with the caveat the questions would make good test questions. In fact I enjoyed posing such questions on my exams. They enabled me to learn which students listened carefully, had good insight, and allowed themselves to get into creative role playing by identifying with the situations runaways encountered and how they dealt with them. (These days I wouldn't be surprised if a student said running away without a GPS would be unthinkable.)

Anyway here's a partial list students offered pertaining to the hazards of running away. One hazard was actually the dilemma of who to trust.

There were instances when a slave planning to flee told another slave only to learn the master or overseer had been informed of the plan. Down through the years the consensus of opinion held it was unwise to tell anyone about fleeing. Another likely issue was the challenge of finding food along the way. Away from the plantation three or four days saw the necessity of finding nourishment become a major priority. Passing a farm growing vegetables not needing to be cooked was good fortune, as was coming upon a tree with low hanging ripe fruit. Only at night might one sneak close to a farm house, hoping not to wake a dog, to draw water from a well. But one still had to be very careful because many counties had armed whites acting as "patrollers" scouring local roads at night hoping to capture a runaway.

Runaways knew the safest time to travel was at night, especially when a bright full moon was useful. Movement during the day along a road with open fields on each side was dangerous. One was vulnerable to be seen by white folks when taking such a route. One had to be careful to avoid population clusters. Coming suddenly upon such a circumstance was dangerous. Appearing out of nowhere, unknown to local whites, meant an immediate challenge regarding identity would be forthcoming. Poor whites were quick to challenge an unfamiliar black person. They were always eager to apprehend a runaway for the sake of collecting a reward which was predictably offered.

Slaves wisely chose not to attempt to cross deep fast flowing creeks or rivers, since most didn't know how to swim. Some slaves who did know how to swim were wise not to let on they could. The fact he could swim, and no one knew he could, enabled Solomon Northrup to plan an escape route his owner didn't expect him to take. There were instances when runaways on the Kentucky side of the Ohio River fortuitously came upon a row boat lying on the river's bank. Runaways were lucky indeed if oars were with the boat. It would then be "borrowed" and easily found on the Ohio side of the river if its owner also made the crossing somehow.

Also noted, respecting the Ohio River, every four or five years a severe cold snap in winter would see temperatures drop dramatically below freezing for a considerable length of time causing the river to solidly freeze over. This occurrence probably made slave owners on the Kentucky side rather anxious. Mother nature thus enabled slaves to simply walk on the ice over to Ohio and continue on their journey for their freedom. However, one was advised not to linger in Cincinnati. It was well known slave catcher agents were numerous in that city.

Owners posted advertisements in various newspapers indicating the reward amounts being offered for capture of their runaways. An outstanding condemnation of slavery, published six years before the narrative of Frederick Douglass, was by Theodore D. Weld. In his *Slavery As It Is, the Testimony of a Thousand Witnesses*, Weld presented the dozens of advertisements for runaway slaves he found in southern newspapers. One feature dramatically revealed by Weld was the southern indifference to breaking up families on the auction block. This book observably increased the intensity of the abolitionist movement.

Did George Washington or Thomas Jefferson break up families with auction block sales? I haven't seen information that would conclusively answer that question. I once read Washington never advertised for his runaways in northern newspapers. Evidently the first president was public relations conscious. He didn't want to remind northerners he owned slaves. In his study *Early American Views on Negro Slavery"* (1934), Matthew T. Mellon of Columbia University said of Washington, "From his birth to his death he was a slaveholder and controlled three hundred and seventeen slaves at the time of his death." Of course this fact isn't something most Americans would now bother to think about. And if they did they wouldn't likely be critical. After all he's our nation's first super hero. So he must be held above reproach - right?

In its first year of publication the majority of the initial subscribers to Garrison's *Liberator* were free blacks living in the North. Also of interest is the fact copies of David Walker's *Appeal* were found in the possession of some blacks living in the South. It would be considered contraband and a severe punishment would be the consequence of its discovery. In his *Appeal,* Walker saw a time, in the not too distant future, when people held in bondage would be inspired to undertake drastic measures to overthrow slavery. Plainly speaking he saw a time when all hell would break loose with blood spilled in the process of the struggle for winning freedom.

Like other informed free blacks living in the North, Walker was aware of what the Haitians had undertaken to win their freedom from their French masters shortly after the beginning of the 19th Century. Within two years of Walker's conjectures about drastic measures, Nat Turner of Virginia lead an uprising (1831) where 50 whites were slain. Though Turner himself was most likely unaware of Walker's prediction about a future bloody slave uprising, it's not difficult to see Turner's revolt as a manifestation of what David Walker envisioned in the not too distant future.

The South saw abolitionist literature as incendiary. Sharing this view was Andrew Jackson, seventh President of the United States. Like Washington and Jefferson, Jackson was a slave holder and encouraged the practice by southern U.S. Postmasters of censoring incoming mail if suspected of having abolitionist content. Such mail was prohibited from delivery by most local southern postmasters. I'm unaware how many northern Congressmen challenged Andrew Jackson for allowing that. Then again, perhaps they were unaware Jackson approved of the practice. As for subsequent Presidents approving of measures Congress is unaware of at a given time, I don't think it unreasonable to assume it happens more often than the public is likely to quickly learn about.

While Jackson was President the House of Representatives passed a resolution prohibiting abolitionist petitions from being read on the floor of the House. The measure became known as the Gag Rule. It was in effect almost thirteen years, though predictably challenged by former President John Quincy Adams, then representing his Massachusetts home district in the House of Representatives. Had Jackson objected it wouldn't have any binding effect on House procedures since the Constitution states the House shall make its own rules. However, it was Jackson's option to go on record, if he chose to do so, and condemn the practice of restricting freedom of speech. He kept silent on the Gag Rule practice to the best of my knowledge. I don't think Jackson cared for freedom of speech in this instance anymore than he cared for non-white people's rights. Should there be something of a similar implication today, I would expect the American Civil Liberties Union to publicize their freedom of speech advocacy for all aspects of public deliberative discourse.

When it came to depictions of slavery, during the cotton boom era, the South made concerted efforts to sway northern public opinion toward a favorable view of the institution. Southern writers of the antebellum period followed what amounted to a party line defense of it. As abolitionist contentions became more widely circulated, the South became even more vehement in offering pro slavery polemics. A common theme, offered by these writers, advanced the belief southern slavery was actually benign. They claimed it was a period of tutelage serving a charitable purpose, namely to engender the uplift of the slaves. I don't get it. How was time spent in slavery, where all endeavors for promoting education and literacy were prohibited, going to promote an appreciation for and adoption of a supposedly higher level of civilization which people of northwestern European ancestry claimed they possessed?

Also, keep in mind the rather self serving religious views of white southerners at this time. These views were too frequently tailored to be compatible with the prevalent secular justification of slavery. One notion, accepted in some quarters regarding uplift, held the widespread adoption of Christianity by slaves was evidence a first step toward their enlightenment was underway. Most white southerners wouldn't want to consider the possibility the institutionalization of slavery might be understood as a giant step away from the basic precepts of Christianity. Obviously New Testament precepts were discomforting and generally ignored by most slave holders, so they had a tendency to refer to Old Testament scripture to get biblical justification for slavery.

In contrast, on the other hand, a close examination of abolitionism reveals a strong emphasis on Christ's admonitions found in his *Sermon On The Mount* and the Golden Rule. Yes, a student once asked, "What's the Golden Rule?" Another quickly informed him, "Do unto others as you would have done to you." The first student then responded, "how could slavery be justified by people calling themselves Christians if they're supposed to practice the Golden Rule?" My reply to his question was most religions try to bring out the best in people, but materialism brings out the worst in them. For most Americans chasing the almighty dollar supersedes abiding by the tenets of their respective religious affiliations. Slavery was the key factor enabling plantation owners to chase the almighty dollar. Obviously southern clergy didn't utilize the Golden Rule as a litmus test for validation of their parishioners commitment to the tenets of Christianity.

Upon asking students what they knew about the Missouri Compromise (1820), only a few indicated some understanding of its profound meaning. The question of statehood for Missouri pivoted on the issue of the extension of slavery. Should slavery be allowed to cross the Mississippi River into Missouri which was within the domain of Jefferson's Louisiana Purchase? This question came roaring onto the national stage in 1819. Earlier in the 1780s, slavery had been prohibited in the territory north of the Ohio River. Now some northerners were interested in establishing another river, namely the Mississippi, as a boundary to contain slavery as the Ohio River had been so designated by the terms of the Northwest Territory Ordnance of 1787.

Southerners quickly pointed to the fact Louisiana had become a state in 1812, and by its geography slavery had already been permitted west of the Mississippi River. Plus, at that time, Congress had not forbidden transporting slaves across the Mississippi into what was then recognized as the Missouri Territory. Proof slaves were already there was supported by the 1810 census indicating 3,000 slaves had been counted. By 1820, the census figures revealed the number had risen to 10,000 slaves in the Missouri Territory. If Congress ruled slavery illegal in Missouri, would the slaves already there then become immediately free? What would then be done to compensate those who had earlier taken slaves into Missouri Territory as their property? Clearly the status of what Missouri should be, slave or free, was the most vexing question Congress had to address since its decision to declare war on Britain in 1812.

The Missouri statehood controversy was "like a fire bell in the night" alarming former president Thomas Jefferson. It appeared like a dagger ready to puncture the fabric of agreeable consensus politics much in evidence during James Monroe's presidency. Monroe was reelected for a second term in 1820. He would have received a unanimous vote in the Electoral College, but a New England elector gave his vote to John Quincy Adams to preserve the honor of electoral college unanimity for George Washington. Before he left office Monroe's presidency had been termed the Era of Good Feelings. The Monroe years, with the exception of the heated Missouri statehood debate, gave the appearance all was well in all regions of the country. However, that era was followed by almost two generations of politicians reluctantly willing to compromise, only after heated wrangling when the ominous issue of slavery couldn't be ignored because of perceived dire consequences.

In 1819, when Missouri petitioned for statehood, the balance in the U.S. Senate was equal. There were eleven free states and eleven slave states represented. If Missouri came into the Union as a slave state the balance of power in that chamber would tip in favor of the South. Southerners saw a Senate majority as necessary to offset the North's representation advantage in the House of Representatives. In that chamber the North's influence was on the rise because its population growth was outstripping that of the

South. Certain proposals initiated in the House began to put the South on the defensive. Southern representatives became agitated when protective tariff proposals or those pertaining to slavery, such as the Tallmadge Amendment, were brought to the House floor and supported by northern Congressmen.

Who in the world was James Tallmadge you ask - as did many students. In my thirty-two year college teaching career, I can't recall any student having knowledge of Congressman James Tallmadge. During the deliberations on the Missouri statehood bill, this rather obscure New York Congressman introduced a resolution that would later gain him mention in various academic publications. The Missouri enabling bill would have passed in the House sooner if Tallmadge hadn't introduced a rider which provoked southern outcries of objection. His proposal prohibited the further introduction of slaves into Missouri. Of more significance, it had a gradual emancipation provision which could have served as a model for the rest of the country to eliminate slavery in a moderately paced fashion. Specifically, Tallmadge's proposal called for all slaves born in Missouri to become free on their twenty-fifth birthday. His amendment to the Missouri statehood bill passed in the House with considerable northern support, but was rejected overwhelmingly in the Senate just before the Fifteenth Congress adjourned.

Whenever the slavocracy perceived a threat to the status quo, it was met by their stiff opposition in the Senate. Not to be overlooked, there were usually a few northern senators the South could count on to vote for what was basically southern interests. Such northern senators justified siding with southern interests in the name of preserving national unity. To avoid sectional discord they sidestepped the issue of the immorality of slavery and supported the southern position slavery was a local question of no concern to the U.S. Congress. In this vein the South frequently invoked the 9th and 10th Amendments to the Bill of Rights.

On the issue of slavery the votes of certain northern senators served southern plantation owners interests as well as those who owned textile mills in northern locations such as Lawrence, Massachusetts. When the Senate thwarted House resolutions on issues pertaining to slavery, in such instances the Senate did indeed act as a check – an implied function of that body envisioned by delegates at the Constitutional Convention of 1787.

By the 1840s, when certain northern senators displayed presidential ambitions, like James Buchanan, Stephen Douglas, and Daniel Webster, they knew the South would carefully scrutinize their voting records. If their records showed support for anything the South opposed, they wouldn't get the necessary southern delegate votes in their party's nominating convention. "Doughface" was the term abolitionists began to use to describe northern politicians who seemed to do the South's bidding. (Dough is malleable and can be shaped into a desired form or shape.) The term was frequently used to describe James Buchanan of Pennsylvania.

Until I took a college level history course I never knew Abraham Lincoln had voiced objection to the war with Mexico. The question he raised in that regard, which he posed to President Polk, was likely a factor explaining his defeat in his bid for reelection to the House of Representatives. How about that? One term Abe thought his political career was finished as he headed back to Springfield, Illinois. The successful outcomes of wars always get top billing in broadly presented historical narratives as opposed to voices challenging the reasons given for engaging in those wars. Given that premise, I understand why students and I never heard of Abraham Lincoln's misgivings regarding the war with Mexico.

When explaining various wars the United States has engaged in, America's mainstream societal institutions actively engage in creating a popular historical narrative intended to have posterity believe all Americans, at any given time, supported the wars the United States became involved in. You have to dig deep to find who the dissenters were regarding disapproval of America's many wars. Too frequently the corporate media sets a tone to shape the public discourse toward acceptance of policies resulting in acts of U. S. aggression. One intellectual who recently exposed the complicity of the corporate media in promoting a go to war political agenda was Norman Solomon. He noted when debate on the issue of waging war became burdened with frantic flag waving, jingoistic rhetoric, and slogans to induce repression of reason, the media was likely to pass on the spin those calling for military action generated. Solomon convincingly made his case explaining the 2003 attack on Iraq in *War Made Easy (2005)* – also available in DVD.

Does history honestly acknowledge those opposing war at a given time? Will it give an unbiased presentation of the reasons opponents articulated in their opposition to wars the United States has engaged in? Why did Frederick Douglass, Abraham Lincoln, and Henry David Thoreau oppose the United States engaging in war against Mexico? Yes, their anti-slavery views were at bottom the reason they opposed that war. They believed a likely outcome would be the acquisition of territory from Mexico, territory the South would want open to slavery. Both Douglass and Thoreau were correct in their conjecture. As mentioned previously about Lincoln and the Mexican-American War, I didn't learn until I was in college that he opposed it for practically the same reason as Douglass and Thoreau.

In mentioning those 19th Century opponents to war, I wonder how many literature majors today know the best read American author of that century, Mark Twain, opposed the United States war against Spain in 1898? I wonder also to what extent future historians will acknowledge the opponents of this era's wars. Will students in the future learn why Daniel and Philip Berrigan, Ramsey Clark, Chris Hedges, Camilo Mejia, Cindy Sheehan, Cornel West, or Howard Zinn, to name a few, opposed the wars of these times? Will they be acknowledged forty years from now in historical narratives? Also, will tomorrow's historians be willing to make some waves as historian Howard Zinn did in his *History of the American People?* Zinn did present those who dissented, those who popular history has traditionally ignored. By 2005, Zinn's work had sold more copies than any other single volume pertaining to American history. Hopefully future historians will not be intimidated by political considerations brought to bear in subtle and not too subtle ways.

More than one occupant of the White House has acted deviously when it came to war - getting the United States involved in one. It's doubtful any students I taught ever had a previous teacher confront them with the question, "Who was the most devious president of the 19th Century regarding the issue of war?" This question seemed to surprise, or was it stun, most students. Really? Well, yes, after all they had been taught by their football coach history teachers, you know the myth cheerleaders, all our former presidents were noble and righteous men - like Thomas Jefferson and Indian killer Andrew Jackson. And, how dare Tom Paine, depicted negatively by Federalists newspapers, pen harsh criticism to George Washington? I got the sense, year in and out, my students never had teachers who posed such a question pertaining to presidential deviousness. I would like to think some had, but I believe that's very doubtful.

In the 1950s, when I was in high school, no teacher would dare pose a question regarding presidential duplicity. After all, at that time the anti-communist hysteria generated by the tactics of Senator Joe McCarthy had teachers fearing they might be called a communist sympathizer if they delved into issues popular history conveniently overlooked. I remember one student rather facetiously responding, "So, O K, who was the war monger president?" My reply was a question too. "Did you ever learn anything about James Knox Polk and how the war with Mexico started?"

As for the Mexican-American War Frederick Douglass joined with many prominent New Englanders who also opposed "Mr. Polk's War." He was dismayed, but not surprised, by the fact only fourteen members of the House of Representatives opposed the declaration of war against Mexico. Most of them came to be known as Conscience Whigs and Douglass applauded their opposition votes. Within that dissenting group was Joshua Giddings of Ohio. He courageously stood by the convictions of his conscience by voting against the declaration of war and then, additionally, refused to vote for appropriations to supply the invading troops. Professor Howard Zinn presented Giddings' objection: "In the murder of Mexicans upon their own soil, or in robbing them of their country, I can take no part.... The guilt of these crimes must rest on others – I will not participate in them." Now if only we had more members of Congress like Giddings, perhaps then the Military Industrial Complex functioning within the Corporatocracy might be curtailed somewhat in its influence.

With the onset of the Mexican-American War, the American Anti-Slavery Society said its outcome would be conspicuously related to the further extension of slavery "throughout the vast territory of Mexico." That prospect foretold the reintroduction of slavery into areas where it had been abolished by the Mexican government a generation earlier. The 36:30 latitude line, established in the Missouri Compromise of 1820, prohibited slavery in territories north of that east to west demarcation of the Louisiana Purchase. However, territory likely to be acquired from Mexico would be south of the 36:30 latitude and had never been a part of the Louisiana Purchase. Since no prohibitions were in place south of the Louisiana Purchase territory, the South believed territory taken from Mexico should be open to slavery.

Generally the South assumed slavery was not at issue pertaining to the Mexican Cession and so it was believed ratification of the peace treaty, the Treaty of Guadalupe-Hidalgo, would move forward in a timely manner. This was evident by the fact the Senate's preliminary approval was by a vote of 38 to 14. By the terms in the treaty Mexico was to receive fifteen million dollars - a token compensation for the transfer of a vast territorial acquisition to the United States. (These days many athletes make more money with multi year contracts.) But, the treaty's final approval hinged on the House of Representatives authorizing the appropriation of that sum, since the Constitution requires all revenue and spending bills to originate in that chamber. Shortly before the topic of appropriating funds began, David Wilmot, a Democrat from Pennsylvania, introduced his proviso. It called for the appropriations bill to stipulate a prohibition against slavery in the territory taken from Mexico.

In various Congressional deliberations down through the years, slavery was the hot button issue most preferred to avoid. Now, however, Wilmot's proviso became the elephant in the room everyone saw clearly. Calling for the prohibition of slavery in the former Mexican territory caused Wilmot's proposal to generate a high decibel furor in the House and was cause for great alarm throughout the South. When mentioning Wilmot's proviso, historians often overlook the fact he was not an advocate of full citizenship rights for African-Americans.

The issue of slavery was once again, as in the Missouri statehood debate, front and center in the legislative discourse of the nation. With Wilmot's proviso attached, the House passed the appropriations bill only to have the Senate refuse to act. In heated debate in the Senate, South Carolina's John C. Calhoun repeatedly offered resolutions stipulating that Congress had no constitutional authority to exclude slavery from any territory.

Wilmot got support from some members of his own party, a portion of whom shortly became known as Free Soil Democrats. Former Democratic president Martin Van Buren also supported Wilmot's proviso. Of no surprise, Conscience Whigs also rallied to support it as well. However, this coalition's support wasn't sustained and his proviso ultimately excluded in the final appropriations bill which facilitated Senate ratification of the treaty with Mexico.

Shortly after Wilmot's proviso became a dead letter, Popular Sovereignty surfaced in the debate on slavery. This idea was accepted by many northern and border states Democrats as a compromise for accommodation with the slave holding South. Essentially Popular Sovereignty meant Congress had no say as to where slavery would be permitted. Senator Calhoun of South Carolina referred to it as "squatter sovereignty." Popular

Sovereignty put the decision of slavery's status in the hands of the people who actually settled in a region about to apply for statehood. This idea was consistent with what the South had maintained for many decades, namely that slavery was a local question of no concern to the federal government's authority. It implied Congress had overstepped its authority when it enacted the Missouri Compromise.

Popular Sovereignty allowed the South to back off for a while from heated expressions acknowledging secession as their ultimate recourse to measures negating states' rights. It also served rather briefly to blunt free soil expressions associated with Wilmot's resolution. It appealed to moderates who wanted to regard slavery, henceforth, as a non-issue. If a Congressional majority agreed to accept the principle of Popular Sovereignty, then slavery would no longer be a topic for deliberations at the national level.

When the Treaty of Guadalupe-Hidalgo was signed by Polk, in February of 1848, Congress then assumed its responsibility for organizing civil governments in the lands wrested from Mexico. Surprise, the question of where slavery would or wouldn't be allowed was again being debated in the halls of Congress. Regarding the Mexican cession the principle of Popular Sovereignty had not kept slavery out of the national legislative discourse after all. Slavery was still an issue lingering barely beneath the surface in the national political arena.

As for the presidential election of 1848, many conscience Whigs acquiesced to their party's nomination of General Zachary Taylor, a war hero. One wonders if those Whigs saw the irony of nominating a man who owned a southern plantation and slaves who worked it. I suppose winning and claiming political spoils was more urgent to those Whigs than commitment to the moral high ground. Classes often commented at this point about how politics rarely rewarded participants to hold the moral high ground. At this juncture I usually offered my understanding of the term "politics as usual."

Politics as usual? Students would ask what I meant by that. O K - here's what I mean. Reform ideas are abandoned when they [the politicians] don't perceive anything advantageous to their political careers to be gained by clinging to them. Compromising is usually associated with cooperating with others. Cooperation is regarded in a positive light. Those who compromise rarely see themselves as hypocrites. You know, those who go along get along - get along with continuing their careers.

Inherent in politics, part of the game, is the understanding by those actively participating that political rewards are their due for cooperating. Rewards most desired are those furthering political careers or having the potential to enlarge bank accounts. Hypocrisy reigns in politics you say? But of course it does. Politicians are actually honest when they acknowledge engaging in political wheeling and dealing. Their engaging thus means pleasing some and disappointing others. Always in the mix is the careful calculation to please those who can give you a bigger reward than those who you disappoint. Sometimes a student responded to this with a statement like, "Hey, Mr. Reiss you're so cynical about everything." To this I might respond, "Tell me something I shouldn't be cynical about. Did you say Richard Nixon's Vietnam peace plan?" This response usually got some laughter, but by the 1990's I had to offer specifics regarding Nixon's career of carefully calculated political opportunism.

Admittedly not all conscience Whigs were hypocrites. Some supported the candidacy of former president Martin Van Buren running at the top of the Free Soil party ticket. This resulted in Van Buren taking votes away from the Democratic candidate Lewis Cass in New York state. So, Zachary Taylor, "Old Rough and Ready," won in New York. The hero of the Mexican-American War, General Taylor, thus became the second Whig to win the presidency. He was the last Whig to accomplish that feat. He stayed quiet on certain outstanding issues, especially slavery. As a slave holder himself he seemed reluctant to offer an opinion on that subject.

It seems when one of the political parties, usually the conservative one, doesn't want to address pressing controversial issues they nominate a military hero. Do political party movers and shakers do this because they assume voters will give a hero a pass on discussing difficult issues - such as slavery? When the public is in a hero worship mode, do advisers believe voters wont expect their candidate to get down and dirty addressing controversial issues?

The irony of 1848 is the candidate of the third party, which had major reservations about slavery, enabled the slave holding general to win the election. A close examination of certain presidential elections reveals third party candidates have affected outcomes which wouldn't have occurred had they not participated in those elections. Third party candidates have played the spoiler role for two incumbents in the 20th Century. In the mid 1990s, before I retired, I frequently commented on the election of 1992. Third party candidate Ross Perot greatly impacted that presidential election in the same manner Martin Van Buren had in 1848. Perot took critical votes away from incumbent President George H.W. Bush, thus ensuring the presidency went to Democratic candidate William Jefferson Clinton. Bill Clinton owes much to Ross Perot for participating in the election of 1992.

In one of my classes, not the African-American course, a student was absolutely certain Ross Perot would win the election. I told him he probably would get close to 20% of the popular vote and spoil things for the Republican George H.W. Bush seeking a second term. After the election I was rather proud of my accurate political prognosis. Later, in my African-American classes, I reminded students Bill Clinton got more votes from African-Americans than the combined support that quarter gave to the two other candidates. In addition to owing much to Ross Perot, Bill Clinton owed much to the African-American community for supporting his candidacy.

So, back to the mid 19th century and the issues which emerged after the Mexican - American War. Just as that war ended a gold rush to California had occurred. Within two years the population there had grown to exceed the required number of persons needed to petition for statehood. Californians did just that. And, they wanted to enter the Union as a free state. So, disputations regarding slavery were again heard and seemed more heated than ever before.

California's petition to enter the Union as a free state was one of the issues ultimately resolved by the Compromise of 1850. There were other issues having to be dealt with and resolved as well. A bone that stuck in the throat of northern sensibilities was the practice of buying and selling slaves in Washington - the nation's capital! Once the Gag Rule had been revoked petitions calling for the prohibition of that practice were coming to the floor of the House with a frequency that dismayed southern Congressmen.

Another issue was the South's demand for a stronger fugitive slave law. Alarmed and outraged by the success of the Underground Railroad whisking an ever growing number of slaves out of the South each year, the South adamantly called for a new rigorous fugitive slave law – one putting all fugitives on notice they were not safe though living in a northern state. Kentucky's Henry Clay, architect of the Missouri Compromise, was hopeful these hotly debated issues could be resolved by compromise as had been done in 1820. Supportive of Clay's efforts to facilitate compromise were other senate luminaries such as Daniel Webster, Lewis Cass, and Stephen Douglas - all northerners.

President Zachary Taylor seemed pleased California petitioned to be admitted as a free state as were various abolitionists in the North. And, he indicated he didn't want slavery extended into the territories acquired from Mexico, but he was opposed to Congress acting to exclude it. His other views, regarding compromise measures being debated, seemed unclear. His Vice President Millard Fillmore presided over the Senate and witnessed the wrangling involved in trying to strike a compromise. Some believed Taylor might resort to using the veto if he saw fit. Also, it was thought Senators Clay, Cass, and Webster wouldn't be able to muster enough support to override a Taylor veto.

Henry Clay played the part of ringmaster in the Senate's deliberations on resolutions which the North might favor and the South disavow and vice versa. Finally, in July the five bills specified within the context of a compromise, known ultimately as the Omnibus Act of 1850, were about to be placed before President Taylor. Then, totally unexpected, Taylor died on July 9, 1850. In less than ten years it was the second time a president didn't live to again become a private citizen. At this juncture, year in and out, I learned some students thought Lincoln was the first president to die in office and John Kennedy the second.

Chapter 6

On July 10, 1850 Millard Fillmore was sworn in as thirteenth president of the United States. He appreciated Henry Clay's laborious effort to achieve compromise and indicated his willingness to sign its five component bills into law. Three of the five legislative proposals were of consequence regarding the institution of slavery. With the admission of California as a free state, the North gained a sixteen free states to fifteen slave states advantage in the U.S. Senate. Also most likely, California's representatives to the House would have free soil inclinations. The political balance of power was thus significantly tipped away from advantages long held by the South for many decades. Secondly, the sale of slaves was prohibited in the nation's capital, and thirdly, most controversial in the North, a very compelling strict fugitive slave law was passed.

Senator Daniel Webster of Massachusetts had added his signature to the bill that became the Fugitive Slave Law of 1850. His popularity plummeted in his home state as a result. Under the law's provisions anyone escaping from slavery was vulnerable to be captured and returned to the South regardless of how long they resided in a free state. Of those living in the North to whom the law was applicable, Frederick Douglass said they, like himself, would "die rather than be returned into slavery." Fully expected also was the denunciation of the compromise by William Lloyd Garrison who called it a "hollow bargain for the North."

As a consequence of the Fugitive Slave Law (1850), Canada became the ultimate safe haven for runaways from slavery. There are various estimates regarding how many fled to Canada from 1850 to 1861. One figure I recall claimed about seven thousand five hundred fled, yet another figure indicated perhaps twice that number at fifteen thousand. (Fifteen thousand is a significant number considering the population of Philadelphia at the time of the Constitutional Convention was roughly twenty-three thousand.) A student asked if I had ever been to Canada and if so had I seen black persons living there? My answer was in the affirmative to both questions.

In the early 1990s, during a summer break, my then wife and I visited Nova Scotia. While checking out an historical site, we encountered a docent who happened to be black. She did a superb job explaining the site's historical significance. After she finished her usual presentation, she seemed to read my mind and went on to explain how blacks came to be in Nova Scotia. I learned they were taken there by the British navy, a few times before the Battle of Yorktown and then again shortly before the Treaty of Paris officially ended the war. I knew slaves had been freed by the British, but until she mentioned it I hadn't given much thought as to where the British took them. They were free in Nova Scotia, as the British who took them there had promised. She estimated the number taken from the American South to Nova Scotia at four thousand, but also indicated documentation was sketchy regarding that number.

Students learned I had discovered Lord Dunmore's "Proclamation" while in the process of preparing to teach the course in 1969. Dunmore promised slaves freedom in return for assisting the British forces opposing the army authorized by the Second Continental Congress. The British made good on their promise to take the former slaves to a place where they would be free. So there were already some blacks living in certain parts of Canada, especially Nova Scotia, long before the Fugitive Slave Law of 1850 went into effect. After that date those who had arrived earlier were joined by those fleeing in the 1850s.

Abolitionists viewed the provisions of the 1850 Fugitive Slave Law with horror. It stipulated anyone apprehended wasn't allowed to testify before the special commission on their own behalf as to their identity. If a slave owner's agent testified the runaway was five foot ten, weighed approximately one hundred and sixty pounds, and was about thirty years old, then anyone fitting this description might be apprehended under the law.

The federal commissioner had arbitrary authority as to who could speak up to indicate a mistake in identity had occurred. Only white persons were permitted to testify. Since African-Americans were most likely to live in an alley or street amongst themselves, they weren't likely to have an ongoing acquaintance or friendship with white persons. Hence, it was unlikely a white person would be involved in a proceeding on behalf of a person charged with being a fugitive slave.

The injustice of how the law worked made the agent the beneficiary. He was capable of getting a reward for returning South with any black person who fit the description he gave to the federal commissioner. Another flaw favored the commissioner himself. If he allowed the person charged with being a runaway to go free, he was paid five dollars. If he ruled a person a fugitive slave and ordered their return South, he was paid ten dollars for such person. After describing this procedure, I would ask my class, "what would the American Civil Liberties Union (ACLU) think of that law?"

That question led to another topic because in the span of my thirty-two year teaching career there were usually only five or six students per semester (out of numbers averaging 120) having knowledge of the American Civil Liberties Union and thus able to respond in a relevant way. Because community colleges have a marginally diverse socio-economic spectrum there was always the possibility some students knew about the ACLU. But why hadn't more students heard about the ACLU? In all fairness, I have to acknowledge my growing up in a blue collar family meant I never heard of the American Civil Liberties Union either. Therefore community college students sharing similar circumstances as mine, and they tended to be the majority, weren't likely to know about the ACLU either.

First generation college students of blue collar backgrounds are usually ignorant about organizations such as the American Civil Liberties Union, Amnesty International, Planned Parenthood, the Sierra Club, the War Resisters' League, and Veterans For Peace. Most, however, are aware there are non Christian Americans such as Jews and Muslims, but have no knowledge of Unitarian Universalism. Many are more likely to have heard of the American Legion, the National Rifle Association and, in rural areas, the Future Farmers of America. An overwhelming majority of students, even those Catholic, had never heard of the *Catholic Worker* newspaper, let alone such periodicals as *Harpers Magazine*, *The Nation*, or *The Progressive*. It wasn't until I was a junior in college that I began to learn of such organizations and publications. So, in addition to working class whites, who else isn't likely to have heard of the previously mentioned organizations and publications? I believe sociologists, black and white alike, would say young African-Americans and Hispanic Americans, especially those dropping out of inner city schools and not going to college.

My classes learned of the ACLU's purpose, that it was steadfastly committed to upholding the integrity of our Constitution's Bill of Rights. One time, after I made this pitch for the ACLU, a student asked if I was a member. Upon my reply, "of course," he expressed an enthusiastic approval by saying "right on brother!" I was pleased to have his enthusiastic approval. I reminded the class that in 1988, George H.W. Bush, the Republican candidate, demeaned the ACLU. He implied it was some kind of subversive organization in which Michael Dukakis, his Democratic opponent, held membership.

Once when discussing the provisions of the Fugitive Slave Law, at the time O. J. Simpson was being tried for murder, a student commented, "Even Johnnie Cochran wouldn't be able to help a suspected fugitive in those circumstances." (Cochran was a celebrity African-American lawyer at the time.) My response was, "How come you know about Johnnie Cochran but not the ACLU?" He then asked if I watched the televised O. J. Simpson trial. I replied, "just off and on." Others in the class, especially the black students, knew about Johnnie Cochran defending former football star O. J. Simpson accused of murdering his ex-wife Nicole and her male companion Ronald Goldman. Actually their knowing about Johnnie Cochran came as no surprise. After all, the O. J. Simpson trial was destined to go down as "the trial" of the 1990s, just as the Sacco and Vanzetti trial became known as "the trial" of the 1920s decade.

Now as for the Fugitive Slave Law of 1850, the *North Star's* editorial content conveyed Frederick Douglass' outrage regarding it. He urged all black men to defend themselves from government sponsored kidnappers. In his biography of Douglass, Philip S. Foner quotes him saying, "Every slave hunter who meets a bloody death in his infernal business, is an argument in favor of the manhood of our race." Implied here is when a slave has an opportunity to become free and resists attempts to deny it, then he is acting manly and thus becomes equal to whites – will earn their respect and gain self respect as well. One can't earn respect by cowering and cringing in submission. The prevalent cultural norm of the time regarding masculine identity is summed up by the admonition to any insulted or wronged male to "take a stand – fight like a man!" For Douglass surrendering one's freedom without a fight was indicative of not truly behaving as a man should.

In some ways that notion of "fight like a man" reminds me of statements embodying the philosophy of Malcolm X. But, then too, that philosophy isn't restricted to advice given by an indignant African-American spokesperson. It was epitomized also by the likes of John Wayne. In the 1940s, '50s, and into the 1960s, Wayne had hero status among white folks because he epitomized the idea of what a "real man" should be like. The movies John Wayne appeared in were very popular. As I see it Frederick Douglass, as well as Malcolm X, would abhor any stereotype depictions showing black men fearfully cringing in submission to white authority. I'll also assume Douglass would have been pleased by the account indicating Nat Turner didn't cringe in fear at the time of his capture and kept a valiant composure during the time leading up to his execution.

Less than a year after passage of the Fugitive Slave Law, the citizens of Boston learned first hand of its consequences. In February of 1851, an ex-slave named Shadrach, working as a waiter, was apprehended. Taken into custody, he was incarcerated in Boston's Courthouse. The authorities underestimated the resolve of his black friends to assist him. Realizing he wasn't being guarded conscientiously, they took advantage of that circumstance and helped him to escape. A few months later a teenager named Thomas Sims was taken into custody. With the example of Shadrach's escape in mind, the authorities made young Sims' confinement virtually escape proof. Sims, in chains and in the custody of U.S. Marshal Charles Devens, was escorted down State Street to the Long Wharf. There he was placed on a boat destined for Savannah, Georgia. Upon arrival there, he was whipped for public show. The entire episode caused Marshall Devens to suffer remorse. To alleviate guilt for the part he played, within the year Devens bought Sims his freedom for the sum of eighteen hundred dollars. (In 2010 that amount would be approximately forty thousand dollars.)

Like Dr. Martin Luther King, Jr., Frederick Douglass kept little of the money he earned from speaking engagements. Douglass used such income to assist those fleeing slavery via the Underground Railroad. One of its many routes came through Rochester and frequently made a stop at his house. In the winter he paid to outfit the fugitives with warmer clothing and shoes, supplied food provisions, and purchased tickets for passage to extreme northern New York locations close to the Canadian border. As for the Fugitive Slave Law, Douglass saw it as the shame of the entire country not just the South.

In his *A People's History of the United States*, Howard Zinn presented selections from various speeches Frederick Douglass gave from Ohio to Massachusetts in the turbulent years after the Mexican-American War. In these speeches Douglass frequently made reference to the fact black communities in the North recognized the first of August as a very special day – one to be celebrated! On that date in 1833, slavery in the British West Indies Islands was officially abolished. At approximately the same time the British navy began to intercept slave ships, in violation of American law, headed to southern American ports. The British justified their actions by asserting the slavers were engaging in piracy. The American navy was supposed to be taking the same action against slavers, but the British navy was doing a better job at striking this blow against slavery.

A student exclaimed, "Wow! The English abolished slavery thirty years before Lincoln's Emancipation Proclamation – right?" I concurred and saw an opening provided by his statement. "On what other issue have the British been ahead of us?" To my surprise and delight a student quickly responded, "That's easy, they have publicly funded health care for everyone." There it was, a critical issue from the past put into perspective of an analogy with a current critical issue. I loved it when this happened. It was the spontaneous teachable moment, so very rewarding to anyone giving it their all in the classroom.

Frequent references to August 1st can be found in Black publications such as *The North Star*. A number of African-Americans, including Frederick Douglass, deemed that date more worthy of celebration than the Fourth of July. As for the significance of the Fourth of July to African-Americas, Frederick Douglass saw the inherent hypocrisy in its celebration. In a speech he made on the Fourth of July in 1852, Howard Zinn presented his righteous indignation: "What to the American slave is your Fourth of July? To him your celebration is a sham; your boasted liberty an unholy license; your national greatness swelling vanity ...for revolting barbarity and shameless hypocrisy, America reigns without a rival...." This statement by Douglass certainly wouldn't find a majority in the white community approving of it today. I would guess Douglass was mindful of who his audience was at the time he made that statement. Were Douglass alive today I think he would be as aware now as he was then that the American public generally exhibits an intolerance of any criticism assailing popular self congratulatory myths.

Douglass also understood how myths of America's popular culture assisted slaveholders in their ongoing efforts to discredit any criticism of the status quo. As for myths of this time, trotted out by politicians trying to capitalize on the ignorance and bigotry of voters, here are five that readily come to mind: (1) Democrats are weak on defense, (2) the United States only goes to war if attacked first, (3) our troops never commit war crimes, (4) no one goes to bed hungry in America, (5) corporations are always near bankruptcy because of union contracts.

Ever notice the tactics defenders of the status quo often use to deflect criticism? Back in Douglass' time I guess slaveholders would quickly point to other places where slavery also existed, but under much harsher conditions. In accepting such convoluted thinking a slave should give up wanting his or her freedom because their master's punishments weren't as cruel or harsh as those given on the plantation down the road. That response is, at bottom, basically the lesser of two evils syndrome. It offers no remedy to a serious inequity. Persons using such dubious logic are basically recognizing the wrong in question, but are doing a political slip slide away from going on record supporting a measure to right the wrong.

The yes but syndrome often plays a part in our choice of candidates. It's seen within the context of our political discourse. Essentially the lesser of two evils choice is embodied in the "yes but" syndrome. You know what I mean - "yes but" this or that candidate is still preferable to so and so. Are we expected to understand the lesser of two evils is somehow a recommendation proving one so perceived ultimately has integrity? The reality I see is most Americans simply have their fingers crossed after a presidential election and are just hopeful the lesser is *somewhat* more truthful and worthy than the defeated opponent. Is one a fanatic for demanding a politician's truthfulness not be qualified in terms of being the lesser of two evils?

What can be said about those compromising with the evil of slavery, such as many of the Founding Fathers? What does their compromising tell us about their character, their integrity, of politicians in general? It seems character and integrity, as understood by most politicians, are relative concepts. At bottom politicians never bite the hand that feeds them. If pleasing the special interests of the Military Industrial Complex for the purpose of receiving huge campaign contributions, so be it. Noble ideas and principles, articulated by the likes of Martin Luther King, Jr. be damned, if such principles become obstacles to being elected.

One of Jefferson's written opinions acknowledged the evil of slavery, the inherent dilemma it posed to society. He observed, "... we have a wolf by the ears." So, yes, Jefferson talked the talk in his Declaration of Independence, but we know he failed to walk the walk. Yet he and other Founding Fathers are usually referred to as men of high minded principles aren't they? Former slave Frederick Douglass was always walking the walk. As for me, I hold in higher esteem those who vigorously opposed slavery, like John Brown, Frederick Douglass, and Thomas Paine as opposed to the presidents who owned slaves.

In 1972, a University of Notre Dame professor named A. J. Beitzinger referred to John Brown and William Lloyd Garrison as fanatics in his textbook *A History of American Political Thought.* Would he also judge Harriet Tubman and others involved in the Underground Railroad as fanatics? I also wonder what Professor Beitzinger might have thought about Muhammad Ali for refusing to fight in the immoral Vietnam War? (Ali took his stand five years before Beitzinger's book was published.) It seems American opinion fluctuates with regard to whom the term fanatic is applied. One political persuasion sees a fanatic while another sees an idealist taking a principled stand. But, as I see it, a principled stand is rarely evident in the lesser of two evils equation.

Frederick Douglass was on to the fact southerners who owned slaves generated certain myths to justify the propriety of slavery's existence. How about the myth of the happy go lucky slave without a care in the world? Oh, that meant an abolitionist would be way out of line if making reference to the suicide rate amongst slaves. Oh, sure, everyone was content, so why would slaves take their own lives? Reminds me of why would any of our troops take their own lives while serving in Afghanistan or Iraq – both military interventions defined by most elected officials as just causes. And, predictably, the mainstream media won't elaborate on those suicides because the notion they served in a just cause might come under scrutiny if greater attention to the causation of those suicides is presented.

During the 1960s scholars started to meaningfully investigate conditions on plantations. However, they seemed to overlook the phenomenon of suicide in the slave quarters. Maybe I missed material having to do with that topic, but I can't recall reading anything about it. Actually, I imagine plantation owners being reluctant to record such instances and not inclined to talk about it with other slave owners, hence not much recorded about it. Also, they were disinclined to talk about a slave or slaves running away and avoiding being retaken. Even if planters did talk about their slaves committing suicide, would they contemplate anything about causation? I seriously doubt they would fault their own treatment as a factor explaining why a slave committed suicide. It's sort of like present day politicians acknowledging terrorists hate us, but they don't want to consider reasons why that's so. That would be risky, too likely to be at odds with popular myth that we, as Americans, are so likeable as a people. A politician calling a spade a spade is always at risk of suddenly becoming unpopular. And, as we know popularity, not the moral high ground, is the name of the game in American politics.

In his early presentations Frederick Douglass followed the Garrison orientation calling for neither recognition or participation in the workings of the government. In the 1830s Garrison called for the North to break away from the South. He objected to the union with slave holding states. You may recall Garrison had on one occasion burned a copy of the Constitution which he considered a compact with the devil. The Garrisonians stayed aloof from the political process which they believed was morally corrupt for sanctioning slavery. They were displeased with Douglass when he broke away from their orientation by endorsing the Free Soil Party ticket in 1848.

Consequently Frederick Douglass examined and assessed various legal and political documents having to do with slavery. His new found interest in the potential for certain actions, within the framework of the Constitution, meant he had rethought the Garrisonian point of view calling for staying detached from the political process. Though Garrison certainly wanted to abolish slavery, it seems he refused to believe it could happen by engaging in the national political process. Douglass, on the other hand, had come to the conclusion there was potential within the national governmental process capable of challenging the legitimacy of slavery. He realized it all came down to getting elected politicians to vote your interest. They would do that when they realized your view was shared by those whose votes they counted on to win elections.

Though Franklin Pierce, the Democratic Governor of New Hampshire, didn't actively seek his party's endorsement for the presidency in 1852, he was viewed favorably by southern delegates because of his strong commitment to the Fugitive Slave Act. Southerners were also impressed because he had defeated a free soil Democrat in obtaining his party's nomination. A dark horse, Pierce was nominated by his party on the forty-ninth ballot. His running mate was William R. King of Alabama who died of tuberculosis barely six weeks after being sworn in as vice president. Opposing Pierce as the the Whig candidate was General Winfield Scott, the other Mexican-American war hero.

In 1852 both presidential candidates attempted to stay away from discussing slavery – perceived as nothing to be gained by doing so. Basically they wanted the Compromise of 1850 to hold, believing it sustained the political middle ground – thought to be where most voters placed themselves at that time. Carrying the South ensured victory to Pierce. He placed southerners in his cabinet, naming Jefferson Davis as his Secretary of War. Like Buchanan, Cass, and Clay, he was committed to keeping things from getting out of hand by compromising whenever possible. But, his opponents viewed Pierce's inclination to compromise as always favoring the South. Most egregious to northern opponents was his wholehearted support of the Kansas-Nebraska Act.

President Pierce probably didn't expect the Kansas-Nebraska Act to rupture the political tranquility supposedly secured by the passage of the Compromise of 1850. Popular Sovereignty was again invoked as an organizing principle for the region in question. Previously, you will recall, it had been offered for organizing the territory acquired from Mexico. However, applying the principle of Popular Sovereignty to a region where Congress, a generation earlier, had prohibited slavery quickly aroused the wrath of abolitionists and others opposing slavery's expansion.

Slavery was not permitted north of latitude 36'30" by the terms of the Missouri Compromise of 1820. In the north a generation had grown up believing the region in question was off limits in perpetuity with no possibility of slavery ever being permitted there. Possible is key here because Popular Sovereignty allowed for the possibility slavery might be allowed if the settlers of the region in question voted to permit it. The South didn't object to Popular Sovereignty because essentially it was an acknowledgment of sorts that slavery was a local question, a principle the South had always argued was substantiated by the Constitution's 9th and 10th Amendments.

President Pierce signed the the Kansas-Nebraska bill into law with the belief it was a significant administration accomplishment. In the North disapproval of the new law was practically instantaneous. Massachusetts' Senator Charles Sumner denounced it as a "swindle." Other northern senators, such as New York's William Seward and Ohio's Salmon Chase, vehemently inveighed against it. By his own admission Senator Stephen Douglas, the sponsor of the Kansas-Nebraska bill, said his trip by train to Illinois was illuminated at night "by the flames of [his] burning effigy."

An additional episode indicating growing anti-slavery sentiment was the public's indignation to the apprehension of Anthony Burns in Boston thanks to the Fugitive Slave Law. A thousand troops were mustered to ensure crowd control. Hundreds booed and screamed along the route he was taken to be placed on board a ship bound for the South. On that infamous day church bells tolled and many buildings were seen draped in black. The federal measure taken against Burns was critically reported in many newspapers across the North. Seething reaction to his treatment indicated previously viewed radical abolitionist convictions had transformed into an opinion of widespread consensus which acknowledged the injustice of slavery. Because of the Anthony Burns affair the Fugitive Slave Law was rendered of little consequence for further meaningful enforcement in New England.

By the mid 1850s, public opinion in the North, especially in New England and certain other regions, such as northern Ohio and Michigan, was perceptively shifting away from indifference to slavery. One indication of this was the surprisingly well received response to the publication of Harriet Beecher Stowe's story *Uncle Tom' Cabin*. It sold ten thousand copies in less than two weeks and within the year three hundred thousand copies were purchased. This was a very positive sign for abolition. More than at any other time people now seemed willing to contemplate a story focusing on the pernicious evil of American slavery.

An American Heritage History referred to this American literary endeavor as the most significant work of the 19th century in view of its impact. "*Uncle Tom's Cabin* was like a burning glass, focusing and bringing to white heat the whole emotional issue of slavery. For all its literary flaws, *Uncle Tom's Cabin* became one of the three or four books besides the Bible that have helped determine the destinies of mankind." Some students said they heard of it in high school, others said they hadn't. Over the years when

I asked if anyone had actually read it, the overwhelming answer was no. Then, usually, without skipping a beat, I would be asked if I had read it. I had to admit my answer was also no.

After admitting I hadn't read *Uncle Tom's Cabin*, I quickly commented I had read *The Autobiography of Malcolm X.*. One student's response was, "That's cool, now how many whites do you think have done that?" Since I had also read W.E.B. DuBois, *The Soul of Black Folk,* I said a few more had probably read Malcolm than had read DuBois. But, to put it into perspective, I said we had approximately one hundred faculty and I doubted any had ever read either book. To go further with the perspective thing, I said out of a crowd of five thousand whites you might get six or seven who could honestly say they've read Malcolm X, but none were likely to have read DuBois' *The Soul of Black Folk.* The student who said I was cool, responded by saying whites saw Malcolm as "a bad nigger – one who won't take poopy from nobody." He continued, "next to Malcolm X, Martin Luther King is looking better all the time to whites." I agreed. Malcolm's demeanor and rhetoric wasn't likely to bring him a Nobel Peace Prize.

As a consequence of reviewing the 1850s decade and its impact on shaping the direction America would take regarding slavery, my classes and I would sometimes get into broader discussions regarding events in other decades. We assessed those that also seemingly changed the course of history. But as for the 1850s, wow, what a decade! It began with the passage of the Compromise of 1850, featuring the immediately despised Fugitive Slave Law. Then came the Kansas-Nebraska Act, which gave rise to Bleeding Kansas, and at roughly the same time *Uncle Tom's Cabin* was released. The next two events were more startling. First came the Supreme Court's infamous *Dred Scott* decision in 1857. Then, just as the decade was almost history, John Brown attacked the federal arsenal at Harpers Ferry in Virginia in October of 1859.

The essence of the Supreme Court's *Dred Scott* decision, of March 6, 1857, was something only vaguely understood by most students down through the years. The Court handed down this decision just two days after James Buchanan was sworn in as president. There's reason to believe President Buchanan had prior knowledge regarding what he hoped the Court would settle once and for all regarding outstanding issues associated with the institution of slavery.

In his March 4, 1857, inaugural address, President James Buchanan alluded to the Supreme Court which he suggested was imminently about to issue a decision laying to rest permanently all issues pertaining to slavery. He implied the legal status of slavery itself was about to be ultimately defined by the Court's decision, which was not subject to appeal. Of course Buchanan was hoping the Court's integrity and usually appreciated wisdom would be acknowledged by all, thus rendering their decision above reproach. If the Court settled all issues pertaining to slavery, then his administration would get a pass on the vexing issue and not have to deal with it again. He was anticipating permanent relief from political turmoil rooted in society having "a wolf by the ears."

Apparently Buchanan was hoping his presidency would be spared from the rancorous issue of slavery, something his three predecessors had great difficulty coping with. However, the Court's *Dred Scott* decision was like poking a stick in a hornet's nest. James Buchanan muddled along with attempts to deflect the greater hostility than anticipated in the public's reaction to the decision, but he had little success. The Supreme Court's decision generated anti-slavery sentiments to observably ascend to new heights.

Classes often wanted to know, "Who was this Dred Scott dude?" They were informed he was born into slavery in Virginia in the mid 1790s. (Most slaves were denied a part of their identities by not knowing the exact date of their births.) In his thirties he accompanied an army surgeon to posts located in Illinois and Wisconsin Territories between 1834 and 1838. At the time he returned to Missouri with his owner he was in poor health. At a later time a sympathetic white acquaintance, who may have been a lawyer, encouraged him to file for his freedom in a federal district court.

Scott's case was based on the fact he had resided in places where slavery was prohibited and, thus, he had become free. At issue was the question: had his residency on free soil bestowed freedom on him or was he still private property incapable of obtaining the status of free person? In one class a perceptive student saw it coming down to whether he was regarded as property and, therefore, not endowed with "inalienable rights." His statement brought the crux of the question into focus and helped clarify why the Court issued the ruling it did.

Though it's been said Chief Justice Roger Taney personally deplored slavery, he was from the slave state of Maryland. (As for this time, it's possible to deplore racism and yet live comfortably in a defacto segregated suburban school district.) The majority on Taney's Court were southerners. They were committed to upholding the institution of slavery by way of the South's assertion it was a local question. Hence, Taney and five other judges ruled Congress lacked authority to legislate on the issue. Based on that premise they ruled the Missouri Compromise unconstitutional. Additionally, they ruled legislation sanctioning the principle of Popular Sovereignty unconstitutional as well. In effect Scott's suit became a vehicle to move the Court beyond the question of whether Scott was or wasn't free.

The particulars of the *Dred Scott* case facilitated the Court's decision to rule against the legitimacy of Congressional authority to legislate on issues pertaining to slavery. (No, the Court didn't rule the Fugitive Slave Act of 1850 unconstitutional.) Also of significant consequence was the Court's decision Scott and all of African ancestry were not citizens as defined by the Constitution. This meant Scott, as a non citizen, was ruled ineligible to bring a suit in federal court. As for Scott's status, the Court ruled he was still a slave.

The next event to occur in that decade of momentous political disruptions came on the night of October 16, 1859. A raid on Harpers Ferry in Virginia was initiated by John Brown leading a band of seventeen whites, including his three sons, and five blacks one of whom was Shields Green. Green had attended the August 20th Chambersburg, PA conclave where John Brown and Fredrick Douglass met. At the meeting Brown presented an ambitious plan to Douglass. He intended to raid into the South to liberate slaves and recruit them to join his force. His followers would then initiate ongoing guerrilla actions in that part of the country. Brown's first objective was to capture the federal arsenal at Harpers Ferry.

In his authoritative biography of Frederick Douglass, Philip Foner said, "Brown was dismayed by the emphatic disapproval registered in Douglass' reaction to his plan." Douglass didn't believe Brown grasped the reality of the bigger picture portraying how widespread a resistance to him would quickly arise. These two had met for the first time ten years earlier and their paths had occasionally crossed in the ensuing decade. Though he respected Brown immensely, Douglass felt in his bones Brown's undertaking was doomed to failure and he didn't see the wisdom of participating in it.

The former slave Shields Green had accompanied Douglass to the meeting with Brown at the quarry just outside Chambersburg, PA. Asked if he would join with Brown, he reportedly indicated he would go with the "old man." In so doing he shortly paid with his life for something he believed in. Shields Green wanted to be included, not minding how far fetched the scheme seemed. He readily joined in John Brown's undertaking at Harpers Ferry to ultimately liberate people held in slavery as he himself had once been. Like many others, Shields Green is an unsung hero rarely mentioned in the annals of history.

Brown's raid on Harpers Ferry, begun on the evening of October 16, ended with his capture early in the afternoon of the next day. In the last minutes of resistance Brown was wounded. The small force laying siege to Brown's barricaded position in the fire house included marines under the command of Colonel Robert E. Lee. Given the opportunity to make a final statement at his trial, Brown's words were intended more for posterity than for those in the courtroom. The brief statement conveyed his belief he would not die in vain. He was willing to give his life "for the furtherance of the ends of justice" by mingling his blood "with the blood of millions in this slave country whose rights are disregarded by wicked, cruel and unjust enactments." Unlike John Brown, the captured Shields Green was not given a trial and was condemned to the gallows as well, but with scant publicity of his fate presented to the broader public.

In his eulogy to Brown one sees in Frederick Douglass' remarks a philosophy suggesting justification for using force. In some respects Douglass anticipates a similar mode of reasoning expressed by Malcolm X. Of Brown's action Philip Foner quotes Douglass saying, "He has attacked slavery with the weapons precisely adapted to bring it to the death.... Slavery is a system of brute force. It shields itself behind might.... It must be met with its own weapons."

Reaction to Brown's execution on December 2, 1859 immediately swept across the North. Within the hour of his last breath bells tolled, flags were lowed to half mast, and buildings were draped in black. Emerson and Thoreau paid homage to him as did many others attending hundreds of memorial meetings held across the North. Initially Henry A. Wise, the governor of Virginia, wanted to commute Brown's sentence to life imprisonment because he saw abolitionists bestowing martyr status on him should he be executed. Overnight John Brown did indeed become a saint in the cause for abolishing slavery. In less than eighteen months Union troops were marching to a tune paying tribute to John Brown.

John Brown's action sent a tsunami wave of political fear washing over the South. Prior to his raid, in the rhetoric associated with the presidential election of 1856, many southerners had voiced the desirability of leaving the federal union if Republican John C. Fremont were elected president. Before Brown's raid, talk of secession was sporadically featured in southern public discourse. (Recall John Calhoun of South Carolina alluding to the idea in the heated U.S. Senate debates of 1850.) In 1856, however, the Democrat Buchanan was elected President, not the Republican Fremont, and the impulse to secede was checked for four years.

To be sure John Brown's raid made contentions by those advocating secession seem even more reasonable than at any previous time to southerners. His aggression at Harpers Ferry was the most emotionally charged final dramatic event of the decade. It was a climactic ending for that boisterous and unsettling decade which, ironically, had begun with compromise. After Brown was hanged most southern politicians were no longer interested in compromise as a remedy to resolve the outstanding sectional differences rooted in the institution of slavery. The outcome of the presidential election of 1860 was the excuse the South needed, was looking for, to proceed with the plan to secede.

It was obvious to students things had spun out of control toward the end of that event laden last decade before the Civil War. It was agreed certain decades are often pivotal in terms of a country going in a new direction, for better or worse, on the continuum of history. We acknowledged the 1850s was such a decade setting the stage for the country about to embark on a course which would ultimately make things better for the millions held in slavery. However, stamping out the evil of slavery saw incredible social upheaval and personal sacrifices in the decade of the 1860s as well. In most respects the impact of the severity of the Civil War overshadows the significance of events which occurred in the three preceding decades.

While discussing the significance of various decades, such as the 1850s, an older woman, but younger than myself, (I was in my mid fifties at the time) asked what decade in my life seemed critical regarding its impact upon the progression of history. She raised this question near the end of the first Bush's presidency, perhaps in 1992. I responded by designating the 1960s as the most critical decade (to that time) in my life. I said it was, for the most part, a watershed for the continuation and progression of democracy as embodied in the particulars of President Lyndon Johnson's

Civil Rights accomplishments and the promise of his Great Society agenda.
She responded by saying, "I thought you would say that." Another student
then asked if I had opposed the war in Vietnam? I indicated my support
for Senator Eugene McCarthy, the first United States senator to publicly
oppose the Vietnam War. I also mentioned concern of colleagues about
my picture in the local newspaper as a McCarthy supporter harming my
chances at getting tenure. (The concept of tenure had to be explained.) Yes,
no doubt, some decades in a nation's history beget more explosive political
events with greater impact than others. In my lifetime the 1960s left an
indelible mark. So much happened to differentiate that decade from the
one preceding it, as well as from the ones following it.

Chapter 7

In 1860, Abraham Lincoln was nominated and then elected to the presidency as the Republican Party's candidate. Regarding that event, Frederick Douglass expressed a qualified optimism. This because he knew of Lincoln assiduously avoiding being identified in the public's mind with abolitionism. Douglass said this of Lincoln, "His political life is thus far to his credit, but it is a political life of fair promise rather than one of rich heritage."

The Republican election campaign slogan was "No more slave states," but Douglass wished it had been "Death to slavery." Political considerations weighed heavily on Lincoln, many of them rooted in the racial attitudes of poor whites living in northern states. He had to carefully fashion tactics to gain the support of those voters which, early on, meant keeping abolitionist ideas absent from his statements. That policy frustrated Douglass. Lincoln wasn't presenting anything to which Douglass might enthusiastically exclaim, ala the 1960s, "Right On Abe!"

Many northern Democrats were sympathetic to the indignation southerners expressed in their responses to the perceived extremist challenges issued by abolitionists. Such Democrats believed the Republicans were kowtowing to the abolitionist element in their party. This is ironic since the abolitionists, including Douglass, believed the party paid scant attention to them and did its best to marginalize them. But the political reality acknowledged by Democrats was essentially accurate. Their mantra during the election was: "Not all Republicans are abolitionists, but all abolitionists are Republicans." For the most part, unacknowledged by political rhetoric, the election was about potential. Abolitionists saw the potential for Republicans to move in a direction they desired and that prospect was also readily perceived and feared by the South.

A few weeks before the South bombarded Fort Sumter, Lincoln reiterated his opposition to the South's assertion its states had a right to secede from the Union – that it was a voluntary compact. Frederick Douglass was pleased by Lincoln's firm stand negating that southern premise and also approved of Lincoln rebuffing proposals to facilitate reconciliation based on compromise. Of the compromise proposals Douglass said, "To attempt them as a means of peace between freedom and slavery is as to attempt to reverse irreversible law." Here it seems Douglass believed a cosmic force was driving events toward a final resolution abolishing slavery. With the news the South had fired on Fort Sumter talk of compromise was out of the question – all bets for avoiding military initiatives were off.

Business interests in the North had hoped compromise might be reached to avert the horror of war. War between the sections was viewed as a major disruptive force likely to curtail the economic prosperity implicit in the dynamic of peacetime business as usual. Back then businesses didn't look to government, i.e., Pentagon spending, to help subsidize the profitability of their enterprises. But now, in the 21st Century, we have a multitude of corporations thriving thanks to appropriations by Congress which sustain their profitability. Specific major industries understand their incredible profits are contingent upon their participation within the context of the Military Industrial Complex.

A vast majority of students I encountered never heard of the term Military Industrial Complex in their high school experiences. They had no idea of its significance. I was never surprised by this. Again, we have to think about football coaches teaching history. Are they likely to teach about the ramifications of the influence of the Military-Industrial Complex - how its influence permeates American culture?

The economic interests of corporations doing business with the Pentagon presently depends on our country engaging in frequent wars – ones in which it's generally believed nuclear weapons won't be used. Corporations so engaged with the Pentagon have no economic interests in having a long period of peace as the norm. Instead of long stretches of peace occasionally interrupted by war, we now have long stretches of war occasionally interrupted by very brief times of peace. However, in the brief lull between wars we see forces engaging in activity to set the stage for another outbreak of war. The Military Industrial Complex relies on the corporate media to promote their expectations, i.e., please give us scare stories about some perceived threat looming on the political horizon. Emphasis on a potential (desired) enemy means spending for the military has become roughly the same whether actually engaged in war or anticipating one to occur at any moment. That's not the way our national economy functioned prior to the South firing on Fort Sumter.

Yes, I digressed away from 1860. But, looking at various aspects of history serves to evaluate, by comparison, other events embedded in the course of history. To my way of thinking the reason for studying history is to sort out what was and what wasn't beneficial regarding the human condition. We evaluate civilizations, their contributions to facilitating human progress, from a knowledge of history. (One ready definition of progress might be that which promotes the greatest good for the greatest numbers.)

Within the context of this evaluation process I always hoped to promote a greater appreciation for history by students. History as a means not as an ends was what I hoped students would grasp. Ultimately knowledge of history should facilitate people being able to think about events and then judge them within a philosophical framework. The first question of which should be: did events in question serve to promote individual well being for an appreciable majority or were they "nasty business" serving no creditable human uplift purpose and benefiting only a very small minority?

After his election, up to the time he was sworn in, and then until the attack on Fort Sumter, Lincoln had to do a soft shoe political dance. He didn't want to initiate anything giving the appearance he was the aggressor and the South a victim. This was critical because the South had issued statements claiming it just wanted to depart the Union in peace. "Let them go," was expressed in various northern newspaper editorials and probably approved by hundreds of thousands who wanted to avoid bloodshed. This was a disappointing time for Douglass who viewed Lincoln's caution as a continuation of policies reminiscent of Buchanan's administration.

At the time I would say Lincoln was carefully assessing his options. But he certainly believed the "vast majority of northern people" would only join union forces for "the sole aim of saving the union." That is to say blood letting wouldn't be acceptable to northern whites if perceived as only for the purpose of ending slavery. Princeton historian James M. McPherson quoted Archbishop John Hughes of New York on this point. The Archbishop was ostensibly speaking for all Catholics who would be "willing to fight to the death for the support of the constitution, the government, and the laws of the country. But if ...they are to fight for the abolition of slavery, then, indeed, they will turn away in disgust from the discharge of what would otherwise be a patriotic duty." With white working class bigotry in mind in his response to a letter from Horace Greeley, Lincoln said, "My paramount object in this struggle is to save the Union, and is not either to save or destroy slavery."

Within the context of Lincoln's caution, during the first year of the war, was his concern that he not alienate the border states. He didn't want to lose Delaware, Maryland, Kentucky, and Missouri to the Confederacy. General John C. Fremont had an army in Missouri and on August 30, 1861, he declared martial law with an unanticipated provision freeing slaves belonging to those bearing arms against the Union. News of this reached various northern locations and was applauded in many quarters. However, Fremont's action alarmed Lincoln. He believed such a policy would negatively impact the other border states and drive them into the waiting arms of the Confederacy. So, he nullified the emancipation order Fremont had issued. Frederick Douglass was extremely disappointed to learn of Lincoln countermanding Fremont's order and said it would "only dishearten the friends of the Government and strengthen its enemies."

The Stars and Stripes might have flown over Fort Sumter, located in Charleston harbor, indefinitely if Lincoln's plan to continually resupply provisions to its garrison was allowed by South Carolina. But that was an unacceptable humiliation to the secessionists of South Carolina. The fort had to fly the Confederate flag as a representation of their belief in the legitimacy of their cause. Hearing the news the South had fired on Fort Sumter on April 12, 1861, Frederick Douglass proclaimed, "God be praised." For him the ensuing war would become a means to an end - namely the end of slavery.

Immediately Douglass urged the War Department to put black men into the blue uniforms of the Union army. His message: "Men of Color, to Arms ... smite with death the power that would bury the government and your liberty in the same hopeless grave." Black women, such as Boston's Josephine St.Pierre Ruffin and Sojourner Truth of New York, joined with black ministers and others calling for the enlistment of free blacks. Prior to the Civil War, Sojourner Truth had crossed paths with Frederick Douglass at various gatherings dedicated to achieving political equality for women. In mentioning Sojourner Truth to students, I brought their attention to the S.U.N.Y. College at New Paltz where the library is named in her honor. Legend has it Sojourner Truth lived for many years in the vicinity of New Paltz in Ulster County New York.

Should blacks serve in the Union army? Frederick Douglass addressed this question. He reasoned such participation would serve as a major stepping stone toward citizenship with political equality. On this topic he said, "Once let the black man get...a musket on his shoulder, and bullets in his pockets, and there is no power on earth...which can deny that he has earned the right of citizenship in the United States." Ironically the first all black regiment in the Union army was raised in South Carolina, not somewhere in the North as one might expect. Congress allowed the army to create the First South Carolina Volunteer Regiment. Commanded by Colonel Thomas Wentworth Higginson of Massachusetts, the regiment was comprised of runaway slaves fleeing to Union army positions for safety.

When slaves first fled to Union army units, early in the war, they were referred to as war contraband. In some instances, early on, some Union generals returned the runaway slaves to southerners claiming ownership. The practice ceased after Lincoln issued his Emancipation Proclamation.

Not quite three weeks after Lincoln's Emancipation Proclamation, the War Department gave its approval to Massachusetts Governor John A. Andrews to proceed with his request to raise two black regiments in his state. Frederick Douglass had been traveling at the time in parts of New England and upstate New York urging young black males to enlist and fight for the cause of the Union. Upon joining in this fight, he told his mostly black audiences, they would be striking a blow against slavery while proving to others they too were as capable and willing to face ultimate sacrifice situations for the same patriotic cause as others. The struggle with the South was their struggle because if the South won it would again initiate measures to suppress their freedom. His two sons, Charles and Lewis, enlisted in the 54th Infantry Regiment of Massachusetts which their father had urged them and others to do.

Prior to being transported to South Carolina, the 54th participated in a stirring ceremony in Boston Common attended by thousands who wished them success. After the ceremony the regiment of one thousand men impressed crowds as it marched smartly along the route taken to the waiting transport ship in the harbor. Frederick Douglass was indeed a proud father. His son Lewis held the rank of sergeant-major. However, like all other black units, their officers were white. The commanding officer of the 54th was Colonel Robert Gould Shaw, whose parents moved in the same social circles as the governor of Massachusetts. Before commanding the 54th, Colonel Shaw had seen action in Virginia. He knew full well what his troops would encounter and had the utmost faith in their ability to meet all challenges they would face.

On July 18th, 1863, the 54th made a gallant, some might say suicidal, frontal assault on the Confederate held Fort Wagner guarding the entrance to Charleston's harbor. Any doubts about the horrors of war should be quickly dispelled upon learning of the fate of the 54th Regiment. Their ranks were decimated in that courageous but futile attack on the fort Confederates zealously defended at all costs. Their heroic effort strengthened the contention calling for the enlistment of black Americans to serve their country in its time of need.

Approximately a week before the 54th's attack on Fort Wagner, there was draft rioting in New York City which included attacks on black folks simply trying to get out of harm's way. Many of the white rioters were recent Irish immigrants who believed the draft law unjust. Rich whites could buy a substitute and avoid the draft. The much poorer Irish didn't have that option and their seething resentment to the draft law dramatically erupted into violence directed against authority and property. Summing up this episode Civil War authority James M. McPherson, wrote, "Every Republican newspaper drew the obvious moral: black men who fought for the Union were more deserving of rights than white men who rioted against it." Toward the end of the following month President Lincoln spoke of reports from his military commanders praising the use of "colored troops." Of those advocating for black troops, he understood them to mean "the use of colored troops, constitute the heaviest blow yet dealt to the rebellion...."

For one hundred and twenty-five years the story of the 54th Infantry Regiment of Massachusetts had long been overlooked – sifted out of the mainstream of American popular history. Then on December 15, 1989 a movie was released which brought the story of the 54th out of the shadows of history. This Hollywood production titled *Glory* was about this black regiment's participation in the Union army and what it symbolized to African-Americans in their quest for full citizenship rights during the Civil War. For the first three months in 1990, there was a noticeable buzz in African-American communities across America about this film. Those who helped shape opinion in black communities enthusiastically designated *Glory* a must see movie and it became a box office smash hit.

When students, black and white alike, claimed to have seen *Glory* twice, I realized it was a film I shouldn't miss. Two African-American actors with significant parts in the movie, namely Denzel Washington and Morgan Freeman, received high praise for their compelling character portrayals. *Glory* took their acting careers to new heights. Both appeared in various movies during the rest of the decade and into the 21st Century.

Though thousands of African-Americans enlisted, the Union army did not at first treat them as equals to white troops. They quickly became aware of a pay discrepancy based on color. Black troops earned three dollars a month less than their white counterparts. Frederick Douglass brought the discriminatory pay difference to President Lincoln's attention in their first meeting. He also urged Lincoln to approve of officer commissions for African-Americans. Another issue was enlistment bonuses. Whites had been receiving them all along, but black enlistees didn't begin to receive them until June 15, 1864. Douglass said, "...merit, not color, should be the criterion observed by government in the distribution of places."

Opinions regarding the status of former slaves still included some proposals calling for their colonization outside the country. Lincoln had himself endorsed a pilot project which sent a group of not quite five hundred former slaves to a small island near Haiti. Things didn't go well in that venture and those who survived the ordeal were brought back to the United States. Many influential African-Americans, including Frederick Douglass, objected to the idea of overseas colonization. Forty years earlier the same idea was promoted by the American Colonization Society of which Senator Henry Clay and Chief Justice John Marshall were founding members. Free blacks weren't inclined to return to Africa and objected to the idea. Some, not free, did participate in the scheme and became free upon reaching Africa. One outcome of the earlier endeavor at overseas colonization was the founding of Liberia in Africa.

Douglass didn't see overseas colonization as an equitable recompense for generations of slavery. Recently freed persons weren't likely to be allowed to file suits in local civil courts for "pain and suffering" endured in slavery. However, he believed Congress should initiate compensatory measures – such as making land grants to former slaves. Was Frederick Douglass aware his idea was first tried when General William T. Sherman issued Special Field Order #15 on January 16, 1865? This order stipulated the creation of a thirty mile wide zone running north to south along Georgia's coast for the exclusive occupation by former slaves. When General Sherman issued this order Secretary of War Edwin Stanton was visiting him in Georgia. There's no evidence he disapproved of General Sherman's order. (Each family formerly in bondage was to receive forty acres.) Also, from January until his assassination in April, there's no indication Lincoln objected to General Sherman's initiative of far reaching implications.

Sherman's Special Field Order #15 could possibly have paved the way for other measures of a similar nature to be initiated across the South whereby former slaves would gain land ownership. However, by the summer of 1865, with Andrew Johnson occupying the White House that wasn't going to happen. (Johnson, from Tennessee, had stayed loyal to the Union and was placed on the ticket with Lincoln in 1864.) Johnson rescinded General Sherman's Field Order #15. A southerner in temperament, statements he made indicate his belief whites were superior to blacks in all respects. Also, as far as he was concerned equality between the races shouldn't be facilitated by governmental agencies. This explains Andrew Johnson's veto of the Freedmen's Bureau Act.

"The Problems of Peace" was the title of Chapter 26 in James M. McPherson's comprehensive book *Ordeal By Fire: The Civil War and Reconstruction*. Indeed, in the decade after Lee's surrender to General Grant there were many considerations posing as problems to putting the outcome of the war aside and achieving a true reconciliation between the sections. The biggest problem, from the white population's perspective, had many economic, political, and social dynamic facets. It was defined broadly and quickly by newspaper editorials across the country as the "Negro question." At bottom, this question was simply how should society at large acknowledge the freedman? What rights, beyond simply no longer being a slave, should be granted to ex-slaves? Were they to have the same rights as white Americans? Would they be allowed to vote, join local militias, serve on juries, go to schools financed by the public, and be treated as equals in public places of accommodation such as hotels, modes of transportation, and restaurants?

A few months before Lee's surrender, in his desire to obtain a non retaliatory speedy reconciliation between North and South, Lincoln issued his Ten Percent Plan for reconstruction. The South, Lincoln asserted, had not seceded from the Union. He said its actions had simply pushed southern states out of their "practical relationship" with the Union. His Ten Percent Plan was minimally punitive, all things considered not as harsh as many southerners had expected, but was considered rather ill conceived as far as the Radicals in his own party were concerned. Under Lincoln's plan if the number of white males not supporting the Confederacy totaled ten percent of the population, then those so qualifying could go ahead and hold conventions in their respective states to reconstruct and implement new state constitutions which had to stipulate slavery was no longer legal.

Radical Republicans could easily envision southern states quickly picking up where they had left off prior to the election of 1860. This implied sending Democrats back to Washington where they, joining with northern Democrats, could become the majority party again. Republicans, especially the Radicals, were not about to allow a policy most likely to result in their losing majority control of Congress. They had to devise a reconstruction plan other than Lincoln's Ten Percent Plan, if they hoped to somehow keep their majority control of Congress.

During the war the Republican Party had fashioned the ubiquitous message they were the party defending the Union and Democrats were the party of disunion. For political purposes in 1864, Lincoln ran for reelection with southern unionist Andrew Johnson on the Union Party ticket and the label Republican was astutely neglected. Once hostilities ended the Republican label became commonplace again and the party's constant message was: "Not all Democrats were secessionists, but all secessionists were Democrats." Republicans had become used to being the majority party in Congress and they didn't want to lose their control.

Since Lincoln wasn't proposing any punishment to the rebels other than being disqualified from participating in conventions to reorganize new state constitutions, the Radical Republicans knew they had to reject his proposal. They countered his Ten Percent Plan with the Wade-Davis Bill. This called for fifty percent of the population to take an "ironclad oath" affirming they had never in any way supported the Confederate cause. Supporters of the Radicals' bill knew it might take fifteen years before fifty percent of the population in the South would be able to take such an oath. Radicals were disappointed to learn Lincoln used the pocket veto on the Wade-Davis Bill. Seven weeks later Andrew Johnson was president and Congress was not in session. Radicals soon learned he favored implementing Lincoln's Ten Percent Plan which they vehemently opposed.

In the fall of 1865, six weeks before Congress reconvened, three northern states held referendums on the question of black suffrage. At the time a majority of other northern states did not permit African-Americans to vote. As it turned out those who went to the polls in Connecticut, Minnesota, and Wisconsin voted to continue denying black Americans the right they had just utilized. In those states the enfranchisement proposals lost by margins of ten percent. Also that fall, the ten percent conventions in southern states were drawing up constitutions abolishing slavery but were withholding the franchise from former slaves. The sentiments of those attending southern conventions can be summed up by South Carolina's new governor. He said, "this is a white man's government, and intended for white men only...."

At this time attitudes of northern white Americans towards black Americans varied. Negativity toward African-Americans was more prevalent in certain regions and amongst certain social classes of white folks. Probably working class whites felt more threatened by recently freed black persons than small business owners. I often asked classes, "To what extent and in what respects were blacks threatening to the whites?" A common response from students was the whites probably thought they might have to compete with blacks for jobs - that blacks would work for lower wages than they would.

A prominent threat perceived by whites, especially those in the South, had to do with, you guessed it, sex. Ironically, in this vein of seeing someone racially different as a threat more than once a black female exclaimed, "most black men really want to marry a white woman." Classes laughed at this. I would try to make a point in response, "What you said is what whites in the South thought and feared – miscegenation." (On many occasions students were unfamiliar with the word miscegenation.) She raised the issue some black women objected to losing their men to white women. Rather humorous was another black student's quick response. She chimed in with,

"It ain't too long before those brothers find out what they're missing. Look at those white boys who've been there. You know what I'm talking about. Once they try black they never go back!" Most white students had never heard that before and had a good laugh. Responding to her observation, I couldn't resist saying, "I suppose Thomas Jefferson might be a case in point." My response gave the class another good laugh.

Of course fear of racial miscegenation was the reason southern states quickly passed laws prohibiting marriage between people racially different from one another. Well past the middle of the 20th Century these laws meant diverse couples born in the South had to relocate to a northern state to become officially married. (We now see gay and lesbian couples relocating to states that permit them to officially marry.) In 1967, in the case *Loving v. Virginia*, the Supreme Court ruled states could no longer prohibit interracial marriage. Thus Mildred Jeter and Richard Loving's marriage would no longer be in violation of Virginia's law - struck down by the Court's decision. They could continue to live in Virginia without the threat of legal prosecution if they chose to do so.

More than in traditional four year college settings, the spontaneity of community college students seems to be a given in the dynamic of classroom student/teacher interactions. In the African-American history class, more often than in other classes, humorous unexpected comments often sparked casual banter. Quite often, to varying degrees, it served a useful purpose by helping to establish a rapport with students which in turn facilitated learning. One consequence of humorous exchanges was my renewed appreciation for the old saying about much truth frequently being said in jest.

White fear of black men putting the moves on white women was a prevalent fear during the aftermath of the Civil War and well into the 20th Century. Fifty years after the Civil War ended, the fear was dramatically reenforced by D.W. Griffith's film, *Birth of a Nation (1915)*. Ironically, the time frame for his film was the Reconstruction Era. Two themes were prominent. First, there was the almost prevalent view recently freed black men would sexually ravish white women refusing their unwanted advances. Were southern white male fears actually an acknowledgment of the possibility of pay back?

Birth of a Nation's second theme was Griffith's presentation of the Ku Klux Klan as a noble righteous organization dedicated to upholding the social mores of the South, which included protecting the "virtue" of white womanhood. The Klan was not reluctant to punish any black person crossing the line pertaining to its understanding of how things should be regarding interactions between the two races. Punishments included killing a share croppers' mule, whippings, humiliating a spouse, and lynchings – often with the approval of whites gathered to witness such spectacles. These crimes rarely saw anyone held accountable and prosecuted under the full operation of the law.

Often politicians courting poor whites, and supposedly addressing the "Negro question," would invoke the question: "Do you want a nigger to marry your daughter?" From what I've read about Andrew Johnson he would resort to racial scare tactics if he thought it would garner a few more votes than his opponent. Scare tactics are such a staple of American politics. Unlike Lincoln, the hill country of east Tennessee president apparently subscribed to the commonly held racist beliefs, all the unfounded fears, held by the people he once represented in Congress. Johnson never challenged his social milieu to examine its fears rooted in negative racial assumptions.

At this time one of the fears great numbers of whites held was rooted in the notion granting certain rights to former slaves might compromise or take some of their rights away. On numerous occasions Frederick Douglass addressed this fear many whites held. Also, before his death he clearly saw those truly economically privileged, in the new industrial age, have a special interest in seeing antagonisms persist between black and white workers. He was well acquainted with the political ploy of many ages - divide and conquer. Douglass knew this tactic was frequently used and worked against the common lot of people in their attempts to live with human dignity.

The concept white privilege wouldn't be accepted or even considered as an explanation for how society functioned in the latter part of the 19th Century. Given the education levels and the deep rooted societal norms of those times, the concept would not be understood. Most people of that time simply thought things were the way they were because that's the way things were supposed to be.

Immediately after the Civil War and for subsequent decades the Democratic Party ran candidates who played upon rather commonplace racial fears of working class whites. One fear whites living in the North had was hundreds of thousands of blacks would migrate to the North to accept work at lower wages, thus taking employment from themselves. In the area of unskilled employment opportunities wages are usually low because of the keen competition for jobs resulting from a surplus of workers often brought about by a large influx of those recently entering the available work force. It's been observed recent immigrants swelling the numbers of a given labor pool were often willing to work for less than what had been a prevailing wage. Economic desperation prompted many workers to take lower wages than those in similar circumstances as themselves.

Super wealthy industrialists of the late 19th Century regularly brought workers over from Europe to suppress local prevailing wages. Each new influx of immigrants tended to lower wages. However, it wasn't too long before workers got wise to the practice. But they knew if European immigration was curtailed the Captains of Industry had another option to swell the ranks of the labor pool in the North. It was to simply bring those already here "up North" to compete with the recent European immigrant workers. Thus, workers of European ancestry feared employers might hire black workers for the same reason they were brought to the country a few years earlier.

Also, capitalist employers weren't adverse to playing on racial antipathies to create barriers preventing working class people from seeing the necessity for making common cause via color blind union organizing. In this era working class whites were lucky to have an eighth grade education - poor whites in the South had fewer years of formal schooling. And, of course, people recently freed from slavery had almost no education in comparison. Ignorance is always fertile soil to plant suspicion of others. Fear and suspicion of others is useful to those having something to gain by hoping those social factors prevail.

One compelling question I can think of pertaining to the Reconstruction Era was: would America's various institutions accept and promote new modes of thinking to challenge beliefs sustaining racism long held by the common lot of white Americans? Obviously that question wasn't raised or acted upon. Initiating challenges to institutionalized racism at that time would probably have been more socially disruptive than it seemed to be almost one hundred years later in the 1960s. Today's understanding of racism's ramifications would be beyond the comprehension of the great majority of white persons living in mid to late 19th century America.

Even at this time many whites can't grasp the meaning of white privilege. In my endeavor to explain it, I kept it quite simple. If you haven't

experienced discrimination based on your race, then you enjoy what others
who are discriminated against don't enjoy. Therefore you have a pass or
privilege based on being white. People challenged to understand that, but
who don't get it, will likely continue to feel somehow alienated.

Basically President Andrew Johnson acknowledged slavery was over.
But, beyond that it was sink or swim for former slaves. He vetoed the
first Freedmen's Bureau Bill which had provisions for economic assistance to ex-slaves. Johnson had no interest in helping former slaves to
their feet with any sort of economic assistance. His attitude is still at the
heart of political conservatism today. To avoid total economic deprivation
most freedmen agreed to engage in sharecropping. However, this quickly
proved very harsh as it fostered a condition of debtor peonage not much
better than slavery itself. Sadly, it was the most realistic option available
at the time.

Prior to the Civil War abolitionists would be hard pressed to find anything to like about Andrew Johnson. After the war those believing society had a moral responsibility for providing economic assistance to former
slaves didn't appreciate Johnson's opposition to their initiatives. Among
other measures proposed to economically assist former slaves, he also vehemently opposed the plan calling for confiscation of fellow southerners'
property thence to be awarded to former slaves as compensation for their
involuntary servitude. Sherman's Special Field Order #15 had never been
legally sanctioned by an act of Congress. So, during the summer of 1865,
when Congress was not in session, President Andrew Johnson rescinded
Sherman's Special Field Order #15.

The idea of granting forty acres and a mule to former slaves as a means
of recompense rather spontaneously circulated in many black population
segments across the South. It became an expectation boosting high hopes.
Yet as some were calling for compensatory land grants to former slaves,
there were others, somewhat sympathetic to the defeated South, articulating the idea of monetary restitution to former slave holders for the loss
of their slaves. Dr. John Rock, a black physician from Boston, called for
compensation to those who endured slavery not to those who profited from
its horrors. "Why talk about compensating masters? ...it is the slave who
ought to be compensated. The property of the South is by right the property of the slave." Congress didn't heed Rock's proposal, instead it passed a
law giving former Confederates priority over former slaves for the purposes

of reclaiming their plantation lands. President Andrew Johnson had no problem signing this bill into law. He never supported proposals calling for ex-slaves to obtain lands at the expense of ex-Confederate plantation owners. Essentially the law was intended to promote reconciliation with the South as quickly as possible.

Also, Johnson opposed Congress giving the vote to African-Americans by way of national legislation. He believed such a measure by Congress was unconstitutional. It was the states, based on his interpretation of the Constitution's 9th & 10th Amendments, who determined the qualifications for voter eligibility. This was a states' rights issue that lingered well into the 20th Century. State imposed poll taxes weren't prohibited until final passage of the 24th Amendment to the Constitution on January 23, 1964 which prohibited the practice.

Every measure the Radical Republicans sponsored, intended to close the civil rights gap between free whites and recently freed black Americans, was vetoed by President Andrew Johnson. Even passage of the 14th Amendment to the Constitution giving African-Americans citizenship, nullifying the Dred Scott decision of 1857, was not supported by Andrew Johnson. For the three and a half years he was president, Andrew Johnson's policies amounted to throwing former slaves under the bus. Along with Radicals, sponsoring legislation for their benefit, freedmen hoped to see things take a turn for the better with the election of General Grant to the presidency and with more Radicals winning seats in Congress in 1868 as well.

The establishment of Radical governments in southern states was assisted by Congress passing certain measures it managed to sustain over President Johnson's vetoes. Radicals who came to hold various state offices were also known as Carpetbaggers by unsympathetic southerners. Obviously in the presidential election of 1868, the Radical or Carpetbag governments in those states did everything possible to get former slaves to the polls to vote for U.S. Grant. In many areas the Ku Klux Klan engaged in unlawful activities intended to intimidate black voters so they wouldn't vote. Much of the Klan's activities would be considered terrorism by 21st Century criteria. But despite the Klan's efforts, thanks to the African-American vote in those southern states, U.S. Grant obtained the electoral college numbers he needed to win the presidency in 1868. This in turn meant a priority of the Republican Party would be to sustain its southern power base for the purpose of getting Grant reelected for a second term in 1872.

On February 25, 1869, a week before Ulysses Simpson Grant was sworn in as the eighteenth president of the United States, Congress approved of the proposed Fifteenth Amendment to the Constitution and sent it on to the states for ratification. This amendment stipulated no "citizen of the United States" could be denied the right to vote "on account of race, color, or previous condition of servitude." It also gave to Congress the "power to enforce this article by appropriate legislation." It became part of the supreme law of the land when Georgia ratified it on March 30,1870. At the time of its passage there were eleven northern states out of twenty-one which barred African-Americans from voting. In some northern states blacks had been disqualified not on the basis of race, but because they didn't meet a property or net worth requirement.

With passage of the Fifteenth Amendment, Democrats North and South supported the contention its ratification completed the post Civil War process of reconstruction. As far as they were concerned additional congressional measures were no longer necessary as requirements on southern states to return to full participation in the nation's governing process. The Democrats embraced the idea the entire business of reconstruction was finally over because of the ratification of the 13th, 14th. and 15th amendments to the Constitution. While vehemently expressing this contention, Democrats were working diligently to overthrow the Radical Republican regimes in the various southern states. Upon achieving that goal, they would immediately devise measures to deny the franchise to freedmen based on passing literacy exams, satisfying a grandfather eligibility clause, or a poll tax. Such measures making many ineligible to vote were not predicated on race per se and, hence, didn't violate the letter of the law inherent in the wording of the 15th Amendment to the Constitution.

Students frequently asked, "Who were the Carpetbaggers?" Some northerners, I explained, saw economic and political opportunities in the South immediately after the Civil War ended. So, they went South and replaced disqualified former Confederates in various levels of government. Their political activities were frequently in conjunction with policies enforced by Union army units stationed nearby. Generally Carpetbaggers were of limited economic means and went South looking to improve their station in life by way of achieving political influence. They were often seen arriving in southern locations carrying their meager possessions in bags made of similar fabric commonly used to make carpets.

Carpetbag Republican governments weren't able to take root in the South once intimidation and disqualification of the suffrage for African-Americans succeeded. The national Democratic party vigorously assisted in portraying the reconstructed Republican governments as being corrupt because of malfeasance in office by elected officials, about twenty percent of whom were black. Most Democratic newspapers in the North would have readers believing blacks in the South were terrorizing former Confederates when in truth it was just the opposite. Like Fox News today Democratic newspapers were adept at putting a spin on what they chose to suit their purposes.

The Republican governments in the South were characterized as bogus because of participation by former slaves portrayed as ignorant and illiterate, therefore incompetent. Democrats emphasized the fact an overwhelming majority of southern blacks were unable to read, thus easily manipulated into supporting unsavory political policies sponsored by Republicans. But what about those recent immigrants from Europe? Most were not literate in English and barely, if at all, better educated than blacks in the South. Yet their voting patterns essentially facilitated the existence of the corrupt Tweed Ring in New York City. As Princeton's James M. McPherson observed, "…the graft that took place in the South must be seen in a national context. All the Southern governments combined…stole less from the taxpayers than did the Tweed Ring in New York."

A legend soon emerged claiming former Confederates were being denied certain rights and systematically oppressed because of "Negro supremacy" being promoted and sustained by Republican sponsored "bayonet rule" implemented by federal troops then stationed in the South. Again, to quote Princeton's James M. McPherson, "This theme of 'Negro Supremacy,' by which the 'barbarous African' exercised 'uncontrolled power' in ten Southern states, was a staple of Democratic propaganda. It became enshrined in many textbooks and in the popular memory of Reconstruction."

As for my high school experience, in the early 1950s, I learned nothing about Confederate general Nathan Bedford Forrest founder of the Ku Klux Klan. Nor did I learn about the Klan's acts of terror such as riding at night to burn schools established by the Freedmen's Bureau - one of many measures taken by the Klan calculated to suppress the black vote. Also, I was never taught sixteen African-American men, most former slaves, served in the U.S. Congress during the Reconstruction Era.

Despite obstacles preventing black participation in the political process, former slave John R. Lynch engaged in Mississippi state politics thence to be elected to the U.S. House of Representatives. Democratic Senators tried to prevent Hiram Revels from representing Mississippi in the U. S. Senate because he didn't meet the Constitutional requirement of being a citizen for nine years. They claimed he was only a citizen as a result of the passage of the 14th Amendment passed just four years prior to his election. As Harvard professor Randall Kennedy noted, Hiram Revels was "born free in North Carolina in 1822 of white, black, and Indian ancestry." (He was filling Mississippi's vacated Senate seat once held by Confederate president Jefferson Davis.) Again, as for the Klan, its nefarious actions were omitted or minimized in popular history narratives for almost a century. A nationwide syndrome of indifference regarding the South's hostile treatment of African-Americans persisted long after the Reconstruction Era was over.

In 1872, Republicans were barely maintaining their authority in reconstructed state governments of the South. Yet they managed to deliver their electoral college votes once again to Grant who won his second term. His popular vote tallied an impressive 56 percent – the highest recorded in presidential elections between 1828 and 1904. His electoral college tally was 286 votes to the 66 originally designated for Horace Greeley who died before the electoral college count was presented to Congress. In many respects Grant's big victory was not indicative of attitudinal changes underway regarding Congressional policies imposed upon the South. Democrats claimed Radical sponsored policies were based on opportunism facilitated by unconstitutional measures.

Grant's popularity in 1872 did not carry over to assist Republicans running for Congress two years later. In 1874, the Democrats gained a majority in the House of Representatives. This indicated a political shift had occurred and was moving Congress away from positions Republicans had espoused regarding the status of African-Americans living in the South. With their new majority in the House of Representatives, Democrats were disinclined to pass any measures to bolster laws previously passed guaranteeing to African-Americans the same rights as white Americans. Circumstances for black Americans in the South continued to deteriorate with the outcome of the presidential election of 1876. In this election the number of blacks voting in the South had fallen off dramatically, thanks to various measures of intimidation, as compared with the numbers recorded in the reelection of Grant four years earlier.

Halfway through Grant's second term there was a public mood swing. Economic circumstances loom large in explaining why this happened. In September of 1873 Jay Cooke's bank collapsed. It quickly precipitated other bank failures. The banking collapse sent panic waves through Wall Street and within six months five thousand businesses failed. Soon hundreds of thousands of workers were out of work and just as many had to accept wage cuts. Enterprises such as mining, the infant steel making industry, and textile manufacturing were hard pressed to stay in business. Workers now began to listen to ideas considered without merit a dozen years earlier. Harsh economic circumstances moved farmers and factory workers in the direction of joining forces - ultimately resulting in the formation of the Populist Party.

Considering the social dynamic of the day, most likely laid off first because of the unexpected economic collapse were small numbers of African-Americans recently added to the workforce. A pattern of "last to be hired, first to be fired," rooted in racist attitudes, thence became a norm which persisted right up to the Great Depression in the 1930s. Seemingly not as hard hit by the economic nose dive of the mid 1870s were African-Americans in the South engaged in agricultural activities. They probably were slightly better off than unemployed white workers living in Pennsylvania, many of whom were going to bed hungry at night. For the most part hard times in the North meant the obliteration of concern for African-Americans losing their civil rights by lynch law terror and political chicanery in the South.

The economic collapse of the mid-1870s took northern attention away from the seemingly unresolvable problems associated with the South's political reconstruction. However, I wonder if opinion in the North was ever, in any profound way, concerned with the manifestations of racism prevalent across the former Confederate states? Were most northerners ever really concerned about the injustices of the Jim Crow era from *Plessy v. Ferguson* in 1896 until the *Brown v. Board of Education* case in 1954? It seems concern for people whose ancestors were slaves now and then occasionally flared up in certain quarters, but was never an overriding concern most whites living in the North had.

To be sure there were some Republicans in Congress during Grant's second term who consistently expressed a commitment to equal rights for African-Americans but they were, at most times, a small vocal minority. Those insistent on providing and sustaining political equality for former slaves, such as Thaddeus Stevens, Charles Sumner, and Henry Wilson were all deceased by 1875. They weren't replaced by persons as dedicated to equal justice for all, regardless of race, as they had been.

Senator Charles Sumner had sponsored a civil rights bill that closed legal loopholes the courts had discerned in earlier legislation of that nature. However it languished in committee and didn't come to the Senate floor until after he died on March 11, 1874. As a tribute to him for his twenty years in the Senate his bill passed, but was not approved by the House of Representatives. The torch light he carried for the rights of African-Americans was essentially extinguished by the new breed of business oriented Republicans winning seats in both chambers of Congress. Philip Foner quoted the compelling tribute to Senator Sumner offered by Frederick Douglass. "Let us…teach our children the name Charles Sumner, tell them his utterances, and teach them that they, like him, can make their lives sublime by clinging to principles."

A new breed of Republicans, considerably less concerned about securing rights for African-Americans, had come into the party's leadership positions. They were more interested in national economic growth than maintaining commitments made earlier by the now departed Radical idealists of the party. Stock jobbing, political favors for "kick backs," and bestowing huge land grants to railroad companies took precedence over commitment and concern for the rights of poor black tenant farmers in the South. These farmers had begun to face local discriminatory practices sustained by local courts where white judges instructed white juries. For example, blacks received harsher jail sentences for crimes such as vagrancy or walking away from share cropper contracts than did their white counterparts.

Also, this new element in the Republican Party didn't care that southern states had begun to give self serving interpretations to the Fifteenth Amendment essentially denying most African-Americans their right to vote. Discriminatory voter qualification laws handicapping blacks were enacted into law. These voter eligibility requirements such as poll taxes or literacy examinations were blatantly structured to keep black participation in elections negligible.

In 1877, the emerging business oriented Republicans wanted to build
political bridges to like minded southerners to facilitate shared understandings necessary for promoting mutual economic interests. The most affluent
class in the South was encouraged to see the economic advantages of moving away from dependency on agricultural enterprises and, instead, cooperate with northern investors interested in industrial development in the
South. Both parties knew labor in the South, black and white workers alike,
was obtainable for much lower wages than were being paid in the North.
Workers in the emerging steel production and coal mining industries in the
vicinity of Birmingham Alabama would not be paid on a par with those
working in Bethlehem or Pittsburgh, Pennsylvania.

Actually, Frederick Douglass' biographer, Philip Foner, indicated
pointed reservations about the Republican Party's motives for implementing reconstruction policies, seemingly to advance justice for black
Americans. He summed things up rather cynically, "The northern capitalist had been interested in the Negro only to maintain political leadership of the national government." By 1877, the Republican Party had
become oriented toward economic policies from which both northern
and southern investors would profit together. With this development
underway questions pertaining to legal and political justice for African-
Americans living in the South no longer had priority in the Republican
Party.

Things had taken a turn for the worse respecting commitment from
Republicans to assist African-Americans as a result of the presidential election of 1876. Rutherford B. Hayes of Ohio was the Republican candidate.
He was a compromise candidate selected to stop the possible nominations
of either U.S. Grant for a third term or James G. Blaine of Maine, recently
charged with a shady deal made with a railroad. Hayes had the previous
year been elected for a third time as governor of Ohio. One observer said
his main qualification was his "availability." Henry Adams said of him, he
was "a third rate nonentity, whose only recommendation is that he is obnoxious to no one." Opposing Hayes was Democrat Samuel J. Tilden. As
governor of New York, Tilden was credited with exposing and ousting the
corrupt Tweed ring in New York City.

The Electoral College number needed for election was 185 votes. After
ballots had been counted the tally indicated Tilden had 184 electors. He
was in need of just one more electoral vote to become president. However,

the votes of three southern states, totaling 19, were in dispute. Hayes had 166 votes and needed all of the disputed votes to be elected.

To resolve the issue of Florida, Louisiana, and South Carolina's contested votes, Congress established a special Electoral Commission of 15 members. The findings of this body claimed Hayes won all the disputed votes. By a straight party line vote of 8 to 7, Hayes was awarded all 19 votes. It was the exact number needed to take his count up to the 185 votes required to be elected president. While he served opposition party critics frequently referred to Hayes as "Rutherfraud" and "Old Eight to Seven" because they believed the election had been stolen. I suppose it might be humorous if we could know what the Democrats of 1877 would say about the role the Supreme Court played in 2000 when it selected George W. Bush to be President instead of his Democratic opponent Al Gore who had the most popular votes.

When the findings of the Electoral Commission were announced there was less than a week until March 4th, the day the Constitution required a new president to be sworn in. Shortly before that date, in mid-February, some Democrats in party leadership positions indicated they might prevent the House from voting acceptance of the commissions' adjudication if it favored Hayes. They would resort to filibuster tactics. Gravely concerned by this possibility Republican spokespersons, influenced considerably by business interests wanting to avoid a potentially violent political showdown, entered into "unofficial" dialogues with influential southern Democrats. It seems they were able to reach mutually acceptable understandings which averted a constitutional crisis.

The final meeting to secure an agreed upon political policy allegedly took place at the Wormley Hotel in Washington. As a result of the agreements reached, Democrats didn't initiate a filibuster tactic to block Hayes from being sworn in. Hayes responded to the trouble free transition by ordering the withdrawal of federal troops from the South less than a month after entering office. His early policies indicated he knew of the deal reached with the Democrats, but he always claimed otherwise – that he had no personal knowledge regarding specific political understandings. As for my summary comments pertaining to the election of 1876, I simply said Hayes gaining the presidency served as an example of "politicians wheeling and dealing and disavowing." That too is as American as apple pie.

It was a pleasure when students asked, "How did Republicans expect to stay in power after turning the South back over to the former confederate Democrats?" (In 1876 South Carolina and Louisiana had elected former confederate army generals to be their governors.) Responding to the question, I indicated Republicans believed they could still win national elections without relying on the military presence in the South to secure election victories. They looked to the West. Colorado was admitted to the Union in 1876, thence to be known as the Centennial State. Congressional Republicans expected more western states to enter the union under Republican control as in Colorado.

The Hayes administration signaled Republican abandonment of their decade long attempt to control politics in the South. In the final analysis this simply meant abdicating responsibility for securing equal rights for African-Americans living there. There would no longer be a meaningful commitment, by either party, to the spirit of the law implicit in the Civil Rights Act of 1875 - later struck down by the Supreme Court in 1883. To be sure former slaves had benefited from early interpretations of the 15th Amendment, but that quickly became a thing of the past. In 1876, the Supreme Court, in *United States v. Reese*, ruled the Fifteenth Amendment did not confer the right of suffrage to everyone, but simply forbade the suffrage being denied because of race or previous condition of servitude.

Southern states immediately saw the implications of *United States v. Reese*. It opened the door for them to deny the suffrage to black Americans based on questions regarding legal residency, literacy exams, or payment of a poll tax, but not specifically because of race. Other contrived barriers were put in place to disqualify blacks from voting. Also, a rather significant implication of not being listed on the voter registry meant you weren't qualified to sit on a jury in most places.

When it came to justice based on equal rights, after 1877 it was like African-Americans had been placed in leaky rowboats, in the midst of a turbulent sea, far from shore, and without benefit of either oars or life jackets. Those who had been slaves, their children as well, were now adrift out of sight of a port offering hope for a commitment to the rights enjoyed by the majority of other Americans. What soon evolved as the norm regarding unequal justice was observed by Thomas Fortune, an African-American newspaper editor. In testimony before a U.S. Senate committee in 1883, Fortune said, "The white man who shoots a negro always goes free, while the negro who steals a hog is sent to the chain gang for ten years." That's how it would go in court for African-Americans for the next eight decades after President Hayes pulled the federal troops out of the South.

Also, in other regions of America there was little concern over the next eighty years regarding how things were for African-Americans living in the South. Whites had put segregation based on race in place there and whites in other parts of the country didn't know or care about how that was achieved. It was enforced by laws rooted in Jim Crow imposed customs. Whites in the North, many recent immigrants from Europe, were struggling with issues related to their own existence, such as working six days a week ten to twelve hours a day. So, they weren't likely to look beyond their own circumstances to see social injustice south of the Mason-Dixon Line.

At the time the Jim Crow system had taken hold, I reminded classes racism was being cloaked in pseudo scientific terms - some based on Darwin's theory. People with needs to believe their superiority to others different from themselves often gravitate to dubious theories to justify their negative behavior to others. This often happens in time of war. Notions of racial or ethnic superiority to one's enemy too frequently allows for horrors to be inflicted on the perceived enemy because they're viewed as less than human.

To this day many believe their race, whatever it might be, is superior to others in the family of humankind. For decades Social Darwinism was invoked by European imperialists when they sought to impose their dominance over other peoples unlike themselves in Africa and Asia. Interestingly, European (British and French) domination in Africa and Asia was coming to an end in the 1960s, the same decade the demise of the South's Jim Crow system was occurring.

The responsibility of all people in this 21st Century is to challenge all ethnocentrism and racial egotism. For myself I try to keep Canadian anthropologist Edmund Wade Davis' observation in mind - "The world in which you were born is just one model of reality. Other cultures are not failed attempts at being you; they're unique manifestations of the human spirit." And, I add here again what I constantly told my classes, "No one group has a monopoly on virtue, virtuous people can be found in all groups, whatever race or ethnicity."

Chapter 8

From the time Rutherford Hayes became president in March of 1877 until the Supreme Court's *Plessy v. Ferguson* ruling, nineteen years later in 1896, the nation as a whole took little notice of the plight of African-Americans living in former Confederate states. The population in the North was rather dramatically outstripping population growth in the South. This was due in part to the hundreds of thousands of European immigrants pouring into northern ports of entry every year from the end of the Civil War until the turn of the 20th Century. Their labor was needed in the rapidly expanding areas of industrial production located in the North.

European immigrant groups were usually competing with each other and certainly didn't expect or want to find themselves competing with black labor. African-Americans, the new European immigrants learned, would not be a threat if they just stayed in the South. These immigrants, from the Austro-Hungarian Empire, Italy, Poland, Serbia, Russia, and other places in Europe were quick to discern and adopt certain values held widely by white Americans – many dubious to be sure because they sustained racist beliefs.

It quickly became apparent to European immigrants African-Americans were on the bottom rung of the social structure ladder. What a break for them. There it is, a manifestation of white privilege. They were fortunate to enter American society, because of being white, a rung above African-Americans. This gave them privileges African-Americans didn't enjoy, especially those living in the South. For example, politicians in the North quickly did them favors like finding them places to live, help them gain employment, locate relatives, etc., in exchange for their support at the next election. Their children went to schools which taught them how to be patriotic American citizens, but that process didn't include admonitions to challenge racism as something un-American. Most likely European immigrants didn't know, wouldn't likely care if they did, that southern politicians weren't doing African-Americans any such favors as they received in exchange for their votes.

Subsequent to the Hayes administration southern states had begun chipping away at laws intending equal rights for African-Americans. In the 1880s and 1890s various local and state laws had been enacted in the South which, by today's standards, were blatantly discriminatory on the basis of race. In effect the laws called for separating the races in most public settings like public auditoriums, courtrooms, schools, parks, etc. Cumulative southern state court decisions, following the Supreme Court's nullification of the Civil Rights Act of 1875, also upheld the right of individuals to discriminate. A general store owner, for example, could prohibit entrance into his store by African-Americans if he so chose. Also, African-Americans could be refused service in many other business establishments such as restaurants and taverns.

This discriminatory legally sanctioned practice was brought to my attention in 1956 while I was in the Air Force stationed near Topeka, Kansas. At the time tavern owners there were permitted to deny service to anyone they didn't want as a customer. I didn't immediately understand this essentially permitted discrimination based on ethnicity or race. There was a bar in Topeka where we went in civilian clothing to have a few beers. It had a sign behind the bar which read: "We reserve the right to refuse service." I asked one of my beer drinking buddies to explain it. He said if someone caused a disturbance, the bartender could then refuse serving additional drinks and order them to leave his premises. Nineteen then, I accepted that explanation until I learned of the sign's real purpose.

As it happened I asked a guy named Rodriguez, who was on the same weapons loading crew as myself, to join me and two others for a beer in town. He asked where we were going and we told him of our usual place. He said he couldn't go with us because he was Mexican-American and wouldn't be served in that tavern. "What? Are you serious?" I asked him.

He responded, "Didn't you guys ever see the sign behind the bar? Don't you know what it means?" When Rodriguez clued us in about what the sign meant for him, that he would be refused service because he was Mexican-American, we became rather angry. We were from the North and never experienced such a policy with its racist implications before. Learning about this was a real eye opener for me. We encouraged Rodriguez to go with us and if he wasn't served then we would all leave the bar together.

We went to the bar in town having the coded meaning sign. It was practically empty, a slow night for sure. We were a bit surprised when the bartender served all of us. Upon sitting down with our beers, Rodriguez leaned over the table and quietly said, "It's because I'm with you guys, he didn't want to lose business. If I was by myself, he wouldn't serve me." Upon asking for reactions to this episode, hands would immediately be raised. The consensus every time was Rodriguez by himself had race liability. And, because of white race privilege, my white buddies and I didn't have to think twice about what Rodriguez or someone like James Meredith would likely encounter. With an occasional dissent, classes agreed minorities have to constantly think twice about circumstances where their race changes the social dynamic – something whites don't have to think twice about.

Oh, as for that bar in Topeka, I'll always remember it. That's where I first heard Count Basie's version of "April In Paris." The powerful blare of that jukebox actually did justice to his rendition of that song. Wow, talk about the impact of air blowing through brass, what a sound! The record in the jukebox had Basie's quirky ending where he said, "One more time" and the band repeated that big ending riff again. Basie actually did that twice. Count Basie was always capable of making an innovative musical statement. So, no surprise, I presently have that version in my rather extensive CD jazz collection.

The last two decades of the 19th Century saw African-Americans excluded from participation in civic and social activities in many places in the North and most places in the South. Basically the process sanctioning racial discrimination was rooted in long held unquestioned readily accepted racist beliefs held by a majority of whites. Segregation policies were sporadically challenged in the courts. But, southern state courts, of which some judges had been Confederate army officers, upheld racially objectionable policies sweeping across the South at the time.

In the post Reconstruction Era the Supreme Court upheld the segregationists contention political parties were private organizations. Thus, they could admit or exclude from enrollment in the party whomever they chose. Essentially racial segregation had taken root across the South because of the accumulation of many local legislative initiatives sustained by judicial activism of the various southern state courts. Then, in 1896, in *Plessy v. Ferguson*, the U.S. Supreme Court gave its blessing to the racially segregated way of life local legislative and judicial actions had imposed on the South. The Court ruled segregation was permissible so long as there was a condition of equality in its public policy implementation.

Upon learning of the *Plessy v. Ferguson* decision, Bishop Henry M. Turner, of the African Methodist Episcopal Church, referred to the United States Supreme Court as a "corrupt conclave." He said, "fool judges distort and debauch the United States Constitution to further degrade the race." However, he praised the minority opinion written by Justice John M. Harlan, who viewed the majority opinion as a perversion of the Constitution. Bishop Turner saw Justice Harlan as the only righteous member of the Court and said black children should forever "revere" his name. In essence Justice Harlan said the Constitution was, and should be, color blind.

Riding the wave of a surging "Negro phobia," legislators in southern states moved to purge the last duly elected black representatives from their legislatures. Ten years after the *Plessy* decision this was accomplished in 1906, the year the last African-American would serve in a southern state's legislative body (Georgia) until the post World War II era. After Booker T. Washington's *Atlanta Exposition Address* in 1895 (followed the next year by the *Plessy* decision) those legislatures readily believed the segregation policies they had enacted were justifiable. Southern politicians were quick to refer to Washington's *Atlanta Address* where he said, "In all things that are purely social we can be as separate as the five fingers, yet one as the hand in all things essential to mutual progress."

A major consequence of Booker T. Washington's 1895 *Atlanta Address* was favorable publicity given to him from significant venues which shaped public opinion. By the beginning of the 20th Century he had gained widespread positive recognition acknowledging him as the preeminent spokesperson for African-Americans. Pleased by his "responsible" views, Washington was accorded a special status by the white power structure. Andrew Carnegie took an interest in what Washington represented.

African-Americans of influence in their respective communities concurred with this recognition of Washington. Black ministers, educators, and businessmen thought of Washington as a key person with great potential to work for the advancement of their race and were supportive of his policy statements.

As founder and president of Alabama's Tuskegee Institute, Booker T. Washington issued various statements assuring influential whites that blacks "were more interested in economic opportunity" than social integration and political participation on the basis of racial equality. Washington's philosophy actually minimized political participation as an end in and of itself. It was not, he reasoned, urgently required to improve the overall lot of African-Americans. Thus, he would most likely be adverse to advice Frederick Douglass gave in the last year of his life (1895) to "agitate, agitate, agitate!" Washington wouldn't want to be perceived as an angry, hence unreasonable, black man to those very capable of shaping public opinion favorably toward him.

The state of affairs for African-Americans at the beginning of the 20th Century was an unmitigated disaster. Black historian Rayford Logan called this time "the nadir of Negro history." In 1900, circumstances for most African-Americans were no better than what they had been twenty years earlier in 1880. Within certain circles of the African-American community there was acknowledgment things had taken a readily discernible turn for the worse. The most prominent feature indicative of how bad things had become was the dramatic rise in the number of lynchings taking place across the South.

At the turn of the century statistical information on lynching was ominous and revealing. In the decade between 1899 and 1909, southern lynching of blacks had risen ten percent. In the first two years of the new century alone, there were 214 reported lynchings! Corresponding to this was a decrease of nearly thirty-one percent in the number of whites being lynched. When assessing aggregate numbers by 1909, it became clearly evident a racially inspired custom had taken hold in southern society.

The muckraker writer Ray Stannard Baker visited the South early in the first decade of the 20th Century. He utilized events he observed as subject material for his book, *Following The Color Line: American Negro Citizenship in the Progressive Era*. The southern justice system came under his close scrutiny. Essentially he reported it was a travesty regarding equal justice for

African-Americans. He noted a black man arrested for the same crime as a white would receive a harsher sentence. In one instance a black man arrested for public drunkenness received a fifteen dollar fine, but a white man was more likely to receive a reprimand or perhaps a three dollar fine. If the black man was unable to pay the higher fine, which was likely, he would be assigned to a chain gang for a month or two. A more serious offense, like violating a Jim Crow ordnance, often meant a higher fine with a longer chain gang sentence if the fine couldn't be paid. (A $15 fine in 1906, would roughly be the equivalent of $250 a hundred years later.)

Baker noted Georgia's chain gang system turned a profit for both the state and various counties. Chain gangs were hired out to private contractors who bid for their services. He observed one bidder in particular, often awarded the services of chain gangs, to be an influential Atlanta banker. This man also owned a very large brick works which utilized convict labor of which African-Americans were overwhelmingly the majority. Baker reported this man saying "…large fortunes in Atlanta have come chiefly from the labor of chain gangs of convicts leased from the state."

Shortly after the turn of the 20th Century the critical question was whether Booker T. Washington's philosophy would ameliorate or exacerbate the everyday circumstances African-Americans had to contend with in their lives? Washington didn't promise pie in the sky. He called for rigorous self sacrifice within the continuum of the ongoing struggle in pursuit of what he perceived as realistic goals for African-Americans.

The idea of pulling one's self up by one's bootstraps was a frequent admonition offered by Booker T. Washington. Some students snickered upon hearing this. Usually a perceptive student would ask, "Suppose you didn't have boots – what then?" Of course I always hoped that question would be asked. It was a question begging a point needing to be made. Most would agree the bootstrap reference was of dubious validity and I added W.E.B. DuBois would likely agree. I would then make an analogy to another dubious observation made by President John F. Kennedy in the early 1960s. With regard to economic growth, Kennedy once said, "A rising tide lifts all boats." His statement, not questioned by the press corps, presupposes everyone has a boat, sort of like the notion everyone has boots with straps.

Washington believed economic gains would come through hard work and attention to careful money management. Whimsical compulsive buying to stay current with the latest fads would likely displease him. I wonder what he would say about this time with so many having burdensome credit card debts? As for impulse buying, Booker T. Washington would likely agree with my father's frequent admonition, "Nothing's a bargain if you don't need it!" If individuals were steadfast in resisting behavior which squandered hard earned economic advantages, then, he believed, progress would be realized by subsequent generations.

Of his generation Washington said, "the opportunity to earn a dollar in a factory just now is worth infinitely more than the opportunity to spend a dollar in an opera house." For him the denial of immediate gratifications would serve as stepping stones for the industrious and talented of subsequent generations to proceed further along the path of progress sure to benefit the race. His beliefs regarding hard work and thrift were reasons why the elites of the white power structure approved of him. Essentially he believed in and endorsed what is known as the Protestant work ethic.

The values of the Protestant work ethic were regularly acknowledged by Booker T. Washington. After all, they facilitated recognition of a person such as himself. Given his early circumstances, Washington certainly made something of himself in accordance with the dynamic the Protestant work ethic represented. Of his influence, it was apparent seventy years later when Rev. Jesse Jackson said, "You may not be responsible for being thrown down, but you are responsible for getting up!" At bottom Washington's views didn't pose a threat to whites. After all they were approved of by those having the most economic and political influence and compatible as well with white middle class sensibilities of that time. The American Dream was yours if you worked hard and kept the devil's temptations at bay. (On a humorous note regarding the devil, classes enjoyed my reference to the late 1960s African-American comedian Flip Wilson. In explaining his indiscretions, he would lament "the devil made me do it!")

Washington also subscribed to laissez faire capitalism, the prevalent economic paradigm at the turn of the century. This belief served as the lynchpin of his relationship with the quintessential capitalist Andrew Carnegie. In large part thanks to Carnegie's financial support, Washington was able to found the National Negro Business League. In Carnegie's published essay, "Wealth" (June of 1889 for the *North American Review*), one view he offered was "Our duty is with what is practicable now … in our day and generation." Washington shared this view. But many of Washington's critics saw Carnegie in a different light than he did. They viewed Carnegie and his

peers as being responsible for exploiting African-Americans as strikebreak-
ers. And, as such, they saw black workers being even more despised by
working class whites.

Any confrontational challenges to the existing socio-economic scheme
of things were to be avoided as far as Booker T. Washington was concerned.
This policy made him acceptable to Carnegie and his super-rich contem-
poraries. They approved of his advice to African-Americans to be "patient."
To the power structure this was "responsible" counsel. He was convenient
to the new industrialists. There would be no wave making sponsored by
Washington. In his time he wouldn't advocate participation in something
akin to the Occupy Wall Street Movement of 2011-2012. For the most part
he acquiesced to the role economic elites expected him to play as spokesperson for African-Americans. In that role Washington was useful to the
plutocrats. But, given that, I also think we can safely assume he and the
financial oligarchy carefully calculated how useful they were to each other.
And, I don't suppose Washington and his supporters would ever readily
acknowledge the part money played in keeping his credibility viable among
the masses, especially black folk. Surely Dr. W.E.B. DuBois was on to this
pragmatic quid pro quo.

Booker T. Washington was invited to the White House for dinner by
President Theodore Roosevelt in October of 1901. To a great extent this
event clinched celebrity status for Washington in most black communities around the country. (However, news of the dinner brought immediate
southern newspaper editorial condemnations.) Basically Roosevelt was acknowledging Washington as an exemplary role model for what he believed
was possible for those who had begun life at the bottom. Roosevelt's recognition of Washington confirmed the white power structure's approval of
him. He was presented, ala Horatio Alger mode, as one exemplifying the
idea it was possible for one to rise up - just follow his example! The power
structure knew Americans often bought into myths. African-Americans
were credited with the same capacity to buy into myth as well – that's
equality of sorts. One African-American who wasn't buying was Dr. W.E.B.
DuBois.

In the first decade of the 20th Century, Booker T. Washington enjoyed
the luxury of not really having to respond to a handful of black critics. He
was, after all, backed by the likes of Presidents Theodore Roosevelt and
William Howard Taft, as well as key influential whites of vast fortunes. In

his *Atlanta Address* of 1895, Washington had assured these industrialists that black workers would continue to be a stable and dependable source of labor. Unlike their recent European immigrant counterparts, black workers wouldn't snap at the hands feeding them. He said black workers, "without strikes and labor wars," would continue to build the country's "railroads and cities." This message was music to the ears of super rich industrialists who saw in Washington an ally for their continued very profitable laissez faire policies. In addition to white industrialists supporting him, by 1906 it was undeniably obvious Washington had a vast network of African-Americans adhering to his philosophy.

Many African-Americans who recognized Washington's special status engaged in initiatives to establish leadership roles for themselves in their respective communities. They quickly learned Washington would respond to them favorably with economic assistance in exchange for loyalty to him. Northern philanthropists frequently funded projects proposed to them by Washington. Portions of sums he received were then funneled to his supporters across the South. Financial assistance received from him enabled supporters to undertake worthy local projects which, in turn, enhanced their status in their respective communities. Those loyal to Washington included men who published weekly newspapers which, as one would expect, obviously praised the wisdom of Washington's leadership. Basically his supporters acknowledged the correctness of Washington's philosophical orientation on issues affecting African-Americans. The network supportive of his leadership was known as the "Tuskegee Machine."

Atlanta's two prominent figures in higher education, John Hope, President of Atlanta Baptist College, and sociologist W.E.B. DuBois, of Atlanta University, expressed opinions that growing numbers agreed with. The desirability of dialogue within the African-American community was seen in a positive light by those impressed with the opinions questioning "King Booker." Also, in 1905, a journal *Voice of the Negro,* published in Atlanta, began to openly criticize Booker T. Washington. The following year (1906) the Equal Rights Association was formed in Macon, Georgia where several hundred black delegates held a meeting to consider policies for advancing racial equality. Those attending called for the restitution of unencumbered voting rights for African-Americans. Also, criticism of Washington's policies were expressed and shared by many.

With publication of his *The Soul of Black Folk*, in 1903, W.E.B. Du-Bois began to achieve recognition as a prominent anti-Washington opinion maker, especially because of his provocative essay entitled "Of Mr. Booker T. Washington and Others." The Washington ideas to which DuBois objected most were: the notion the current generation of African-Americans shouldn't pursue higher education in the liberal arts, but should focus on industrial skills instead, and, secondly, shouldn't initiate challenges to restore the franchise. When it came to the right to vote DuBois was as adamant as Frederick Douglass had been on this issue. Both were insistent African-Americans should have the franchise as did immigrants just off the boat from Europe. DuBois said African-Americans shouldn't forfeit or give up political equality or their civil rights for the sake of "domestic harmony."

Early in 1905, W.E.B. DuBois invited a "few selected persons," like minded to be sure, to meet at Fort Erie, Ontario, in July. This invitation was nothing less than an unmistakable call to those who opposed Washington to come together to establish an alternative philosophical agenda to the one espoused by Booker T. Washington in his 1895 *Atlanta Address*. This gathering in Canada, near Niagara Falls, incorporated itself as the Niagara Movement and its participants agreed to holding annual meetings. The following year, in 1906, they met at Harpers Ferry, West Virginia. At these meetings delegates debated the course of action to challenge the Jim Crow system and Washington's philosophy which they viewed as accommodating to it.

The unofficial publication sponsored by supporters of the Niagara Movement was *The Horizon*. DuBois was a major contributor and with others they lampooned "King Booker" and his allies. *The Horizon* was published in Washington, D.C. From 1907 until 1910. Washington sponsored publications featured counter charges to the ones made by pro-Niagara Movement writers.

When the 20th Century began, Washington's leadership was at its zenith. By the time it was half over, many significant African-Americans were saying things about him that would have dismayed black folks living at the turn of the century. For example Harlem Congressman Adam Clayton Powell, Jr. said, "When viewed as a leader of the black masses, he must be judged as one who did more to retard the progress of black folk than any other single individual." Powell's assessment was something DuBois believed at an earlier time.

Now a brief digression in conjunction with mention of Adam Clayton Powell, Jr. He was still a member of Congress representing Harlem at the time I taught my first class in African-American history. First elected in 1944, he served until 1972. Most students knew little about him, but a few older ones knew he had been investigated a few times but didn't exactly know why. Another student responded by saying, "if you're black and in politics you have to be more honest than white politicians or they'll come after you before they'll go after the most corrupt one of them." He didn't hold back on that opinion. Spontaneous responses such as his made my classes especially enjoyable. I always told students they had a part to play if they didn't want class to be dull and forgetful. Back to Powell, I felt obligated to mention he played a major role in getting New York City's retail stores, such as Macy's, to hire African-American sales persons in the 1940s.

With the horrendous Springfield, Illinois race riot of the previous year (1908) still fresh in their memories, many progressive whites and participants of the Niagara Movement, including Dr. W.E.B. DuBois, came together on May 30, 1909 for an informal reception at the Henry Street settlement house in New York City. The next day they assembled, with some interested parties from the general public, at the Cooper Union. They had gathered to address the issue of unprovoked "lawless attacks upon the negro," as well as the indifference in the public at large to the plight of African-Americans. Conference participants were hopeful they could coalesce as a positive force to promote a "renewal of the struggle for civil and political liberty" for African-Americans.

The names of those responding to "the call" are recognizable to anyone familiar with the activists of the Progressive Era. In attendance were Jane Addams, Ida Wells Barnett, John Dewey, W.E.B. DuBois, William Dean Howells, Lincoln Steffens, Rabbi Stephen S. Wise, and Mary E. Wooley, President of Mt. Holyoke College, to name just a few. Before adjourning participants of this special assembly called for chartering an organization to be known as the National Negro Committee. This organization proposed and then sponsored another conference to be held the following year – 1910.

Early in deliberations the following year a new name was decided upon. The organization was to be known as the National Association for the Advancement of Colored People, soon generally referred to as the NAACP. According to Mary White Ovington the goals announced by the NAACP, in 1910, were "denounced by every white man who gave to Negro institutions." Across the South local black leaders dependent on Booker T. Washington's largess, to sustain community activities they played prominent roles in, were generally negative in their reactions to the formation of the NAACP. Many other informed African-Americans, such as the clergy and teachers, discreetly reserved judgment about the newly formed NAACP.

Named as Director of Publicity and Research for the NAACP, DuBois wasted no time in pressing the board of directors to allow him to publish a periodical. They agreed to sponsor a magazine of which DuBois was designated editor. It was named *The Crisis* and DuBois edited this publication for almost twenty-five years. It was the vehicle for "Association propaganda, news, and his own personal views." Within a decade its circulation rose to 100,000 subscribers. Just after World War I, at the time of the Red Scare, *The Crisis* came under intense scrutiny by a New York Joint Legislative Committee investigating "revolutionary radicalism." It seems advocating equal rights in all phases of American life was considered a radical threat by many New York politicians at that time.

The Progressive Era is a term historians apply to the period between the years 1900 to 1915. Many notable worthy reform measures had been initiated and came to pass in that time span. However, a closer look reveals this period offered few benefits to America's black population per se. After all, what good was the primary election, the initiative, the referendum or the recall, if one wasn't permitted to participate in the election process? The progressive political climate of this era conceded very little to African-Americans.

In the South the Democrats were in control and their electability was facilitated by white only primaries. The system allowed the South to continue men in Congress for extraordinary lengths of time compared to their northern congressional counterparts. Because Congress functioned on a seniority basis, southern Congressmen were able to become chairpersons of select committees. In those capacities they were capable of killing any bills placed on their respective committee's agendas viewed as having potential to undermine the South's Jim Crow system. Their significant political positions enabled them to stymie any proposals calling into question southern racial policies. Throughout the first half of the 20th Century, their strategy was to effect a holding action to preserve the status quo in race relations south of the Mason-Dixon line.

The presidential election of 1912 was the first the recently formed NAACP had to assess. Looking to the Progressive Party of Theodore Roosevelt, running as this third party's candidate, the NAACP sent a draft of proposals to the party's platform committee. Mostly by the hand of W.E.B. DuBois, it called for a meaningful civil rights plank to be included in the platform. However, it was brushed aside with an indifference that dismayed Joel E. Spingarn, the dedicated white NAACP trustee, who knew Theodore Roosevelt personally. Spingarn was taken aback when the former president warned him of his "dangerous" association with W.E.B. DuBois. Since Theodore Roosevelt didn't object when the convention refused to acknowledge and seat black delegates, many blacks, initially favoring his candidacy, lost interest in him.

The Virginia born Democrat, Woodrow Wilson, won the election of 1912 because of the split in the Republican Party. (In 1992, President George H.W. Bush, seeking a second term, lost many Republican votes to third party candidate Ross Perot, thus enabling Democrat William "Bill" Clinton, in similar fashion as Wilson in 1912, to win the presidency.) Wilson had received endorsements from some influential African-Americans including Booker T. Washington who said, "Mr Wilson is in favor of the things which tend toward the uplift, the improvement, and advancement of my people." In less than a year Wilson disappointed most black voters who had initially supported him.

The Crisis reported Wilson failing to appoint blacks to the ministerial posts in Liberia and Haiti. Both were positions African-Americans held in the previous five Republican administrations. Wilson also permitted certain department heads to reduce the number of black appointees from thirty-one, as retained by the Taft administration, to just eight. Wilson also approved of implementing racial segregation in eating and toilet facilities in federal office buildings. To make matters worse, Wilson didn't object to the Civil Service Commission instituting a policy requiring photographs of persons taking examinations. This policy seemed blatantly racist. It would too easily facilitate race bias in hiring decisions.

In many respects of more long term significance than the legacy of Booker T. Washington, who died in 1915, was the birth that year of *The Association for the Study of Negro Life and History*. This worthy organization came into existence thanks to the dedication and perseverance of its founder Carter G. Woodson. It immediately added a renewed sense of purpose for black scholars doing research and writing on important previously neglected topics pertinent to the African-American experience. Beginning in 1926 it called for a week long presentation of events in Black History every February. Fifty years later, in the Bicentennial Year of 1976, the celebration of Black History was expanded to the entire month of February.

Also, in 1915, the Supreme Court finally struck down the "grandfather clauses" in the state constitutions of Maryland and Oklahoma. In *Guinn v. United States,* they were ruled in violation of the intent and scope of the Constitution's Fifteenth Amendment. Two years later, in *Buchanan v. Warley,* a residency restriction ordinance, passed just a few years earlier by Louisville, was declared a "denial of property rights under the due process clause of the Fourteenth Amendment." *The Crisis* widely publicized both NAACP victories. The Supreme Court seemed to be moving in a direction away from *Plessy v. Ferguson.* Perhaps these recent decisions caused some to speculate about whether the days of Jim Crow were numbered.

Though the aforementioned judicial victories were very significant, attention to them by most African-Americans was probably of short duration. After all, mainstream newspapers, widely read, were reporting events associated with the war in Europe begun in August of 1914. In the greater scheme of things consequences of the war might bring about change, for good or bad, having greater impact on African-American communities. The essential question, implicit in speculations by African-American intellectuals, was: how will this war affect us? To be sure this was a compelling question the significance of which was understood by many who were staying abreast of the news from Europe.

Chapter 9

As a consequence of the European war, later designated World War I, the countries at war, especially the Allies, placed unprecedented war materials orders with American manufacturers. These orders generated great demand in the North, especially in cities of the Great Lakes region, for additional manpower. Since the war stopped European immigration, which had long satisfied northern industrial manpower needs, the industrialists now turned to workers of African-American ancestry as a cheap alternative labor source. They saw the necessity of encouraging southern poverty stricken blacks to migrate North. This endeavor was boosted by northern African-American newspapers, such as the Chicago *Defender*, which encouraged northern migration to enjoy better living conditions. Black workers, in turn, informed family members back home their wages were appreciably higher than those paid to workers anywhere in the South.

During the first half of the 20th Century, white workers with special skills, learned through apprenticeships, belonged to locals of the American Federation of Labor (AFL). White members of these unions were not interested in bringing young black men into apprenticeships their union locals sponsored. Union members would readily vouch for sons, nephews, and brothers-in-law before sponsoring an African-American to begin an apprenticeship. For the longest time the AFL national leadership steered clear of issuing directives to challenge local policies that basically sustained racial discrimination in apprenticeship programs.

Shortly after John F. Kennedy took the presidential oath of office, on January 20th of 1961, a few enlightened national AFof L leaders began to evaluate apprenticeship policies pertaining to the union's locals. When acknowledging those pushing for change in local union policies, we shouldn't overlook the participation by progressive white union leaders in the enormous gathering in Washington on August 28th of 1963. The crowd of 250,000 rallied to implement the theme - "Jobs and Freedom." Black and white progressive union leaders had joined with black civil rights organizations to co-sponsor this massive rally where Martin Luther King Jr. gave his memorable "I Have A Dream" speech. Among prominent union leaders attending were A. Philip Randolph and United Auto Workers head Walter Reuther. The orientation change by the unions could be seen as a small step pointing toward the giant steps taken in the middle of the decade when the Civil Rights Act of 1964 and the Voting Rights Act of 1965 were passed by Congress and vigorously endorsed by President Lyndon B. Johnson.

At one time African-American labor leader A. Philip Randolph subscribed to certain anti-capitalist tenets found in Marxist ideology. For him, early on, the Marxist view best explained causation for racial discrimination rooted in economic injustice. However, shortly after the war, by the mid 1920s, Randolph apparently came to the conclusion no single ideology offered ultimate answers for African-Americans struggling to gain fair wages and achieve true civil and political equality. However, his one unwavering belief, quoted by his biographer Daniel S. Davis, was "when no profits are to be made from race friction, no one will any longer be interested in stirring up race prejudice."

Randolph understood the American Federation of Labor's locals enabled their members to earn wages and have benefits the unskilled workers could only dream about. Thus, the unions of skilled workers tended to stay aloof from issues affecting unskilled workers of which a very large portion were black. The white skilled workers rarely bothered themselves with questions pertinent to just compensation for non-skilled workers. Of course Randolph also realized many better paid white skilled workers became conservative in proportion to the rise of their standard of living. As he saw it the notion of we, as in we workers, was rarely understood by members of

AF of L locals to mean anything transcending priorities established locally by themselves.

In contrast to the local mentality of the AF of L was the International Workers of the World (IWW) popularly known as the Wobblies. A. Philip Randolph believed the IWW had more to offer to black workers. Its dual function was to promote one big union and expose the exploitative nature of capitalism. He also acknowledged the IWW's worthy commitment to "change society." For Randolph this meant elimination of minority exploitation. But, the Wobblies didn't meaningfully survive the Red Scare in the immediate aftermath of World War I.

The IWW's radical ideology was a threat to the corporate sponsored political status quo. So, they were blacklisted and harassed constantly by trumped-up criminal charges. Their organizers received death threats when they arrived in certain locations and attempted to recruit new members. Some were murdered! The Red Scare hysteria caused many IWW members to abandon organizing activities and, instead, seek the cover of anonymity. Also a factor, when considering why the IWW's message became less compelling to workers, was the observable across the board rise in the standard of living brought on by the unprecedented prosperity of the 1920s.

Upon going into more detail about the IWW and how it was systematically maligned by a sensationalizing corporate media, a few brighter students were quick to make an analogy to the Black Panthers. Of course there's an element of truth to that analogy. Those condemning Black Panthers never mentioned their free breakfast program for elementary school kids. Likewise the IWW's endeavors to take care of workers' widows and children were not publicized by corporate interests out to discredit them.

When Congress declared war, in April of 1917, W.E.B. DuBois called for the African-American community to "close ranks" and support President Wilson's wartime agenda. Wilson justified America's entry into the European conflict by saying the war would be "the war to end all wars." Wilson's other stated objectives called for the liberation of subject peoples and to secure for them the democratic principle of "self determination." This, of course, had anti-imperialist implications. Logically it should have meant the indigenous peoples of Africa and Asia would gain independence from British, French, and German colonial authority. That's what W.E.B. Dubois understood Wilson's idealistic pronouncement to mean.

Additionally, Wilson had urged Americans to join in the fight to "help make the world safe for democracy."

In marked contrast to DuBois position supporting Wilson's wartime agenda was that of A. Philip Randolph and Chandler Owen. In their publication, *The Messenger,* they denounced Wilson's erstwhile idealism as a "sham, a mockery, a rape on decency and a travesty on common sense." They labeled the war an imperialistic struggle. As they saw it, World War I was a consequence of capitalistic rivalry. Which ever power survived would gain a larger share of the world's markets and resources by taking possession of the defeated powers colonies in Africa and Asia.

At the time America declared war there were four African-American regiments serving on active duty. The units were: the Ninth and Tenth Cavalries (historically known as the Buffalo Soldiers) and the Twenty-fourth and Twenty-fifth Infantry Regiments. Also, at the time there were eight all black National Guard units. Within a week of the declaration of war the black guard units were up to full organizational strength. The War Department then prohibited further black enlistments until a policy update was agreed upon within the department.

While the Selective Service Bill was being debated in May of 1917, Secretary of War Newton D. Baker went on record favoring its passage without restrictions preventing African-Americans from being drafted. A majority of northern Congressmen supported Secretary Baker's position. However, they favored the continuation of organizational structure along racial lines as was the case during the Civil and Spanish-American Wars. This meant again having units comprised of black enlisted men with white officers. Adamantly opposed to drafting black men under any circumstances was Mississippi's Senator James K. Vardaman. He said such a policy was foolhardy and would create a "menace to the South."

Educated African-Americans were indignant about being denied the opportunity to obtain commissions. General Leonard Wood promised to initiate a black officers' candidate school if a list of two hundred college educated men could be compiled. When this occurred, an officers' candidate school was set up at Fort Des Moines in Iowa. By October of 1917, 639 men had received commissions. There were one hundred and six captains and the rest were first and second lieutenants.

One year after the declaration of war almost 200,000 African-American troops were in Europe. Approximately 150,000 of them were assigned to labor battalions and food service units. Most in the navy served as mess attendants on board troop transport ships. Army non-combatant units did such work as unload navy supply ships docked at LeHavre, thence to load railroad box cars with supplies destined for the front. Near the front other black troops unloaded the railroad cars and placed the materials onto pack mules. Mule team drivers, most of whom were black, took the pack mules to regimental compounds near the front for a final unloading and distribution of the supplies to combat units.

My father had an older sister who was married to a man who served in World War I. He had two years of college and was given a commission. I suppose because of racial attitude assumptions, he was assigned to an African-American labor battalion based on the fact he was a Virginian. It seems the army believed he knew better than white northerners about how to get along with African-Americans. I asked a class what they thought of that. One comment coming out of the discussion took me by surprise. "Hey, professor, you're white and you know how to get along with us better than the other white professors." I didn't quite know how to respond to that and told him so. "That's no offense," he said. Another student chimed in, "it's really a compliment Professor Reiss." There it was, as I've said before, you never know what kind of comments might pop up during a community college class.

Most African-Americans would have preferred serving in combat units. Many believed they had been racially pigeon holed into the old stereotype situation of "tote that barge and lift that bale." Resentments flared up on occasions and were manifested in what psychologists today would characterize as passive aggressive behavior. One extremely unpleasant task some black troops performed was taking the bodies of men killed in combat to certain places behind the lines for death certification registration. At these locations black carpenters made the thousands of simple coffins in which their slain fellow Americans were eventually buried.

In southern towns near military installations where blacks were stationed, the white townspeople resented their presence. Black troops in their midst seemed to place an extra burden on their local Jim Crow way of doing things. At Houston, Texas, in August of 1917, some black soldiers tried to board a trolley car which the passengers claimed was reserved for whites. An altercation ensued which brought police to the scene and they immediately began clubbing the soldiers. Black civilians entered the fray as did whites which then precipitated a race riot. By the time violence had subsided seventeen whites had lost their lives. Ultimately, thirteen black soldiers of the Twenty-fourth Infantry were convicted of murder and hanged. Additional numbers were punished for their participation and some received life sentences.

The previous month on July 2nd, a calamitous race riot had erupted in East St. Louis. It grew out of friction between white and black workers in a factory doing war contract work. Scores of African-Americans were stabbed, clubbed, and even hanged. Responding to this odious event the NAACP office in New York sponsored the now famous silent protest parade along Fifth Avenue on July 28, 1917. To the sound of muffled drums hundreds of participants carried signs and placards, one of which read: "Mr. President, why not make America safe for democracy?"

Though President Wilson knew of his cabinet members' concerns on racial issues, he maintained a silence on the subject. As the distinguished African-American historian John Hope Franklin observed, he was "unwilling to make…statements that would seem to ally him with black leaders – perhaps to do so would identify him with their demands for racial equality as quid pro quo for their wartime efforts." When it came to race matters the southerner Wilson wasn't about to allow what might give the appearance he was pressured into making concessions. When I was inclined to give Wilson the benefit of doubt, I reminded myself he had a private showing of D.W. Griffith's racist movie *Birth of a Nation* in the White House and commented favorably on it.

Of the black troops permitted to see combat in France, the 369th Regiment established an enviable record. In the opinion of many military historians, their battlefield accomplishments were unequaled by any other American units engaging the enemy. They had moved up to the front in April of 1918 and were under enemy fire in the trenches for 191 consecutive days. No one in this unit was ever captured by the Germans. The 369th never allowed the Germans to retake any position they had taken from them. The Harlem Hellfighters were cited for braver on eleven different occasions. The *Croix de Guerre*, France's coveted highest military decoration, was bestowed upon the entire regiment.

The 369th's gallantry made the front pages, on many occasions, of New York City's newspapers. As might be expected southern newspapers seldom publicized accounts of their exemplary service to their readers. On the other hand, African-American newspapers extolled the heroic exploits of Harlem's "Fighting 369th." The unit's impressive reputation was soon shared by its regimental band.

Prior to America's entry into the war, James Reese Europe led an all black band that was constantly being booked to perform at New York's high society affairs. Some influential people became familiar with his talent directing the Clef Club Band. With America's entry into the war and the formation of the 369th infantry, they arranged for him to head the regiment's marching band. Once the 369th was in France the popularity of its band, led by Lt. James (Jim) Europe, spread quickly to other American army units and to the French public as well.

Perhaps performances by Jim Europe's regimental band whet the French appetite for jazz music. (After the war many African-American musicians went to France to satisfy the demand for jazz.) At a given event Lieutenant Europe initially had his band play songs in a traditional manner, but then it moved on to music with noticeable jazz riffs. The French loved it when his band swung into music with upbeat renditions. The Andrews Sisters had a smash hit in World War II with their song about the "Boogie-Woogie Bugle Boy of Company B." Now who do you suppose had trumpet players ahead of that curve? I suspect you would find them in Jim Europe's 369th Hell Fighters Band doing their thing in France during World War I.

At war's end a promising career in music lay before Jim Europe. On April 22, 1919 his band performed in Philadelphia's Academy of Music where he introduced soon to be acclaimed singer Marian Anderson to the audience. His band was booked in Chicago and then in New York before another engagement in Philadelphia on May 8th. From Philadelphia they took an all night train to Boston where they were scheduled for a 2:30 matinee concert and an evening performance as well in Mechanics Hall on May 9th. During intermission of the evening performance Europe was in his dressing room talking with a few band members. Drummer Herbert Wright then entered the room. He seemed upset and expressed grievances to Europe. Evidently he didn't think Europe properly acknowledged him and he became angry. To everyone's surprise, Wright then lunged at Europe with a knife and stabbed him. Taken to hospital, he passed away at 11:45 P M on May 9, 1919.

Jim Europe was back from France and out of army uniform barely six months when he died. He had already achieved celebrity status in Harlem as the crowds on the streets for his funeral procession indicated. The circumstances of his death plus the fact his talent was just becoming known beyond Harlem made him a tragic figure by any reckoning. Of the music Europe played in France, his biographer Reid Badger quoted him as saying, "We won France by playing music which was ours and not a pale imitation of others, and if we are to develop in America we must develop along our own lines."

Another all black unit, fighting in France in WW I, was the 92nd Division. It's tenacity under fire was acknowledged by General John Pershing. As for Pershing, he commanded an expedition into Mexico to capture the bandit Pancho Villa prior to America's entry into WW I. He held the all black 10th Cavalry Regiment in high esteem and requested it be included in his force to hunt down Villa. Because of this, it seems some officers and then enlisted men started referring to the general as "Black Jack" Pershing. This nickname became public knowledge when it was reported in newspapers having correspondents present during his command's hunt for Villa.

On the surface General Pershing seemed confident in the abilities of black troops, but African-American Harvard law professor Randall Kennedy expressed reservations about General Pershing. In his *The Persistence Of The Color Line* (2011), on the topic of black officers, Kennedy quotes Pershing saying, "We must not eat with them, must not shake hands or seek to talk or meet with them outside of the requirements of military service." If Pershing were President I suppose he would never have invited Booker T. Washington to dine at the White House as President Theodore Roosevelt had done.

At war's conclusion, fair minded people realized African-Americans had played a significant role in the endeavor to "make the world safe for democracy." Blacks, of course, wondered if their patriotic sacrifices meant they would finally be able to fully participate in their own country's democracy, the country they had proudly born arms for since its inception at Philadelphia in 1776.

As the year 1919 began Americans at home felt a sense of relief the stress associated with the war was behind them. Other Americans, in uniforms in Europe, were excitedly looking forward to their return to loved ones. All were jubilant about the war being over. Did any have premonitions about what the year 1919 might bring? History has revealed wars frequently generate unpleasant socio-economic circumstances in their immediate aftermath, but most Americans probably didn't anticipate this happening in their country. Americans simply wanted things to return to normal, be the way they were before the war as soon as possible. However, societal anxieties and stresses were not abated in 1919 simply because the war was over. New stresses emerged resulting from sporadic violent confrontations between big business and organized labor. Also, societal tensions were manifested by race riots in the summer of 1919. In African-American history that period is known as the Red Summer because racial violence caused much blood spilling in the streets of many American cities.

In 1919, there was the issue of the expectations of returning African-American servicemen. Of course white folks in the South assumed things would go back to the way they were before the war. To a large extent they didn't see attitudes had dramatically changed in black communities. But, of course, they never were inclined to address black grievances before and were in no hurry to do so after the war. So, how would attitudinal changes in black communities of the North manifest themselves? Keep in mind that in the North, as in the South, most white folks believed blacks would still show deference to them as they had basically done before the war. However, what the war had changed was the willingness of many African-Americans to unthinkingly comply with old societal expectations based on previous race based social conditioning.

Newspaper editors, white elected public officials, religious leaders, as well as educators rarely questioned or challenged racial attitudes up to the time America entered World War I or in its aftermath. Before the war and into the 1920s popular culture was constantly depicting black Americans as ignorant, happy go lucky, water melon eating buffoons. In entertainment venues, especially vaudeville shows, many white comedians in blackface used stereotype characterizations in their acts. Even West Indies born Bert Williams applied soot to make his complexion darker to play a role he created more convincingly. As the first featured black artist in the Ziegfeld Follies, just prior to WW I, Williams sang the song "Nobody" which he wrote. The implication of the song's title meant that if you were black you were a nobody in American society.

Eddie Cantor, a Jewish vaudeville comedic song and dance man, did his routine in blackface. (Most white vaudevillians never gave this ploy a second thought.) Cantor wasn't in blackface when I first saw him on Milton Berle's weekly televised comedy hour in 1951. However, he did sing his vaudeville theme song - "If You Knew Susie Like I Know Susie." Then there was Al Jolson, in blackface, singing what became his signature song, "Mammie," featured in Hollywood's first sound film, *The Jazz Singer* released in 1927.

But 1919 wasn't to be like previous years before the war. Now many African-Americans, including the hundreds of thousands recently moved to the North, were unwilling to play the second class citizen role historically expected of them. The knowledge they too had enthusiastically rallied 'round the flag, had faced the enemy's bullets, etc., was a motivating factor prompting demands for equal legal and political rights as enjoyed by other Americans. The preceding plus more extensive activities undertaken by such groups as the NAACP and the Urban League were facets of the phenomena altering the African-American community's sense of self at this time. The post war assertiveness came under the "New Negro" rubric - a concept advanced on many fronts and reenforced by African-American newspaper editors.

A prevalent theme at the core of race riots, in 1919, was the apparent lack of commitment by local police to initiate measures indicating black lives and property had equal priority for protection as was afforded to the white community. In the riots of the Red Summer of 1919, as in previous riots, rarely were state militia units called out in time to help local police keep matters from getting worse. Again and again, eyewitness testimony said National Guard units were called only after matters had dramatically taken a turn for the worse. Too frequently the attitude of local authorities was to let violence "run its course." Consequently this meant casualties in black communities increased as property damage also became more extensive.

Of the numerous race riots in 1919, Chicago's came to represent the most reprehensible. To be sure racial antagonisms boiling over into violence elsewhere exhibited causation common denominators. However, it seems the fury exhibited in Chicago was of greater socio-pathological intensity and magnitude than revealed in the riots of Longview, Texas, Knoxville, Tennessee, Omaha, Nebraska, or Washington D.C. Erupting on July 27, the riot in Chicago resulted in thirty-eight persons dead, hundreds injured, and probably scores left with permanent disabilities. The fury ran its course for almost five days and resulted in property damage causing near a thousand people to become homeless.

As 1919 drew to a close, African-American spokespersons expressed their indignation with clarity and vehemence not frequently seen by these figures of authority before. An unprecedented militancy was evident in these many spontaneous eruptions of anger. A. Philip Randolph cried "Enough!" Unfortunately, most whites, especially those still expecting continued black servility, wouldn't, couldn't, comprehend the nature of this new assertiveness phenomena. Some white officials simplistically viewed the new behavior as a consequential symptom of a perceived international Bolshevik revolutionary conspiracy. African-Americans saw the absurdity of that assertion. Such an explanation amply indicated just how out of touch many white politicians were regarding black public opinion. In October, 1919, a *Pittsburgh Courier* editor wrote: "As long as the Negro submits to lynchings, burnings, and oppressions – and says nothing, he is a loyal American citizen. But, when he decides that lynchings and burnings shall cease, even at the cost of some bloodshed…then he is a Bolshevists."

The NAACP estimated seventy-six lynchings had occurred in the year 1919 alone! At a meeting in May, delegates from around the country agreed this was of paramount concern to the organization. A commonly held belief, in the broader culture, was an assumption black men accused of raping white women was the prime reason for certain communities allowing lynching to occur. To refute this notion, the NAACP supplied its Congressional supporters with data demonstrating "rape was a cause in only 17% of the lynchings of record and that in thirty-three years, 64 of the lynch victims were women." The NAACP decided the federal government had to take responsibility and initiated an intensive lobbying effort for Congress to pass the Dyer Anti-Lynching Bill. This endeavor was directed by James Weldon Johnson who had recently become the NAACP's first non-white Executive Secretary. This bill would pass in the House but was predictably defeated in the Senate where the South had more influence.

With regard to James Weldon Johnson, he collaborated with his brother Rosamond to compose the song "Lift Every Voice and Sing" which has become a special anthem to African-Americans. During his life James Weldon Johnson engaged in many significant undertakings the sum of which gave him recognition as a "Renaissance Man" by his biographer Arlene Clift-Pellow. His poem titled "50 Years" commemorated the time since Lincoln issued the Emancipation Proclamation, and was published in the *New York Times* in 1913. His insightful prose included the following titles:

The Autobiography of an Ex-Colored Man, Along This Way, and *Black Manhattan* published in 1930 as a source of information regarding New York's black history before the Harlem Renaissance era began.

By 1920, probably a majority of African-Americans had heard of the NAACP. They also likely understood it was fighting on their behalf to end segregation and other institutionalized forms of injustice based on race prejudice. However, active participation in the organization, i.e., paying dues and attending chapter meetings, was estimated at only two percent of the total black population. Nonetheless, in its first decade, the NAACP had promoted the idea of African-American patriotism during a time of national crisis and then, at war's end, had met head on the challenge from a refurbished racism as expressed by a revived Ku Klux Klan movement. Recall the Klan had gained impressive new numbers in part because it was portrayed as a noble and worthy organization by David W. Griffith's movie *Birth of a Nation*, released in 1915.

Strident messages presented in *The Crisis* editorials, often written by DuBois, were notable departures from the apparent docility associated with earlier articles written elsewhere by Booker T. Washington and his apologists. Readers of *The Crisis* were persistently reminded Washington's philosophy had always been questionable and was now, in this era of the "New Negro," understood as an outdated feature of the past.

The third decade of the 20th Century set the stage for Americans of African ancestry to break away from ideas originating in the late 19th Century. Also, there no longer seemed a need to designate one person as sole spokesperson for black America per se. And, both sexes articulated the dreams and hopes of black folk for a brighter equitable future. In this watershed decade one sees a new generation of creative individuals honing their talents while stridently defining the essence of America's black experience. Acknowledged by many, black and white alike, these individuals were in many respects the innovative "talented tenth" W.E.B. DuBois had envisioned the African-American community would ultimately bring forth. Much of their endeavors contributed to the essence of what became known as the Harlem Renaissance.

Philip Reiss in Air Force Uniform at 20 in 1957

*Philip Reiss (center) with NY Congressman John
Dow at college commencement in May of '68. Both
opposed Lyndon Johnson's Vietnam War policy*

Chapter 10

I n the 1920s the rhetoric of democracy, so audible during the recent war, had taken firm root in the African-American community's political consciousness. Thus, new initiatives for dignity and self respect were emanating from black communities throughout the nation. The language of democracy helped to propel these initiatives. A "New Negro," more politically aware and active than in the past, was emerging. The method of challenging old injustices seemed more direct than at previous times. This "New Negro" alarmed many white Americans who saw an assertiveness not evident prior to the war. DuBois and others were not going to forget war time propaganda regarding making the world "safe for democracy." Initially the phrase was applicable to Wilson's foreign policy goals, but now black leadership began utilizing it as a challenge for democracy's realization on the home front.

Vast numbers of whites now began to perceive blacks as brooding, sullen, and, worst of all, often acting uppity. The latter was probably most offensive to whites who expected African-Americans to never forget "their place," as defined by those whites of course! As the 1920s began many whites, especially poor whites, thought they were losing their white privilege in various aspects of social circumstances between the races. Many whites responded to that belief as the growth of a resurgent Ku Klux Klan seems to indicate. The Klan pandered to white fears of societal changes not readily understood by them.

Released in 1915, two years prior to America's entry into the European war, D.W. Griffith's film *Birth of a Nation* made a dramatic impact on white audiences across America. This film dubiously portrayed a critical era in American history, namely the Reconstruction Era which followed the Civil War. Back then the Ku Klux Klan shamelessly intimidated southern blacks by invoking violence. However, in his film Griffith portrayed that era's Klan in a most favorable light. Klan activities were presented as justifiable and necessary. The mission of Griffith's Klan, as was the mission of the original Klan, was to secure white supremacy. Regrettably, that objective was regarded as worthy by millions of whites who saw his movie.

We may reasonably assume Giffith's movie influenced the Atlanta part time insurance salesman, fundamentalist preacher, William J. Simmons. He envisioned a revival of the yesteryear Klan to cope with forces he saw undermining societal premises for keeping African-Americans subservient. Simmons relegated unto himself the title "Emperor of the Ku Klux Klan." During World War I, just prior to its phenomenal growth, the Klan was responsible for harassing African-American soldiers stationed in the South. The Klan had a network of spies in many southern communities which reported any breach of the traditional etiquette of racial segregation. Most likely to challenge Jim Crow rules were black soldiers who had grown up in the North. The same thing more frequently occurred during World War II, because at that later time there were more in uniform who had grown up in the North.

As the Klan grew the number of reported Klan inspired atrocities kept pace. A *New York World* investigation, published in 1921, alleged the Klan in one year was implicated in forty odd floggings, five kidnappings, four murders, a castration, and a multitude of tar and feather episode. This news story was a contributing factor in prompting Congress to investigate the Klan's activities. William J. Simmons was summoned to testify before Congress where he unabashedly defended the integrity of the Klan. He attributed the cited atrocities to imposters intent on defaming the Klan's good name!

During thirty-two years of college teaching I used various textbooks. In many texts a huge early 1920's Klan march in Washington was documented with photographs. One particular photo showed a group carrying a banner indicating they were from Bucks County Pennsylvania! Internal squabbles and scandals, one of which involved a well publicized sexual behavior impropriety, helps to partially explain the decline of the Klan. By the mid 1930s, most Americans had come to see the Klan for what it was - a hate group opposed to African-Americans, Catholics, Jews, and immigrants.

By the mid-1920s there was an unprecedented prosperity. It produced a wealth "spill-over" responsible for workers becoming consumers in heretofore unprecedented numbers. Unemployment was at an all time low. The capitalist payout of dividends, salaries, and wages was of an unprecedented dimension. Many became convinced the fears they formerly held regarding big business in the Progressive Era were unfounded. Also, Congress had drastically restricted immigration from Europe, but an industrial labor shortage in the North was averted because black workers migrating from the South were filling jobs never before offered to them.

Because the pool of employed black workers had appreciably expanded, they became the paying clientele of black doctors, dentists, and attorneys. With more money in their pockets, black workers were able to buy life insurance policies from black agents and even spend more for funerals at black owned funeral parlors. Also benefiting from the enlarged wage earner base were recently opened black owned stores selling clothing, household goods, groceries, furniture, appliances, and items associated with home entertainment. Thanks to the booming national economy of the 1920s, the black middle class expanded. This, in turn, facilitated more African-Americans attending college.

Economic forces in the 1920s prompted hundreds of thousands of southern blacks to give up the hardships of tenant farming and move North. Raising cotton had became quite trying anyway because of the infestation of the cotton boll weevil. Prospects for employment and more dignity pulled people to cities like Baltimore, Chicago, Cleveland, Detroit, New York, and Philadelphia. By 1930, approximately half of the entire African-American population living in the North resided in those cities.

By the mid 1920s Harlem had become recognized as a unique all black community. It had quickly become a city within a city. A partial explanation regarding how this happened can be found in Gilbert Osofsky's *Harlem: The Making of a Ghetto* published in 1963. Those moving to Harlem were proud to become part of a community taking on a special identity for African-Americans across the country. Black businesses quickly emerged.

By 1926 there were two African-American newspapers located there. Billy Strayhorn, associated many years with Duke Ellington's band, even wrote a song "Take the A Train," which told people how to get to Harlem from downtown. While Harlem was taking on its special identity, a movement promoting racial pride found it hospitable for its purpose.

In 1914, the Universal Negro Improvement Association (UNIA) was organized by Marcus Garvey in his native Jamaica. Two years later he was in New York's Harlem recruiting more followers. By 1922, branches of his organization were thriving in other northern urban centers as well. His weekly paper the *Negro World* carried a message of racial pride. It soon had a circulation rivaling the NAACP's *The Crisis*. Garvey often expressed contempt for the NAACP. After all, the NAACP's stated goal was integration, while he promoted the virtues of Black Nationalist separatism. Garvey believed the NAACP's leadership was "ashamed" of their African ancestry and primarily motivated to "amalgamate with the white race."

Garvey viewed America as a white man's country. He believed blacks would be better off living in an independent Africa - the ancestral homeland. In 1921 he gave himself the title "Provisional President of Africa" and established the organization of the "Empire of Africa" over which he would preside once the time was right for driving the European colonial powers off the continent.

Garvey's supporters paraded in New York and other large cities early in the 1920s. On such occasions dedicated followers donned uniforms. Officers wore regalia, which often included plumed hats, indicative of their rank. Hundreds paraded and spectators often numbering in the thousands lined the streets to watch. Other members moved along the parade route passing out information leaflets about the organization to the multitude of parade onlookers.

Shortly after the turn of the century Garvey had come to the United States to meet Booker T. Washington. He had subscribed to Washington's belief it was essential for blacks to generate and maintain self reliance. Garvey emphatically believed blacks had to break away from a demeaning and too frequent dependency on whites. Black dignity would be achieved only in proportion to success gained from black initiatives not dependent on white charity. However, when Garvey learned Washington had accepted large sums of money from the likes of Andrew Carnegie, he believed Washington had compromised himself and the black race as well.

Marcus Garvey encouraged the founding of all black businesses for the purpose of proving blacks could be successful entrepreneurs. He said such enterprises should only accept money, for investment purposes, from black people. One such initiative he sponsored was the shipping company known as the Black Star Steamship Line. In this undertaking, as in most of the others he inspired, no one sought outside business expertise to resolve complex operating issues which constantly arose. Thus, the Black Star Line was in the red approximately $500,000 for years after it had first been organized.

There's a legend, maybe some truth to it, that another black leader blew the whistle on Garvey due to envy of his movement's recruiting success. Who went to the federal authorities to bring attention to certain irregularities in Garvey's financial operations? This question is sort of like did Lee Harvey Oswald act alone in the 1963 assassination of John Kennedy? We'll probably never know about that or the identity of whoever informed the government regarding the legitimacy of Garvey's financial practices. Anyway, Marcus Garvey was found guilty of perhaps the easiest charge to prove of wrong doing - mail fraud. The judge gave him a five year sentence. However, after not quite two years, President Coolidge commuted his sentence and he was released in 1927. However, he was then quickly designated as an undesirable alien and deported.

The nationalism manifested in Garvey's movement was not purged entirely from the African-American community's consciousness with his arrest and deportation. There were cultural identity ramifications in many of Garvey's image evoking propositions. For example Garvey proposed a flag colored black, green, and red to represent his Pan African movement. These same colors were frequently displayed forty years later, in the late 1960s, by those asserting racial identity pride. And, to this day, these colors are often evident in association with Black History Month events. Within the context of the Harlem Renaissance, artists, playwrights, poets, and novelists often selected themes originating in Garvey's movement. Many artists embraced, without apology, African themes for creative expression initially acknowledged by Garvey.

Harlem Renaissance writers frequently conveyed anger, cynicism, and instances of biting sarcasm in their works. This was a consequence of the hypocrisy they saw resulting from the frequently articulated noble ideas of democracy being out of sync with the everyday racist behavior of millions. They were keen observers of the injustices rooted in racist attitudes and behavior. Did their anger serve a useful purpose? Perhaps it did. Through their writing their anger was often channeled toward bringing hypocrisy into sharper focus, thus more likely to be acknowledged for what it was.

Writers of the 1920s disdained writing in the so called Negro dialect. Blacks and whites alike had utilized that style from the 1880s to the turn of the century. The best known African-American writer of that time was Paul Lawrence Dunbar. He frequently utilized Negro dialect prose. But, by the 1920s, that technique was like a relic from the past - dated and assiduously shunned.

Observable in the 1920s was prose on a par with featured white writers. The best African-American writers now capably presented human emotions which readers, regardless of race, readily recognized and understood. There was universality in anger, hatred, love, jealousy, and disappointments. These emotions, realistically delineated and featured, were convincing to readers capable of understanding black folks were no different from whites when it came to their shared humanity.

Within the African-American experience, the Harlem of the 1920s gave rise to and promoted unprecedented expectations. Harlem, vibrantly alive, had become like a magnet to those believing they possessed artistic talent. Those allowing themselves to feel its pull were not inclined to resist. Within the pages of black periodicals, such as *The Crisis* and *Opportunity*, writers stylishly portrayed the rapidly emerging uniqueness of Harlem. When their descriptions reached the hinterlands, they fired the imaginations of many already totally dissatisfied with their local circumstances.

In 1924, *The Crisis* and *Opportunity* began to offer prizes for literary creativity. This stimulated an increased amount of submissions from all over the country. If restless souls in Alabama, Arkansas, or Missouri were published two or three times in either publication, the net effect was equivalent to sending them bus fare to Harlem. Classes often laughed at this. Brighter students quickly acknowledged creative people want to be where the action is. A reasonable assumption is most struggling writers, who thought of themselves as talented, would rather live in Harlem than in some dusty southern town employed as an assistant editor for a weekly newspaper having a circulation of ten or twelve thousand readers.

One restless soul was James Mercer Langston Hughes, son of Nathaniel Hughes whose success was vintage Horatio Alger. Hughes' father held significant jobs in Mexico, one of which was director of an electric utility power company. His fluency in Spanish served him well. While engaged in his career in Mexico, Nathaniel Hughes divorced Langston's mother. Carrie Hughes remarried just as Langston was entering puberty. His mother and his step-father struggled to make ends meet and they lived in Kansas and Illinois. As Hughes later said, he was able to cope with less than ideal living circumstances by writing and this kept him from bottoming out emotionally.

Though his father wanted Langston to study engineering at a German or Swiss university, he was allowed to take such courses at Columbia University as a compromise. He attended classes for two semesters, but spent little time on campus as he preferred to spend more time in Harlem. When his father learned he failed to register for his second year, he stopped sending money and they never saw each other again. Hughes never regretted his withdrawal from Columbia.

In June of 1923, Langston Hughes served as a mess attendant on board the *S.S. Malone* which sailed for Africa. Upon arrival he was disappointed he and fellow crew members were not permitted to go ashore as often as he would have liked. None the less, his limited encounters with things African served to inspire some poems. These poems reveal his emotional affinity for what Africa represented to him. However, he was careful not to romanticize Africa to the point his writing seemed puerile.

Less than a month after returning from the African voyage, Hughes shipped out again. This time his ship was destined for Rotterdam. Upon arriving in the Netherlands, he traveled on to Paris which he reached in March of 1924. His first impression of the French was they didn't "like Americans of any color." But, before long, he was enjoying jazz played in Parisian cafes by African-American musicians in exile and put his first impression feelings behind him.

The time Langston Hughes spent on board ships interacting with mixed crews, as well as his African and European experiences, were factors shaping his worldly perspective. During those times he had jotted down his impressions and reactions to them. To a large extent those experiences became the basis of what appeared under the title *The Weary Blues* in 1925. In this work one sees his cosmopolitanism facilitated by spontaneity and his ability to transcend questions of race as well as conventions of form.

Hughes believed black poets shouldn't restrict themselves or anticipate because of race. As he saw it black folks should be presented in the totality of good and bad, not just in keeping with preconceived representations. His philosophy is apparent with his observation, "An artist must be free to choose what he does, certainly, but he must also never be afraid to do what he might choose." In the mid 1990s, a female student picked up on the fact this quote had three masculine pronouns and said, "He sounds like a male chauvinist." What could I say, other than point out she and her classmates were almost three generations removed from his time.

Other black writers, as dedicated to artistic freedom of expression as Langston Hughes, also contributed to the literary component of the broader construct of what the Harlem Renaissance represented. A few who stood out from among various talented writers were: Countee Cullen, Jessie Fausset, Zora Neale Hurston, Frank Horne, Alain Locke, Claude McKay, and Jean Toomer. Of these most had strong inclinations for penetrating social commentary. (A generation later James Baldwin did likewise.) Often going back to slavery, they evaluated the causes that shaped society's racial attitudes. In so doing they revealed the cynicism rampant among African-Americans because of the multitude of unfulfilled promises made to them as a people for such a long time. However, for the most part these writers were not, as John Hope Franklin observed, "revolting against the system" as much as "they were protesting the unjust operation of the system."

Writers of the "renaissance" portrayed Harlem as a multifaceted community. One facet often commented upon was the music. Langston Hughes and other writers acknowledged the significance of jazz. They knew it was a unique contribution African-Americans were making to America's culture as perceived by the rest of the world. (In 1985, with my son Andy, I attended a jazz festival in Stockholm Sweden and saw first hand how much African-American jazz musicians were appreciated by a European audience.) I suppose Hughes would readily admit if you walked along a Harlem street in mid summer, when windows were open, you were more likely to hear Bessie Smith, thanks to an RCA Victrola, than hear someone reading aloud one of his poems. Hughes was well aware of leisure time preferences of Harlem's residents.

It's been estimated by 1921, five million Americans owned phonographs and one million records had been sold in that year alone. Americans, black and white alike, wanted to listen to music. Putting music in private homes became big business. People in Harlem, for the most part, wanted to listen to what was being referred to as jazz. It seems the designation jazz, as a type of music, started to come into popular usage about 1910. Jazz, however, did not originate in Harlem. Its place of origin was New Orleans – the Big Easy.

Aware I grew up in Philadelphia, a student once jokingly said, "O come on professor, are you saying jazz didn't come from Philly?" I took the opportunity to inform him the 1940s and early '50s jazz vocalist Pearl Bailey considered Philadelphia home. As for Pearl Bailey he and the others never heard of her. A few, however, had heard of singer Lena Horne from the same era. Lena's popularity survived to some extent beyond the time when Pearl Bailey had all but been forgotten. Neither gained the same level of celebrity status in jazz circles that Ella Fitzgerald and Billie Holiday had achieved by the mid 1950s.

As a consequence of her progressive politics, which included standing up for Paul Robeson, Lena Horne's career slumped briefly thanks to being blacklisted in the Joe McCarthy era of the 1950s. Fortunately, her career got back on a somewhat successful track as she reached her sixtieth birthday. Her audiences usually called for her to sing "Stormy Weather," her signature song since singing it in the 1943 movie of the same name. *Stormy Weather* featured an all black cast including legendary dancer Bill "Bojangles" Robinson. Lena Horne was one classy lady until she passed away in May of 2012, about six weeks shy of turning 93. An irony for me was the fact I didn't have a CD by Lena in my collection of women vocalists until one month before she died.

Key jazz musicians, such as Louis Armstrong, took the music up the Mississippi River to Chicago in the late teens and early 1920s. The music found receptive audiences in speakeasies, a few of which were owned by mobster Al Capone. Jazz evolved from music originally played by New Orleans street bands at the turn of the century. These predominantly brass bands frequently played in funeral processions. As such they played mournful dirges en route to the cemetery with the mourners. After the burial, as family and friends began leaving the cemetery, the band would symbolically remind everyone life goes on by picking up the tempo and playing life affirming exuberant music. Similar upbeat music was played outdoors for special occasions such as weddings, anniversary parties, neighborhood festivals and, of course, Mardi Gras - all eagerly looked forward to by the musicians.

The required mobility of street bands precluded use of the upright double bass, so tubas played the bass lines. Pianos, the instrument associated with rag time music, were obviously not on the street. However, once bands more frequently played indoors the piano was utilized extensively, especially for composing and arranging purposes. Also, the upright double bass replaced the tuba for indoor performances. Banjos, long associated with minstrel shows, were also part of street band music (as in Philadelphia's New Year's Day Mummers' parade), but they fell out of favor with bands no longer playing in the streets. Banjoes were rarely evident with jazz groups playing indoors after the mid 1920s. Earlier in the decade Black Swan Records, founded by African-American entrepreneur Harry Pace, hired up-and-coming band leader Fletcher Henderson to be its recording director. Black Swan's biggest hit was their recording of *Down Home Blues* sung by Ethel Waters.

Students often snickered when I mentioned pianos were usually found in the parlors of bawdy houses. Rag time music was played and the johns were served drinks as they waited for a favorite "girl" to join them. Eubie Blake, recognized in professional musical entertainment circles for more than a half century, earned money as a sixteen year old, money his mother didn't know about, playing piano in a Baltimore bordello. When asked what ragtime sounded like, I referred students to African-American Scott Joplin's music. His compositions were featured in the popular 1970s movie *The Sting*, starring Paul Newman and Robert Redford.

By 1926, Louis Armstrong, Eubie Blake, and Duke Ellington had all taken up residence in Harlem. Blake had preceded the others to New York. In 1915, he teamed up with Noble Sissle to do a vaudeville act. They were known as the Dixie Duo. When prohibition began it didn't adversely affect their fortunes. They were part of the Keith Orpheum vaudeville circuit, as opposed to being a night club act. Their well developed act featured them singing popular tunes of the day with improvisations of their own creation interspersed for humorous effect.

In 1920, Eubie Blake, Noble Sissle, and two other black vaudevillians, Flourney Miller and Aubrey Lyles, (Miller and Lyles knew each other as students at Fisk) decided to collaborate on a Broadway musical production. They called it *Shuffle Along*. Its success went far beyond their expectations. First staged in late 1920, it had a run of 504 performances. Blake and Sissle only wrote three songs for *Shuffle Along*'s production. Others used were written earlier and were in their portfolio. Ironically, many of these same songs from their hit show had been rejected by Tin Pan Alley song publishers.

Songs written specifically for *Shuffle Along* were: "Bandana Days," "Love Will Find A Way," and "I'm Just Wild About Harry." (Twenty-eight years later "I'm Just Wild About Harry" became the Democrats theme song as they envisioned Harry Truman's election to the presidency in 1948.) Josephine Baker and Florence Mills would go on to have long careers in show business after their performances in *Shuffle Along*. Five dollars bought a ticket to see the show. Keep in mind five dollars then bought dinner for two at a mid-town desirable restaurant.

The tempo of *Shuffle Along* was quickly set by the first number - "I'm Just Simply Full of Jazz." Here was a song that aptly reflected the emerging new musical taste of New Yorkers as jazz music was quickly becoming the rage. The 1920s are frequently referred to as the Roaring Twenties with jazz music a prominent feature in descriptions of that decade. Two men who became legendary jazz performers at a later time were born in the 1920s. Miles Davis was born on May 25, 1926 in Alton, Illinois and John Coltrane, born the same year on September 25 in Hamlet, North Carolina.

The rapidly growing interest in jazz soon created a demand which musicians Louis Armstrong, Duke Ellington, and Fletcher Henderson were eager to satisfy. Jazz became associated with Harlem where it was featured at the Cotton Club and other places having similar musical venues. Duke Ellington brought his band, at first called The Washingtonians, to New York City in 1926. They played in a few downtown locations, such as the Kentucky Club at Forty-ninth and Broadway, before opening on December 4, 1927 at the Cotton Club, thence to be known simply as the Duke Ellington Orchestra. At that location he gained his reputation as the leader of a premier jazz band.

Since Reconstruction ended, thus allowing states' rights Democrats to control the politics of the "solid South," the response of African-Americans had been to predictably vote Republican – in the North as well as the South in places where they might be allowed to vote. The presidential election of 1928 was no exception. Herbert Hoover received an overwhelming majority of African-American support. However, after the stock market collapse in October of 1929, and the ensuing depression, African-Americans ultimately came to realize Hoover had never addressed any issue arising from racial bigotry. He was silent on the issue of lynching and his indifference to the fate of the Dyer Anti-Lynching Bill, often introduced to Congress, was disturbing to thinking African-Americans.

Hoover's administration sponsored a trip to Europe for Gold Star mothers to visit graves of their sons killed in World War I. Black and white mothers crossed the Atlantic together on board a luxury liner. However, the black women believed they had been discriminated against regarding accommodations. They reasoned Hoover should have addressed their complaints but instead chose to ignore them. That was strike one against Hoover. Strike two was his attempt to place John J. Parker, of North Carolina, on the Supreme Court. Parker was on record upholding various Jim Crow legislation and approved of continued African-American exclusion from the election process. Blacks took some satisfaction when Parker was rejected by the Senate, pressured, in part, by a strident NAACP lobbying action. Strike three was Hoover's apparent indifference to the plight of those standing in soup lines as a consequence of the stock market 'Crash of '29.

A critical event highlighting the travesty of southern justice, while Hoover was President, came to the public's attention in the Scottsboro Boys trial begun in 1931. In Alabama that year nine young black men were found guilty of raping two white woman. Alabama police had arrested the young men for unlawfully bumming a ride in a railroad train boxcar. The authorities then pressured Ruby Bates and Victoria Price to press the much more serious charge of rape against them and all were found guilty. Eight were sentenced to be executed and Leroy Wright, the youngest at 13 years, was sentenced to life imprisonment. (Bates later recanted her rape charge, but it was of no consequence.)

The burden of the first few years of appeal was carried by the International Labor Defense (ILD) and the Communist Party (CPUSA). After two years the NAACP joined in the appeal endeavor and it became known as the Scottsboro Defense Committee. The case went to the Supreme Court in 1937 and resulted in none being executed, but certain lengths of jail sentences were allowed. The last defendant was released in the mid 1950s. The communists gave much publicity to the case as an example of American injustice rooted in racial bigotry. In the mid 1930s, the communists were making a strong pitch to African-Americans to join the party. To this day little credit is ever given to communists for being on the right side of an issue, but in the Scottsboro Boys case they were. You say shush, because we're not supposed to give communists credit for anything – right? (Remember not for profit healthcare for everyone?)

As for the Scottsboro Boys case, I find it curious there's no mention of it in Juan Williams 1998 biography of Supreme Court Justice Thurgood Marshall. (Marshall was the first African-American appointed to the Supreme Court.) It seems unlikely Marshall had no opinion regarding that particular case. Was Williams side stepping this case because of the communist involvement with it? Did Marshall see the communist involvement in a positive light? If so, was Williams concerned reporting a favorable opinion by Marshall might taint his reputation somehow? Perhaps Williams didn't mention Marshall's view of the Scottsboro Boys case because he believes commie phobia still lingers in many quarters. Anyone who can document Marshall's view on the case, please share the information.

I suppose I'm inclined to give the devil his due regarding certain positions the communists took in the 1930s. They were ahead of the curve on some critical issues. And, because of that, some African-Americans were sympathetic to specific communist proposals – certainly those denouncing racist legal formulas. Persons such as Angelo Herndon knew the communists consistently supported the anti-lynching bills introduced into Congress only to predictably fail because of southern opposition. Other more prominent African-Americans, such as Paul Robeson and W.E.B. DuBois, agreed with the communists' condemnation of military aggression against Ethiopia by Mussolini's Italy. Their concern was not shared by U.S. Senators from the South who were basically indifferent to Italy's bombings, invasion of Ethiopia, and killing of thousands who in no way were a threat to the Italian people.

As A. Philip Randolph noted, in the mid 1920s, should the hot economy cool black workers would be laid off first. Black business owners would then see their sales plummet because they depended on purchases by black workers having jobs. Folks out of work, short of money, stop buying anything above required necessities. The African-American community had a definite stake in the prosperity of the 1920s. So, as the prosperity of the 1920s abruptly ended, there was little cause for celebration on January 1, 1930, as the new decade began.

In addition to the hundreds of thousands of black workers being laid off, most black entertainers saw their bookings fall of dramatically in the

early 1930s. Though he lost a lot of money in the 'Crash of '29, Duke Ellington managed to get roughly the same number of booking when he went
on tour. Thus, Ellington's sidemen were more fortunate than those playing
for lesser known bands, some of which broke up. Ellington seemed to take
the hard times in stride and even performed a number he wrote called the
"Wall Street Wail." While Ellington was on the road for a month or two,
Cab Calloway's band frequently filled in for him at the Cotton Club.

Hoover justified his refusal to sponsor action to alleviate mass misery
by paying homage to the philosophy of laissez faire. This economic philosophy came under close scrutiny by various African-American intellectuals.
They began to question its validity regarding economic policy. And, politicians who addressed economic issues forthrightly and didn't ignore those
affecting African-Americans also received their attention. Hoover didn't
give much thought to out of work people, black or white, as newspapers
printed pictures of him speaking at expensive Republican fund raising din-
ners wearing a tuxedo. In New York City thousands were sleeping in parks
using those newspapers, which came to be known as "Hoover blankets," to
keep warm.

Alarming numbers of people found themselves living in shantytowns –
called "Hoovervilles." Often the shantytowns were randomly integrated.
Some black families occupying tar paper shacks had white families in the
same kind of make shift dwellings living next door. Sometimes an astute
student would make the observation poverty can be a great equalizer.
There's truth to that. I raised the question, "how can desperately poor people convincingly act superior to others also desperately poor?" A student
once replied, "if they tried, they got laughed right out of the shantytown."
I agreed with his observation. Another said, "No one could act uppity in
those places - that's for sure!"

African-American writer Arna Bontemps knew firsthand of the consequences the Depression had on blacks in America. Because some of his
writings had been published, he left Los Angeles for Harlem just before
the Crash. Within a short time, he had to cope with greatly diminished
prospects. He realized he shared this fate with many other aspiring black
writers. The Crash, he said, "promptly wrecked the flimsy little world of
the Negro newcomer in New York, Chicago, Los Angeles, and all the other
centers of migration...."

Relief was the responsibility of the states was Hoover's answer to those suggesting the federal government should offer it. But, as we now know, the states then didn't have systematized welfare departments. In 1931-32, two thirds of the states had no funds at all for welfare purposes. Hoover insisted no one was going to bed hungry. Historian Milton Meltzer said otherwise: "The welfare figures showed they starved in the mountains of Kentucky and on the plains of Kansas. They starved in the cities and in the villages." A conservative estimate of the number of children who died from starvation was over ten thousand. Of those who starved in the cities, we can reasonably assume African-Americans were affected in numbers greatly out of proportion to their representation in the population as a whole. I suppose those minimizing or rejecting information about people starving in the Depression are the same mean spirited types who would claim hurricane Katrina, in 2005, didn't cause any widespread hardships for residents of New Orleans.

The impact of the Crash of 1929 on America's black population was profound. For black separatists it brought many unpleasant facts clearly into focus. For example, to those who had been drawn to Marcus Garvey it showed just how dependent on society at large African-Americans actually were. In the aftermath of the Crash, African-American newspapers reported prevalent hardships experienced throughout the land. Hoover's inaction and apparent indifference was also commented upon in black publications.

The Depression prompted African-Americans to closely examine their traditional political behavior since Reconstruction. Intellectuals raised the question: "What have Republicans done for us lately?" The old "gratitude vote" predictably going to Lincoln's party was becoming less predictable. With the election of Franklin Roosevelt, in 1932, African-Americans sensed significant change might be forthcoming. Though most were probably pleased with FDR's victory, at the same time, however, many exhibited a justifiably warranted attitude of "we'll wait and see" while Democrats celebrated.

Chapter 11

The Wall Street debacle of 1929 created serious economic setbacks and ensuing hardships for a majority of Americans. Regardless of their race, millions of Americans could still hear Hoover's promise "two chickens in every pot, two cars in every garage" ringing in their ears as they stood on · soup lines. African-Americans had been the last to be hired to participate in the prosperity of the 1920s, but with the economic collapse were first to be fired. Thus, when Franklin Delano Roosevelt said his concern was for the "forgotten man," a responsive chord in the psyche of African-Americans was struck. Who but African-Americans had been forgotten, neglected, and made invisible since the end of the Reconstruction Era?

Some African-Americans were reluctant to vote Democratic. This was to be expected and understandable. They could envision a Democratic victory conceivably translating to mean the ascendency of southern politicians with greater political muscle in a Democratic administration than in the three previous Republican administrations. It was understood southern Democrats would do their best to resist any change in the racial *status quo*. They would stay committed to the continuation of the Jim Crow system throughout the South.

For implementation of his New Deal policies, Roosevelt selected capable administrators, many of whom had worked for him when he was governor of New York. His key administrators wanted their agencies to proceed with their assigned tasks on a color-blind basis. Roosevelt himself, however, had to keep one ear to the ground to detect any southern disaffection which might lend comfort to his political opposition. Keep in mind his political base was a coalition that necessarily included southern Democrats and many of them were chairpersons of significant Congressional committees. Benjamin Quarles made a reasonable assessment of FDR's policy. He said, "Roosevelt did not design his program with the Negro in mind…but he was opposed to any racial discrimination implementing it."

Roosevelt readily scored many points with African-American organizations because his appointments to offices were based on merit not race. More black Americans were appointed to positions of responsibility by Franklin Roosevelt than done before by either Democratic or Republican administrations. Though numerically not in proportion to the larger black population, the significance of these appointments was their "breakthrough" value. These positions were filled by people eminently qualified, not because they were black. Sixty years later, in the administration of Democrat Bill Clinton, an even greater number of African-Americans were appointed to meaningful administration positions. Clinton's appointments represented a higher percentage ratio of African-Americans to the population as a whole than had ever been done before.

FDR's biggest asset in winning favor with African-Americans was his wife Eleanor. The first lady had shown her admiration and respect for Mary McLeod Bethune, college founder and president. She brought her to Washington for a meeting that was publicized. Eleanor Roosevelt spoke to more black audiences than all previous first ladies combined. One newspaper photo showed her being escorted by two Howard University R.O.T.C. students wearing their uniforms when she arrived at their campus to speak. Southern newspapers took her to task for this as well as for her other "offensive" transgressions of familiarity with African-Americans.

Projects initiated by the Public Works Administration (PWA) stimulated competition for jobs which was especially keen in the South. Unable to make a living wage sharecropping, thousands of blacks had hoped the PWA would have something better to offer. PWA head Harold Ickes, concerned that the federal government not reenforce the Jim Crow system, issued a directive on September 21, 1933, prohibiting racial discrimination in PWA sponsored projects. A positive result of this order was not consistently achieved however because frequently the PWA's role was simply to approve projects proposed by state and local governments retaining authority for implementation.

Within the first One Hundred Days of Roosevelt's administration, Congress, at his urging, passed many reform measures intended to provide relief from economic dislocations and hardships. One of these measures was the Agricultural Adjustment Act passed on May 12, 1933. It created the Agricultural Adjustment Administration. However, blacks in the South were soon subjected to deceptive practices concerning allotment checks intended for them from that New Deal agency. As John Hope Franklin noted, "Many landlords took advantage of the illiterate sharecroppers and tenants and kept the checks intended for them." Numerous poor whites also experienced this corrupt practice as well.

Sharing similar grievances disgruntled tenant farmers of both races organized the Southern Tenant Farmers' Union. Alarmed by this, white southern power brokers predictably charged Communist Party involvement in the formation of the "Union." By applying pressure to the Agricultural Adjustment Administration through their new organization, tenant farmers began to get the allotment checks directly. However, many white landowners began to refuse new lease arrangements which meant all their acreage was credited to them. So, they then received the allotment checks directly instead of former tenants. For the land owners the checks became a sure thing as compared with collecting rents which had frequently become less predictable in the hard times.

In the North on the labor front, the 1930s saw the emergence of the Congress of Industrial Workers (CIO). Its mission was to organize unskilled labor, something the American Federation of Labor had declined to do. The local craft unions of the American Federation of Labor (AFL) were mostly dominated by second and third generation white ethnics who refused to enroll African-Americans into their apprenticeship programs. Hence, black workers were more likely to be part of the unskilled labor pool which the CIO wanted to organize. A boost to the CIO's organizing endeavors came from passage of the Wagner Labor Relations Act. Regardless of skill this New Deal measure permitted workers to organize for the purpose of collective bargaining.

African-Americans were permitted to join the CIO almost three decades before the national AFof L mandated their local craft unions to accept African-Americans into apprentice programs. I recalled my father's membership in an American Federation of Labor's local union. Before I could go into details someone would immediately ask, "Was it all white?" My answer was always yes because that was the way it was in his union at that time. He worked forty-five years (1925 to 1970) for the Bell Telephone Company of Pennsylvania. Luckily for our family during the Depression he was never out of work. When he retired his union was the Communications Workers of America, an affiliate of the American Federation of Labor.

My father retired the same year (1970) I first taught African-American history. That year there were no African-Americans employed where he punched the company's time clock. I remember going to some union sponsored family picnics in the late 1940s and early 1950s, but never saw African-Americans at those events. In 1950, his work place softball team won their league's championship. His team and all other teams were white - no blacks, no Hispanics. Dad was forty-four that summer and put in games to play first base or right field when his team had a comfortable lead in the score.

In some respects I suppose my father was a typical white blue collar worker of his time, but he didn't easily fall into the ethnic white category. Though his parents were Alsatian immigrants he never spoke to me or my siblings indicating we should know anything about that fact as we were growing up. Of his parents cultural or national origin he took no special interest. The name Reiss appears to be German (gentile and Jewish alike) and probably is in most instances. Dad once told me he was teased during WW I "for being German." However, many Alsatians have German sounding names, think of Albert Schweitzer the noted humanitarian of the early 20th Century. Then too there's American labor leader Eugene Victor Debs, his parents were Alsatian immigrants. My mother's father voted for Debs for president in 1912. In the last 20 years French wines of Alsatian origin have gained favorable recognition and the major labels have names giving the impression the wines are of German origin.

I didn't learn about Dad's parents immigrating from Alsace until I was near age forty as a consequence of some family documents turning up. At the time his parents left Alsace in 1889, it was occupied by Germany as a result of the Franco-Prussian War. The Treaty of Versailles returned Alsace to France in 1919. My sister and a brother have visited some distant relatives in France with the same last name and have been in touch with them. These relatives are quite proud Alsace is again a part of France and are as patriotic as those living in other regions of France. A distant relative with the same last name was recently elected to the French National Assembly to represent his Alsatian district. Another distant cousin, Pierre Reiss, is a retired art teacher.

On my mother's paternal side her father, named John, was the son of a Catholic German named Stuhltrager who came to the United States in 1867. Her mother was the daughter of a man named Erastus Carleton Anderson who was born near Rockland in Maine. His lineage goes back to the 1740s in New England and prior to that Ireland. At sixteen, young Anderson enlisted in Maine's 20th Infantry Regiment and served with Company K. My mother knew he was at the Battle of Gettysburg. In his late twenties he came back to Philadelphia in 1876 for the Centennial celebration where he met a woman from Baltimore and they married. She didn't want to live in Maine and he didn't want to move to Baltimore, so they comprised and stayed in Philadelphia where they started a family. Their daughter Anna Anderson married John Stuhltrager the son of the immigrant of 1867, hence my mother's maiden name was Stuhltrager Her younger brother, my Uncle John, served in World War II and was seriously wounded shortly after the Normandy invasion, but he survived and had a family of six children.

Getting back to my father, he quit high school in 1921 to get a job because the economy had begun to boom. He was 16 at the time. He had briefly attended the "old" Central High School in Philadelphia, not the one at its current location that Noam Chomsky once attended. I remember asking him if any black students attended the "old" Central in 1920. He responded, "not to my recollection." After leaving high school, somewhere, somehow, he learned the requisite skills to become an electrician. In that capacity he wired my grandparents row house for electric service. When he went with his parents to visit relatives in Alsace, in May of 1923, electrician was indicated on his passport as his occupation. I have his passport and the signature of then Secretary of State Charles Evans Hughes appears to be authentic by his hand.

My father grew up in all white neighborhood known as Brewerytown. I was eleven in 1948 when his mother died. After the funeral, I recall hearing my aunts saying their old neighborhood was "changing." They didn't offer an explanation for my sake regarding what they meant by "changing." The word was used in a context I didn't grasp at the time. Of course, it meant the once white neighborhood was becoming a black one.

After the story about my family background, a student once asked if my father had racial prejudices like many of his blue collar co-workers most likely had. I responded if he did he never voiced them as such to me or my siblings. I know two things for sure. He never made a disparaging racial remark in my presence. Also, I recently asked my older sister, if she ever heard him use the "N" word. "No," she said, "never." I agreed. I never heard him do that either. Once, after seeing a ball game that Jackie Robinson played in, I recall Pop saying, "there are other colored ball players as good as him and they'll be in the major leagues soon." His generation used the word "colored," instead of black, and its usage wasn't intended to be derogatory. Also, as for racial question issues, about 1951 or '52, the radio show "Amos and Andy," popular in the 1930s and '40s, was tried on television. It bombed! I recall my father saying "it was ridiculous," after watching just one episode.

Ah yes, I again digressed. Now back to the 1930s and labor issues. John L. Lewis of the miners' union met with Sidney Hilman of the Amalgamated Clothing Workers Union and David Dubinsky of the International Ladies Garment Workers Union in November of 1935. They envisioned organizing endeavors of their planned Congress of Industrial Organizations (CIO) to be on a non-discriminatory basis. A few years earlier miners in West Virginia and eastern Kentucky had integrated some locals of the United Mine Workers.

Assembly line workers in the auto making industry were considered unskilled by the AFof L. The CIO believed they were in desperate need to be unionized; hence they were vigorously recruited. Walter Reuther and his associates knew Henry Ford had used black workers as strike breakers in earlier attempts by auto workers to unionize. They clearly understood the importance of recruiting African-Americans into the CIO's auto workers' union.

A. Philip Randolph of the Brotherhood of Pullman Car Porters and Herbert Hill of the NAACP believed it would be advantageous for the CIO to present the benefits of unionism in African-American communities by utilizing black workers already affiliated with the CIO to make the union's case. This was done with impressive results in the auto industry and other assembly line intensive industries. Before the decade was over, CIO membership had reached four million workers. Henceforth, when strikes occurred, black workers were on the picket line with white co-workers and not trying to cross them.

As indicated previously, Eleanor Roosevelt spoke out far more often for racial justice than any other prominent New Dealer. She was on record for supporting the Dyer anti-lynching bill languishing in Congress because of filibustering tactics by southern senators. She also lent her support to the proposal to have black domestic workers covered by Social Security. And, at the beginning of her husband's third term, when Congress passed legislation authorizing a draft, she forthrightly called for ending racial segregation in the armed forces.

Impressed by the extraordinary talent of black opera singer Marian Anderson, Eleanor Roosevelt supported the proposal, first sponsored by Howard University, for Anderson to give a concert at the Daughters of the American Revolution's Constitution Hall. When the DAR refused to allow the concert in their building, Eleanor Roosevelt then lobbied Secretary of the Interior Harold Ickes to allow the concert on the steps of the Lincoln Memorial. On Easter Sunday, April 9, 1939, the free concert was attended by seventy-five thousand, half of whom were white, and included members of Congress and Supreme Court justices. This episode had two outcomes. The Daughters of the American Revolution lost a member, since Eleanor Roosevelt resigned from the organization, and America took a significant step toward overcoming racial bigotry. Many saw Marian Anderson's concert as a sign America had come a long way in twenty years since 1919 – the year of the Red Summer race riots.

Perceptive African-Americans liked what they saw in FDR. His programs were viewed as inclusive as opposed to exclusive. His policies, and the demeanor of his wife, generated an enthusiasm in the black community which northern Democratic Party leaders astutely observed. These leaders soon rightly concluded African-Americans were about to jump ship from the party of Lincoln to the redefined Democratic Party of Franklin Roosevelt. Neighborhood Democratic committee persons had been suggesting to African-Americans that Roosevelt, with their support, would do as much for them as Lincoln had in the previous century.

Before the 1930s, turn of the century European immigrant groups had resorted to ethnic bloc voting. This tactic facilitated the exchange of votes for jobs and other forms of assistance. Able to elect many of their ethnicity to office, the second generation of European immigrants had gained enough power whereby they could check impulses targeting their respective group for discriminatory injustices. Politicians had come to realize if they voted in any way offensive or not in the best interest of the ethnic blocs, their opponents were likely to pick up those votes and accrue a political advantage. The black political leadership, emerging at this time, realized African-Americans had to resort to the same political methods as the white ethnics. This had to be done if they were to ever rise up from the bottom socio-economic rung which past political impotence had, in part, relegated to them.

Historically African-Americans had never been called upon to join with any other ethnic group to form a political alliance. This had been done by the Irish who allied themselves with those of Polish ancestry when it came to issues touching on their shared Roman Catholicism. Who could African-Americans ally themselves with to make common cause? Though overwhelmingly Protestant blacks had little affinity with white Protestants, and certainly none at all with the poor ones from the South who were die hard segregationists.

In a similar, but not identical, situation with blacks were recent East European Jewish immigrants. As with African-Americans, this group had no political affinity with either White Anglo-Saxon Protestants (WASPs) or Roman Catholic ethnics such as the Irish, Italians, and Poles. Basically those groups shunned both African-Americans and Jews. However, the social ostracism against Jews wasn't as severely institutionalized as it was against African-Americans. Case in point, in World War II Jewish-Americans served in units with other white Americans, but black troops were required to serve in segregated units. Jewish baseball player Hank Greenburg played in the major leagues ten years before black ballplayers, like Larry Doby, made it. Most students knew who Jackie Robinson was, but had no clue about Larry Doby. I had to inform them he was the first black player in the American League when he played for the Cleveland Indians.

Democratic politicians in northern cities, frequently Jewish committeemen, saw urban blacks as wielding potential political power. As part of the New Deal bandwagon, these committeemen functioned as recruiters to get African-Americans to register as Democrats. This engendered what amounted to a symbiotic political relationship between African-Americans and Jewish Americans. Astute observers noted Jewish Democratic politicians going out of their way to solicit favorable black opinion. Of great importance was to make common cause with African-Americans against all forms of bigotry and prejudice directed at both groups. After WW II, in the early 1950s, some northern cities were forming Human Rights Commissions. African-Americans and Jews often served on them together to resolve issues arising from racial or religious bigotry. These semi-official entities often included prominent rabbis and high profile black ministers.

Despite the Depression, Hollywood's film making industry was booming during the 1930s. Though many people experienced economic hardships, they usually managed to put some money aside each week to go to a movie. At this time, however, the content of films, how blacks were being portrayed, started to come under review by black intellectuals. The radical expression of the late 1960s is appropriate here. "If you're not part of the solution, then you're part of the problem." The problem was Hollywood continually portraying black characters in ways which essentially reenforced stereotype assumptions.

The NAACP and other organizations believed the time had come to turn the Hollywood legacy of *Birth of a Nation* around. Though the 1930s would not be the decade of Hollywood reform, it was the decade when African-Americans served Hollywood notice they would be holding the movie industry accountable. Hollywood movie producers had long excused themselves when using racial stereotype roles by claiming they were just giving the public what it wanted. The movies of the 1930s never prodded white audiences to engage in any socially introspective thinking.

In the 1930s African-Americans generally got movie parts depicting them as either treacherous or, more often, as someone never to be taken seriously. Stereotype parts presented them as a loyal mammy or equally loyal Uncle Tom. They were featured in roles as cooks, house servants, newsboys, shoeshine boys, stable boys, or busboys. And, white actors, appearing in the same films, referred to them in those roles as "boy." They were condescendingly presented as loyal, happy go lucky, and most content with their lowly lot in life. African-Americans never got parts as legitimate businessmen, doctors, lawyers or corporate executives, but rather as the janitor the white executive said goodnight to as he left his office to go home to the suburbs.

Hollywood of the 1930s approved of society's racial arrangement – how it seemed to function. Studios never called into question roles imposed on individuals by society at large because of racial identity – identities based on values rarely questioned or seriously examined. Producers shied away from anything challenging the racial status quo. Their films would not convey a political/social message such as conveyed in the 2010 hit *Avatar*. As one famous producer of the 1930s exclaimed "Messages are for Western Union."

Perceptive whites living in northern cities noticed African-Americans seemed buoyant on the day following a victory by heavyweight boxer Joe Louis. His prowess in the ring infused pride within black communities across America. He first came to national prominence on September 24, 1935 when he defeated Max Baer in New York City. This fight saw Louis become the first black boxer to participate in a match drawing a million dollar gate. To African-Americans this son of Alabama sharecroppers became a symbol for all that was worthy in their race. However, early in his career, in 1935 and 1936, many sports writers described his abilities in unthinking racial stereotype terms. A few southern writers even hoped he would lose his title to the German Max Schmelling in their 1938 rematch. But that didn't happen. Louis knocked Schmelling out in the first round, thus making amends for his earlier lose to the German.

Dubbed the "Brown Bomber" by sports writers, his wins in the ring in 1940 and '41 helped many Americans to momentarily forget the ominous news associated with Adolph Hitler's Germany. As heavyweight champion, Louis was more acceptable to mainstream white America because his personal life didn't challenge society's racial taboos of the time. Unlike Jack Johnson, the black heavyweight champion twenty-five years earlier, Louis didn't associate with white women or stand over a defeated opponent and gloat. While Joe Louis was champion, bigotry in the form of an urgent search to find a "white hope" to defeat him never reached the intensity exhibited at the time Jack Johnson was champion.

Joe Louis gained additional acceptance when mainstream newspapers presented pictures of him in his army uniform performing duties associated with defeating the Axis Powers. Of course African-American publications showed similar photos of him in uniform as well. By the time Joe Louis quit fighting shortly after WW II, his fan base was well beyond the African-American community. Prominent sports writers paid homage to his positive character as well as to his great ability in the ring.

As for black sports heroes in the 1930s, one person I happened to personally meet, in the fall of 1963, was Jesse Owens. He spoke at a New Jersey education symposium at Atlantic City and faculties from public schools across the state were in attendance. Regarding Owens students usually asked, "who was he?" From 1970 to 1999, the year I retired, an

overwhelming number of students drew blanks when I mentioned his
name. In that time frame basketball, baseball, and football had greatly
eclipsed interest in track and field.

Jesse Owens was born on September 12, 1913 to a couple engaged in
share cropping in Oakville, Alabama. In the 1920s, at his mother's urging, the family moved north to Cleveland, Ohio. While he was unable to
attend school on a regular basis in Alabama, in Cleveland he attended an
elementary school located just three blocks from where his family lived. By
the time he was in junior high, his athleticism in track was observed by a
white coach, named Charles Riley, who took an interest in developing his
apparent natural ability to run very fast.

At Cleveland's East Technical High School, the faculty took more interest in Owen's athletic achievements at the expense of making his classroom experiences truly worthwhile. His high school mentors wanted him
to enroll at the University of Michigan where, apparently, there was less
racial discrimination. However, Owens decided to go to Ohio State located in Columbus. After his enrollment at Ohio State, Owens constantly
struggled with academics, while excelling in track and field performances.
Movie theaters in Columbus, at the time, made blacks sit in the balcony.
Also, he was not permitted to live in a campus dormitory. Coinciding with
his enrollment, Ohio State was being sued by the NAACP on behalf of
two black students who were refused dormitory housing. Though the Ohio
State track team voted him captain, he never completed a bachelor's degree.
However, Ohio State awarded him an honorary degree in 1972.

Owens made the 1936 U.S.A. Olympic team after finishing first in the
100 meter, 200 meter, and long jump final trials. There's a legend stating
German dictator Adolph Hitler refused to shake Owen's hand after he won
gold medals. However, according to Nagueyalti Warren's account, presented
in *Black Heroes* (1988) edited by Jessie Carney Smith, Hitler wasn't in the
stadium the day Owens won his gold medals. Did Owens himself sustain
the myth when he said, "I wasn't invited up to shake hands with Hitler,
but I wasn't invited to the White House to shake hands with the President,
either." In 1976, forty years after he won his gold medals, Jesse Owens did
get invited to the White House. President Gerald Ford awarded him the
Presidential Medal of Freedom. What's that old saying - "Better late than
never?" (Warren's assertion in Smith's *Black Heroes* contradicts noted American news correspondent William L. Shirer's claim he personally witnessed

Hitler in the stadium, turning his back on Owens below him on the field, and then not interacting with Owens. See William L. Shirer, *The Nightmare Years 1930-1940*, p. 234, published in 1984.)

Responding to Nazi Germany's aggressions in Europe, President Franklin Roosevelt said the United States would be the "arsenal for democracy." Orders for weapons, pouring in from Europe, dramatically stimulated the U.S. Economy. By mid 1940, unemployment figures showed an impressive decline. However, African-American workers didn't figure in the dramatic decline in unemployment as did others. Almost 90 percent of companies receiving defense contracts had no African-Americans on their payrolls, save for a few on some auto assembly lines thanks to UAW pressures. The African-American press brought this issue to the attention of its readers. In making their sentiments known to the administration, black leaders were, in turn, told Roosevelt wanted to remedy the unacceptable situation.

A. Philip Randolph convinced other black leaders something out of the ordinary had to be done to seek redress for defense industry discriminatory policies. He received enthusiastic approval for his proposal to hold a massive march on Washington, D.C. Randolph with others organized a "March On Washington Movement" committee. They targeted July 1, 1941, as the date for their demonstration. Some on the committee anticipated 100,000 African-Americans participating in this event.

New York's mayor, Fiorello LaGuardia, Eleanor Roosevelt, and some members of Congress, tried to persuade Randolph to call the march off. They argued it would bring latent hatreds to the surface putting the marchers in grave physical danger. Another concern was for the safety of African-Americans who might be abused in their respective communities by whites resenting the march took place. I had to remind students this could conceivably happen. At the local level many black Americans were physically abused, especially in the South, as a consequence of Theodore Roosevelt inviting Booker T. Washington to dinner at the White House forty years earlier.

Meeting with President Roosevelt, Secretary of War Stimson, and Secretary of the Navy Knox, Randolph remained adamant in his determination to continue with the march. President Roosevelt then proposed he would issue an executive order which would prohibit discrimination in the defense industry, if Randolph would call off the march. Upon learning FDR had issued "Executive Order 8802," on June 25, 1941, Randolph in turn called off the march. In the 20th Century Roosevelt's order was, to that date, the most far reaching policy implementation for the purpose of redressing workplace racial discrimination. The President's order prohibited discriminatory hiring practices in all defense related industries. It also authorized the establishment of the Fair Employment Practice Commission, which quickly came to be known as the FEPC.

President Franklin Roosevelt's executive order signified the end of presidential aloofness in matters of major concern to African-Americans. The Randolph-Roosevelt meeting was indicative of an emerging new political reality regarding African-Americans. Henceforth, the Presidency itself, in addition to the Congress, was viewed as capable of being pressured successfully to take action in the political arena where black Americans had struggled for so long to gain a fair hearing of their grievances. As a result of FDR's action, many African-American leaders sensed America's black community had taken a significant step toward joining America's mainstream.

As war clouds gathered, many African-Americans believed FDR's administration would sponsor additional measures to facilitate recognition of equal rights for them. The wise also realized a war against Nazi racist ideology would serve to challenge racism on the home front. Patriotically serving in the armed forces, as in past wars, would mean demands for freedom and justice could not so readily be ignored and denied in the war's aftermath. With the U.S. declaration of war on the Axis Powers (Germany, Italy, and Japan), African-Americans would be in a better position to challenge America's racial policies. As the war progressed that challenge correspondingly gained momentum as well. As other Americans wondered what the war might bring, many African-Americans viewed the war as likely, somehow, to bring better days for them.

Chapter 12

M uch of the Fair Employment Practice Commission's activities early in the 1940s were expedited by a small but dedicated staff investigating complaints usually brought to its attention by local NAACP organizations. These NAACP chapters, some more diligently than others, monitored the hiring practices of various companies doing government contract work in their respective communities. Empowered to hold hearings, the FEPC was also authorized to subpoena parties suspected of discriminating in their hiring practices on the basis of "race, creed, color, or national origin."

Southern Congressmen were quick to implement roadblocks to stymie the effectiveness of the FEPC. It was also constantly challenged and harassed by various business lobby groups wanting to maintain the racial status quo in America's multitude of workplaces. Those objecting to FEPC's activities usually claimed it was yet another New Deal example of "big government" meddling in the private sector of the economy. Liberal Congressmen would point to their supportive voting record, while southern conservatives proudly publicized their opposition to funding requests made by the FEPC. Congressional opponents also initiated extensive filibustering tactics when the scope and specific powers of the FEPC were at issue.

Supporters of the FEPC didn't want it to become just another paper, do nothing, bureaucratic agency. The NAACP, the Urban League, the

recently organized Congress of Racial Equality, as well as A. Philip Randolph's lobby, all lent their support to staging public "Save FEPC" rallies.
Such rallies were timed to coincide with lobbying efforts undertaken by the
aforementioned groups. Local NAACP chapters petitioned their respective
Congresspersons to give their support to keep the FEPC meaningfully viable.

As during World War I, economic opportunities of sorts were presented to southern blacks if they moved to northern industrial centers such
as Akron, Buffalo, Gary, Milwaukee, Pittsburgh, and Toledo. The wartime
demand for labor also brought sporadically employed whites from Appalachia to those cities for employment. They, with white ethnics, resented
newly hired blacks put on payrolls thanks to FEPC initiatives. Hearing rumors some blacks might be considered for promotions made white workers
anxious and resentful. Most blue collar whites at this time never thought
the day would come when they had to take orders given by a black foreman! The attitude of many of these whites is revealed by a frequently heard
mindless saying, mimicked by their children, "I'm free, white, and twenty-
one." It revealed much about southern attitudes then evident in certain
northern locations.

When three black workers were upgraded at Packard's Detroit plant,
in May of 1943, 25,000 white workers walked off their jobs in protest.
The United Auto Workers Union leadership was embarrassed. Its leader,
R.J. Thomas, said the "wildcat" walkout was in no way condoned by the
union. He claimed the Ku Klux Klan had protested the promotions and
agitated for the walkout. Walter White, of the NAACP, claimed to have
heard one of the strike leaders say to a large group, "I'd rather see Hitler and
Hirohito win than work beside a nigger on the assembly line." This episode
at the Packard plant in Detroit was symptomatic of deep seated prejudice
harbored by many whites now required to work with those of whom they
knew little beyond the popular culture's stereotype depictions.

In August of 1944, white employees brought the entire Philadelphia
transit system briefly to a standstill because roughly a dozen African-American employees were upgraded from menial jobs to motormen. Army units
were deployed to ensure orderly transit service to Philadelphia's citizenry.
During this occurrence I remember boarding the route 59 trolley, which
ran on Castor Avenue, with my parents and wondering why there was a
soldier wearing a helmet and holding a rifle sitting in the front seat near the

motorman. I noticed the soldier immediately. Going on eight and aware we were at war, it seemed curious to me to see a soldier on our trolley car. Though the motorman was black, I wasn't aware of that until my father explained the soldier was there to protect him.

During World War II, racial tensions erupted into serious rioting in Detroit, Los Angeles, and New York City. The riot in Detroit, in the wake of the Packard plant walkout, was the most severe. Before the lawlessness ended 35 people were dead, 29 of whom were African-Americans. In addition to the 35 fatalities, there were approximately 600 people, mostly black, who were injured. Walter White, Executive Secretary of the NAACP, observed if Detroit's Police Department had taken appropriate measures early on with billy clubs and fire hoses, it could have "broken the back" of the calamitous rioting before casualties went into double digits. Among many photo journalist witnesses, one captured the spectacle of two white police officers pinioning an elderly black man's arms, fully restraining him, thus allowing a young white rioter opportunity to strike the black man full in the face.

Next, a riot erupted in Harlem on August 1, 1943, occurring little more than five weeks after the much publicized Detroit race riot. New York City's mayor, Fiorello LaGuardia, had the benefit of knowing how ineptly Detroit's mayor had reacted to circumstances there. The contrast between the two mayors in their responses was duly noted by the NAACP's Walter White. Detroit's mayor was unable to inspire confidence, while New York's mayor took charge on the streets in close proximately to dangerous situations. Mayor LaGuardia was readily seen at locations where he was at risk to be injured. However, during Detriot's riot that city's mayor was rarely seen and black citizens had been assaulted on the steps of City Hall itself!

New York's Mayor LaGuardia and Police Commissioner Valentine met with Harlem's community leaders to solicit ideas about how to most effectively deal with the violence at hand. (No such comparable meeting took place in Detroit.) One decision was to call for military police units including African-Americans. Another recommendation, also carried out, was to have Harlem's recognizable community leaders urge the crowds, from sound trucks, to stay off the streets and refrain from participating in lawless acts. To control the rioters, billy club force had to be used which resulted in 300 injuries. Since restraint in the use of firearms was shown, only five lives were lost compared with the death toll of 35 in Detroit.

The Japanese attack on Pearl Harbor (Dec. 7, 1941) did not prompt the War Department to make any changes in its personnel policies. This fact was of prime concern to members of the Associated Negro Press. Many black newsmen went to Washington to confer with War Department officials to express their opposition to the War Department's continuation of segregation in army organizational policies. As a first step toward ending the army's segregation, the black newsmen proposed the creation of a racially integrated division of volunteers. The War Department put this proposal on hold for many months before rejecting it in September of 1943.

A perceptive student observed the War Department's rejection came shortly after the summer riots in Detroit and New York. She asked if I thought there was a negative connection to the riots influencing the War Department's decision not to authorize the volunteer integrated unit. I indicated a discussion considering the riots was likely to have taken place, but to what extent the riots determined the War Department's decision we weren't likely to ever know. If there's a record of the discussions it probably wouldn't be easily found either.

At the time of the invasion of Normandy, on June 6, 1944, all units of the United States Armed Forces were still officially segregated. This fact was verified to me personally by two African-American veterans of World War II with whom I had coffee on many occasions in the 1990s. At the time both were living in Middletown, New York, but had come of age in New York City. Bob Horton was a WW II army veteran. He was admitted to a C.U.N.Y. College (I can't recall which one.) in 1939, but only finished two years because he was drafted. Bob was very proud of the fact his admission was long before open door admissions. He once said, "dummies didn't get in back then."

The second veteran with whom I was acquainted was Leonard Blake, who had served in the navy in World War II. Some called him Leo, but because Bob called him Lenny so did I. He said it made no difference. Lenny was enrolled in courses at the community college, but his friend Bob wasn't. He was a delight to have in my African-American history course. During the times we had coffee in the cafeteria, I insisted he call me by my first name. He reluctantly agreed to do so, but "not around students."

The three of us had a few things in common. First of all, we were military veterans, secondly, they shared my enthusiasm for African-American history, and lastly, we liked the jazz of the late 1930s until the mid 1970s.

Favorite musicians included John Coltrane, Miles Davis, and Art Tatum. I was surprised, but probably shouldn't have been, upon learning the three of us were familiar with the fantastic trumpet playing by Clark Terry on Duke Ellington's version of "Perdido." Though living in Middletown, New York, we could tune in the Newark, New Jersey jazz station WBGO (88.5 FM) at our respective living quarters.

African-Americans in segregated units were assigned to duties essential to the war effort, but in terms of commanding respect or boosting self esteem were of less significance. Bob Horton said black troops weren't generally given training required to carry out tasks associated with imminent personal danger. As such, their training didn't emphasize combat readiness, but usually only prepared them to function in low status duty assignments. He said the army made him a supply inventory clerk because he had two years of college. Our friend Lenny Blake was a navy mess attendant which included much KP chores.

Since Bob Horton and Leonard Blake had served in segregated military units in World War II, I learned what it meant to them and other African-Americans of their generation. With my retirement in 1999, and in the process of a divorce, I regrettably somehow lost contact with these two special men. So you guys, wherever you are, know you're not forgotten and were never invisible to me as so many of your generation were to most other Americans at one time. Thanks for the memories!

In late December of 1944, at the time of the Battle of the Bulge, Harvard Professor Randall Kennedy noted black units numbering four thousand troops responded to General Eisenhower's call for volunteers and were quickly moved to the front to help repel the German counter offensive. Some of these units, such as the all black 183rd Combat Engineer Battalion of which Dr. Leon Bass was a member, pushed into Germany in the Spring of 1945. His unit was among the first to enter Buchenwald - one of the most notorious Nazi concentration camps. At this camp Bass and others saw first hand the "unmitigated horrors of racism carried to its logical ends."

As for black engineer battalions, often overlooked is the fact during WW II they engaged in constructing the Alaska Highway (Alcan) which went from the States north through Canada to Alaska. Thus engaged in this enormous critically important strategic undertaking, these unsung heroes experienced many weeks on end of the harshest sub zero weather experienced anywhere else by American troops during the war.

Black navy personnel were again utilized, as in WW I, to load and unload cargo ships. In many instances black sailors loaded munitions, six days
a week, on board ships headed to the far Pacific. At Port Chicago, oddly
named since it was located in the vicinity of Oakland, California, a docked
munitions ship exploded and many black sailors were killed. This incident
and its consequences are presented in Studs Terkel's book *The Good War.*

After much concerted lobbying by the NAACP, and others, the War
Department finally agreed to establish an aviation training program per-
mitting African-Americans the opportunity to become pilots. The site
proposed for the pilot training was Tuskegee Institute in Alabama. The
program graduated 994 aviators. Four hundred and fifty graduates were
deployed to North Africa. As the war progressed and their reputations as
excellent pilots spread, they were assigned as fighter escorts for bombing
runs to Polesti and, near war's end, Berlin itself. Their mechanics, parts
inspectors, ordnance loading crews, and other support personnel proved
themselves most competent as well. They made sure every red tail P-51
Mustang was in excellent performance condition and ready to carry out the
dangerous assigned missions. However, the War Department made it clear
this Tuskegee airmen program was not intended to alter the department's
overall segregation policy.

During the war southern whites strenuously objected to racial integration in the military. If African-Americans, in integrated units, proved
themselves worthy under enemy fire, they knew it would become extremely
difficult to insist on continued segregation policies in other aspects of society. They also realized meritorious wartime service would likely become
a basis for black Americans to make certain demands on the government
after the war was over. They feared the war itself might undermine the
racial status quo. Thus politically influential southerners did their best to
make sure news about black units acting heroically were not reported in
the South's newspapers. In the same vein Gilbert Osofsky noted, in his
The Burden of Race, southern Congressmen always tried to "eliminate the
appropriations for domestic activities" of the Office of War Information,
because it had published "a booklet relating Negro contributions to the
winning of the war."

As the war progressed African-American newspapers kept assailing Jim
Crow practices as being hypocritically undemocratic. Due to their wider
circulations the role they played was more significant than what it had

been in World War I. All African-American newspapers promoted the idea among their readers they were fighting for a "double victory." This idea was expressed by making two "V" signs with the first two fingers of both hands. (In the 1960s the first two fingers forming a "V" came to represent peace by opponents of the Vietnam War.) For African-Americans in WW II, the first "V" represented the effort to win the war, the second "V" represented endeavors to win equality and justice on the home front. Lenny Blake and Bob Horton, my WW II veteran friends, confirmed this practice.

Adam Clayton Powell, Jr. said the circumstances for African-Americans had to improve as a result of their actual participation, as well as their demand for more participation, in the war against fascism. However, he noted, it was conceivable for the United States to win the war but lose the peace. If African-Americans were not permitted to share in the realization of America's wartime goals, often articulated by President Franklin Roosevelt, then Nazi racism had not truly been defeated. Regarding race issues in post-war America, if attitudes harboring bigotry were still as prevalent as before the war then the legitimacy of the wartime rhetoric would be seriously questioned.

As minister of Harlem's Abysinnia Baptist Church in the early 1940s, Adam Clayton Powell Jr. embarked on a crusade, via the "Greater New York Coordinating Committee," to challenge discriminatory hiring practices at various businesses in Manhattan. This group, essentially directed by him, organized demonstrations on sidewalks in front of businesses practicing discriminatory hiring practices. Use of the boycott was one of various tactics advocated by Powell. Astute careful planning indicated violence was never contemplated in conjunction with tactics utilized by the organization.

In his effort to bring Con Edison to change its discriminatory hiring policy, Powell called for a total lights out on a designated night during the week. This tactic ultimately caused the electric company, and the telephone company as well, to begin hiring African-Americans. His organization also brought attention to the fact most of Harlem's white merchants didn't employ black help. At one picketed corner drugstore, accustomed to having almost two hundred customers an hour, the number of sales was reduced to only six during an entire Saturday because protesters carried signs exhorting "Don't shop where you can't work." The role Powell played in bringing about significant changes in hiring practices ensured his election to the city council of New York. Of course his priority in that capacity was to look after the interests of his constituents living in Harlem.

Harlem essentially became a United States Congressional District unto itself as a consequence of redistricting in 1944. This proved to be a fantastic opportunity for the politically ambitious Adam Clayton Powell, Jr. Upon learning A. Philip Randolph was not interested in running for the seat, Powell announced his candidacy and then received Randolph's endorsement. In his first term in Congress Powell advocated the continuance of the FEPC as a permanent agency after the war was over. Southern Congressmen opposed the permanence of the FEPC. From Congressional session to session in the late 1940s, Powell battled for the passage of the FEPC bill. Many opposing its passage as a permanent agency claimed it was part of, you guessed it, the communist conspiracy. Students laughed at this.

As for the FEPC being a communist idea, I always made a point to inform classes anytime something new is introduced, something that threatens the *status quo* which influential corporate interest profit from, then the new idea will predictably be assailed as un-American or communist inspired. A wave of a fear of communism was assisted by the media and alarmingly splashed into many dimensions of American culture in the late 1940s and well into the 1950s. Hollywood itself produced many films with plots and sub plots which presented "the menace of communism." This resulted in fear of communism becoming embedded in the American psyche for two generations. One dimension to that fear required teachers, upon being hired, to sign so called "loyalty oath" documents. At one time I had to sign one stating I was not a communist or sympathetic to communist causes. The post World War II anti-communism paranoia lingered much longer than the Red Scare hysteria in the immediate aftermath of World War I.

Though the FEPC bill languished in Congress, none the less, there were other events which heartened informed African-Americans. The Supreme Court had rendered a series of favorable though not very well publicized decisions. In one instance the Court nullified residential restrictive covenants. In another decision it called for school authorities to pay black and white teachers the same salaries. The proceedings in these favorable decisions, as in other cases involving segregation, were long drawn out expensive affairs for the national NAACP. Also, the national press wasn't inclined to give these decisions front page coverage. And, as one would expect, in the deep South the Supreme Court's decisions favorable to the NAACP received scant news coverage.

The rather low profile favorable Supreme Court decisions of the late 1940s served as stepping stones toward the more dramatically publicized and profoundly consequential decisions of the 1950s – culminating with the *Brown v. Topeka Board of Education* decision of 1954. The apparent extreme caution exhibited by the Court in the 1940s can largely be explained by noting its concern for the risky political implications for the government per se. In order to minimize negative political repercussions, in the wake of its decisions, the Court believed the legitimacy of its decisions would be difficult to assail if the decisions were unanimous. This explains why some cases were deliberated at great length. To achieve unanimity in a legal proceeding takes time. My wife Ellen, a law school graduate, has frequently explained procedures within the judicial process, from the federal down to county levels, can sometimes seem of indeterminable lengths of time.

Often overlooked in the realm of African-American history is the story of the origin and purpose of the Congress of Racial Equality. CORE as it came to be known was a spin-off, in 1942, from the Fellowship of Reconciliation's Department of Race Relations. The six who founded CORE, including the twenty-two year old James Farmer, were basically acquainted with each other because of their interest in the philosophy of the Fellowship of Reconciliation. That organization had begun to take a keen interest in American race relations in 1940 when the radical reformer pacifist A. J. Muste became its chief executive.

With reference to A. J. Muste as a radical in mind, on occasion a student would ask what the word radical meant, since I used it sometimes. This term has some elasticity in its meaning - there are variables involved here. In many instances it simply means thinking outside the box of mainstream consensus opinion. For example there's my idea Frederick Douglass should replace Andrew Jackson on the twenty dollar bill. It would most likely be viewed as a radical idea by most Americans at this time. Also, considering society at large for many decades before the Civil War didn't object to slavery, it's fair to say abolitionists were radicals given what they stood for. Then too, it's a given most Americans in the aftermath of the Civil War didn't believe in racial equality. So, those who did would be viewed as radical. And that's exactly what Republicans wanting racial political equality after the Civil War were called – Radicals! They, as radicals in other times, favored what wasn't acceptable to most Americans at a given time.

Yes, it was said CORE seemed radical compared with the NAACP in the 1940s and 1950s. Core's early members, much younger than most NAACP members, initiated activities the NAACP didn't care for. In their published study of CORE, August Meier and Elliott Rudwick said A. J. Muste wanted the Fellowship of Reconciliation to go "beyond ... opposition to war to experimenting with non-violent direct action for social justice." This new orientation was to be initiated at the local level by various "peace teams." One team was established at the University of Chicago in October of 1941. It committed itself to "applying Gandhian principles to racial problems." About the time their numbers reached a dozen they began calling themselves "the Chicago Committee of Racial Equality." This, in effect, became a nucleus from which the Congress of Racial Equality (CORE) emerged. They rejected the word "for" as in Congress "for" Racial Equality. As far as they were concerned the races were equal, which is the assertion of the name they took. They also liked the term CORE because they believed America's core problem was racism.

Meeting in the Fall of 1946, CORE's Executive Committee evaluated a proposal calling for a two week journey, the following Spring, into the South aboard a bus engaged in interstate travel. This trip was to see if the recent Supreme Court decision *Morgan* v. *Virginia* (1946), invalidating segregation on buses engaged in interstate travel, was being complied with by bus companies and local authorities. CORE's national office approved of the proposal and planned coordinated activities to implement what was to become known as the Journey of Reconciliation. It was hoped this undertaking would garner some positive publicity for CORE in the media. Overall black leaders in communities around the country, if aware of CORE's existence, weren't inclined to view CORE's initiative favorably. It's fair to say, given societal circumstances of this time, this action CORE planned was viewed as radical.

CORE decided to restrict this project to the upper South. It was agreed any penetration into Alabama, Mississippi, or Louisiana was fraught with risks not worth taking at that time. In January of 1947, George Houser and Bayard Rustin made a preliminary tour to arrange for lodgings and speaking engagements at stops along the route they intended to take. They also investigated gaining access to legal assistance.

In the planning stage of the Journey of Reconciliation those designated to participate spoke on more than thirty occasions before black church congregations, black college groups, and various NAACP chapters. Though some local NAACP chapters were enthusiastic in their support of CORE's undertaking, at the national level NAACP Executive Secretary Walter White was one of many prominent individuals who declined an invitation to financially back the journey. Prominent African-Americans were wary of this first major post war civil rights exercise because of its obvious negative confrontation potential. Thurgood Marshal, apparently not realizing CORE's activity was restricted to the upper South only, feared it "would result in wholesale slaughter." Because the NAACP had shunned the bus trip project, many in CORE expressed disappointment by claiming it was no longer relevant as a force to promote the change required for ending institutionalized racism in America.

The Journey of Reconciliation was undertaken by sixteen men, eight black and eight white. Among the black men, leaving Washington D.C. on April 9, 1947, were Bayard Rustin, William Worthy, an official of the New York Council for a Permanent FEPC, and Conrad Lynn, a black attorney who was active in civil rights causes in New York. There was no attempt to challenge segregation policies applicable to bus station waiting rooms, rest rooms, or luncheonette counters. CORE focused solely on the seating arrangements in the buses. Twelve CORE riders were arrested for not sitting where the still recognized Jim Crow laws required them. These laws were being locally enforced despite the fact they had been voided by the United States Supreme Court the previous year.

At their respective trial in Asheville, North Carolina, the black attorney for Dennis Banks, a black man from Chicago, and the white James Peck, showed his copy of the Supreme Court's *Morgan* decision to the presiding judge and prosecuting district attorney. It made no difference to either and they continued with the trial. Despite the ruling of the Supreme Court, the judge found the defendants guilty and sentenced them to thirty days on the road gang. However, with one exception, charges in Asheville were later dropped. Not so in Chapel Hill, charges there were processed and all four arrested were found guilty. Bayard Rustin and the others were sentenced to thirty days at hard labor. During appeal the four were allowed to leave the state on bail. Upon learning their sentences had been upheld by a higher court, three of the four returned to serve their sentences. Fortunately,

Bayard Rustin, Joe Felmet, and Igal Roodenko were released for good behavior after twenty-two days.

What was accomplished by this CORE sponsored project – the Journey of Reconciliation? In terms of gaining favorable responses from either
the bus companies or authorities in the southern states, which were ignor-
ing the Supreme Court's *Morgan* decision, little had been accomplished.
Events associated with the Journey failed to stir southern blacks to continue
with CORE's strategy by way of local initiatives. In more practical terms,
this initiative by CORE didn't seem to have an up side. It received no attention to speak of in America's major daily newspapers and barely any
mention in black owned weeklies. Also, unfortunately, it didn't stimulate
an interest boosting membership in CORE's struggling chapters as had
been anticipated.

In terms of media coverage CORE's Journey of Reconciliation was a
non-event. It wasn't page one news anywhere, but, then too, Martin Luther
King Jr's Montgomery bus boycott was mostly omitted from front page
coverage when it was initiated eight years later. (However, at this same time,
the national media was giving much attention to Jackie Robinson breaking
into baseball's major leagues as the first African-American player.) Yet, on
the positive side, this CORE undertaking served to boost the morale of
its small cadre of members and they continued to keep their "eyes on the
prize." From the perspective of some, at a later time, it served a useful purpose none the less. This 1947 event was brought back into focus by those
who planned the much better publicized Freedom Rides of 1961. During
the 1950s and into the 1960s, CORE's activities, which included sidewalk
picketing, continually challenged the negative ways Americans historically
perceived and treated fellow Americans of African ancestry.

Momentum for positive change, somewhat observable during the war
years, faltered a bit in 1946. But, then, the following year African-Americans were again inspired to believe change was coming. Baseball, America's
national pastime, became the venue where a breakthrough in race relations
would occur. On opening day of the 1947 season, the Brooklyn Dodgers
placed a proud African-American in their starting line-up. By season's end,
Jackie Robinson won the Rookie of the Year award and then played in the
World Series, both firsts for an African-American. Two years later, in 1949,
he won the National League's batting title and was named the league's Most
Valuable Player - two more firsts for an African-American. Jackie Robinson

was also the first of his race elected to the Baseball Hall of Fame in Cooperstown, New York.

In 1948 the political stage was being set for the Democratic Party to make a dramatic break from its past. In its presidential nominating convention, held in Philadelphia, Mayor of Minneapolis Hubert H. Humphrey urged his fellow delegates to address the issue of racial injustices. Thus, he offered a civil rights proposal to be incorporated into the party's platform. Paul Douglass and Adlai Stevenson, both of Illinois, also supported including a civil rights plank in the Democratic Party's platform.

Humphrey's proposal was the most forthright civil rights plank either party had ever considered in the 20th Century. President Harry Truman, seeking the convention's endorsement, made clear his approval of the civil rights proposal. This proposal was adopted as a plank in the party's platform by a delegate vote of 651& ½ to 582 & ½. The Republican Party also held its convention in Philadelphia. However, its platform and Thomas Dewey their candidate offered nothing to challenge the racial *status quo*.

Chapter 13

The death of Franklin Roosevelt in April of 1945 took many Americans by surprise. The not well known Harry Truman then became president. In 1944, he had been placed on the ticket with FDR then running for his fourth term. Insiders knew Roosevelt's health was precarious, but the public wasn't generally aware of that. The media hadn't drawn attention to his failing health, just as it never reminded the public he had been crippled by polio in the early 1920s and had to wear leg braces.

Upon Truman assuming office many Democrats hoped progressive domestic policies, having roots in FDR's New Deal, would be supported by him and taken up again at war's end. In 1946 Harry Truman wanted Congress to enact a universal health care plan. His request for Congress to act on this proposal stalled and never reached the House floor for a full vote. It was eclipsed as a priority because Congress began calling for greater spending on defense in response to corporate media continually suggesting the Soviet Union was intent on expanding its base from its eastern European "satellite" countries into the rest of Europe. By the fall of 1948, in addition to raising defense appropriations, Congress reinstated the military draft which had ended in 1946. This was the draft law A. Philip Randolph said African-Americans wouldn't respond to if military units continued to be racially segregated.

Truman abandoned many domestic spending proposals and went along with those calling for more appropriations for defense. It appeared to many Truman did this in response to Republican allegations the Democrats were "soft on communism." The emphasis on dramatically beefing up the military and then the subsequent deployment of military units to Korea meant Truman had to abandon his initial support for universal health care similar to what Canada now has in place. A measure of notable reform in health care didn't come until almost 20 years later with passage of the Lyndon Johnson inspired Medicare Act intended to benefit senior citizens.

However, of consequence on the domestic front for African-Americans, most Democrats, but not those from the South, supported Truman in his endeavor to promote equal rights and facilitate true justice for African-Americans. Early in 1948, President Harry Truman decided to initiate measures based on findings by the Civil Rights Study Commission, established by him the year before. The commission's report was entitled *To Secure These Rights*. It inspired Truman to deliver a "Ten Point" civil rights message to Congress in February. Truman called upon the government to fulfill its obligatory responsibility of guaranteeing and protecting the rights of all citizens, regardless of race, color, or national origin. Though Congress didn't immediately respond, nonetheless, ideas calling for long overdue measures of reform to secure equality for African-Americans had been brought to the public's attention.

Truman's message indicated his desire for the Democratic Party to make a break from its past. After all, up to the administration of Franklin Roosevelt, his predecessor, it had done little and wasn't known for a commitment to equal rights and justice for black Americans. The record shows Democrats had basically ignored their plight for almost seventy years prior to Franklin Roosevelt's election. But now, in this election year 1948, Truman was set to push for some far reaching positive changes African-Americans had called for through many decades.

Most Democrats would support Harry Truman, others, mainly from the South, wouldn't. The latter would, before summer's end, break from the Democrats supporting Truman. The disaffected southern Democrats chose a candidate of their own in the 1948 presidential election. Senator Strom Thurmond of South Carolina was the choice of the states rights Dixiecrat Party. (On December 14, 2003 the *New York Times* featured the story of a bi-racial woman claiming Strom Thurmond was her father. She reported her mother was a sixteen year old maid in the Thurmond household when she got pregnant back in the late 1930s.) Many political pundits thought Truman didn't stand a chance with the loss of southern Democrats. But, to their surprise Truman won the presidency in 1948. As the decade drew to a close, conservative southern Democrats in alliance with stand pat Republicans stymied Truman's civil rights legislative proposals.

Many white southerners, voting for Dixiecrat Thurmond in 1948, wouldn't vote for the Democratic candidate Hubert Humphrey twenty years later in 1968. They recalled his role at the Democratic Convention of 1948, as well as his role as Lyndon Johnson's Vice President energetically endorsing civil rights legislation of the mid 1960s. Instead of Humphrey, in 1968, southerners were most likely to vote for either Alabama's governor George Wallace or Richard Nixon, who had lost his bid for the presidency to John Kennedy in 1960. Nixon initiated a southern strategy to check Wallace's candidacy.

Before the 1940s decade ended, differences between the United States and the Soviet Union over access to Berlin and other post war issues affecting Europe were facilitating the development of alarming tensions between the former WW II allies. Newspapers capitalized on stories of growing mistrust and suspicions regarding supposed Soviet foreign policy goals. Underlying these stories was the constantly reiterated theme of the "evils of communism." These factors resulted in the emergence of a political climate of fear. That fear prompted Congress to again authorize a military draft.

A. Philip Randolph let it be known a reinstated military conscription law based on segregation would be strongly opposed by various African-American interest groups. He announced a plan calling for non-compliance by the African-American community to any new draft law authorizing continuation of segregation in the various branches of the U.S. Military. Randolph subsequently met with White House officials for exploratory "informal" discussions on this issue. The outcome of these meetings resulted in President Truman issuing Executive Order 9981. This order called for implementation, as quickly as possible, for equality of treatment for all in the U.S. Military regardless of race, color, religion, or national origin. Essentially the military services were ordered to integrate by Commander In Chief Harry Truman. Thus, my Air Force enlistment in 1955 came six years after racial segregation in the military officially ended.

A committee to oversee Truman's Order 9981 was quickly established. The committee to evaluate military personnel policies published its recommendation in 1950, under the title "Freedom To Serve." That year also saw President Truman send integrated military units to assist South Korea, invaded by its neighbor North Korea. The Navy and the Air Force were the first to initiate steps to phase out segregation. And, by the time a truce ended the fighting in Korea, in 1953, all branches of the U.S. armed forces had abolished segregation and quota policies.

Also, during the Truman administration the numbers of African-Americans employed by the federal government in positions designated civil service, located in Washington D.C., rose to almost half of what their percentage in the population as a whole was. As an employer the federal government was doing a much better job at hiring non-whites than private sector employers. Of special note also, in 1953 African-American organizations were pleased by the report indicating no lynchings had occurred in 1952. This was a first in 71 years of recorded data in that regard. So, many might say things seemed to be looking up for African-Americans in the early 1950s, but some, with good reason, were entitled to ask would they continue to do so?

In the early 1950s, the Supreme Court revealed the direction it was taking toward ending racial discrimination by a series of decisions nullifying segregation in interstate commerce and higher education, as well as ruling against white only primary elections. But, the decision sending shock waves across the South was made public on May 17, 1954. In *Brown v. Topeka Board of Education*, the Court ruled "separate educational facilities are inherently unequal," and were, in effect, generating a feeling of inferiority within black school children. Chief Justice Earl Warren cited psychological studies, pioneered by African-American psychologist Kenneth Clark, indicating a prevalence of low self esteem among black students who attended segregated schools. Warren's court ruled segregation in public education violated the equal protection clause of the Constitution's Fourteenth Amendment. In many quarters the *Brown v. Board of Education* decision is regarded as the most significant Supreme Court decision of the 20th Century.

Die hard segregationists, in a state of shock, mobilized and quickly delineated a strategy indicative of their determination to resist the Supreme Court's *Brown v. Board of Ed.* and subsequent follow up decisions.

In Virginia's Prince Edward County closed its public schools entirely to deprive black children of education. Many parents laid plans to organize private schools which soon became known as "segregation academies." Non-compliance of the Supreme Court's decision meant the burden of redress fell on black students' parents who often let the subterfuges go unchallenged. Initiating law suits was an expensive proposition few African-American families could afford at that time.

Before 1954 was over highway billboard signs began appearing in many regions of the South bearing the admonition: "Impeach Earl Warren!" Also, just one month after the momentous decision, a group of fourteen men met at Indianola, Mississippi to organize themselves as the "White Citizens' Council." It was dedicated to resisting the Supreme Court's decision. Soon other parts of the South had similar organizations and, by 1957, an organizational federation came into existence known as the "Association of Citizens' Councils."

Other groups with similar objectives, such as the States' Rights Council and the Tennessee Society to Maintain Segregation, merged together on December 29, 1955 under the leadership of Mississippi's Senator James O. Eastland to form the Federation for Constitutional Government. Membership included at least three dozen politicians then holding either state or federal offices. This organization quickly sponsored a document known as the *Southern Manifesto* which they introduced into Congress on March 12, 1956.

The *Southern Manifesto* included familiar assertions such as claiming southern blacks were satisfied with their lot in life and were being duped by outside agitators. In many quarters southern gossip conveyed the belief the agitators were communist sympathizers and liberal Jews from "up North." Included among those signing the *Manifesto* were United States' Senators J. William Fulbright of Arkansas, Richard B. Russell of Georgia, Strom Thurmond of South Carolina, Allen J. Ellender of Louisiana, Harry F. Byrd of Virginia, and Sam J. Ervin of North Carolina. (Senator J. William Fulbright was later a thorn in the side of President Johnson regarding his Vietnam policy and Senator Sam J. Ervin became known to Americans beyond North Carolina when he chaired the Senate's nationally televised Watergate Investigation Committee in 1974.)

One often overlooked consequence of the end of segregated schools was the fact approximately 31,000 African-American teachers lost their positions. Teaching was a very important occupation enabling many traditional black college graduates to utilize their degrees. These teachers couldn't readily get teaching jobs again for quite some time. At the time most whites couldn't abide the thought of their children sitting in classrooms with black children, let alone being taught by black teachers.

An appreciable majority of black teachers in the South were women. So, the end of Jim Crow's dual education system presented an irony for college educated African-American women in particular. They lost teaching jobs in disproportionate numbers. I suppose one might say their livelihoods were sacrificed for the promise a better day was coming. Deep South school districts desegregated at a leisurely pace and were in no hurry to hire black teachers for integrated schools. In 1965, blacks were decidedly underrepresented in the teaching profession, not just in the South, but nationwide as well. They were certainly underrepresented in the New Jersey school district where I taught at that time.

As for African-Americans holding teaching positions in the North, in the 1960s, perhaps my personal experience reflects one dimension of that reality. My first full time public school teaching position began in September of 1963, in the City of Burlington, New Jersey. There was only one black teacher in the junior high where I was first assigned to teach. Actually I believe he was the only African-American teacher in the entire district, but since I didn't know much about the elementary schools I couldn't swear to that. Also, as I recall, a black women worked in the junior high's cafeteria with four or five white women. This staff profile is significant when considering the fact the student body population was roughly twenty percent black. However, no surprise, the five starters on the high school basketball team were African-Americans, including students I taught - cousins Cornell and Reggie Hutton. Bill Burr, the coach, who also taught in the junior high was white.

Horace Gibson was the junior high's only African-American teacher. He taught mathematics in a room directly across the hall from my classroom. He claimed to be related to Ken Gibson - then making a name for himself in Newark, New Jersey politics. (In 1970, Ken Gibson become mayor of that city. The first African-American mayor of a major eastern city.) We were expected to go into the hall, between classes, and monitor student behavior as they moved on to various classrooms. Horace Gibson and I would stand side by side between classes and chat. He had a droll sense of humor which I didn't grasp at first. He used the terms "black kids" and "white kids" to describe our students.

Horace asked if I ever taught black kids before. "No, I hadn't," was my reply. He responded I would "learn a few things not included in college education courses." Horace Gibson contributed to my understanding black students frequently had different needs, because of socio-economic circumstances, than white students. He once said, "Our black kids won't be going skiing in Vermont over the holidays, but some of the white kids will." His comment was right on target regarding differences of economic circumstances between the black and white students. For the most part his observation regarding economic inequality is still presently relevant.

In the North, in the early 1960s, the term "ghetto" was coming into common usage by the media and certain politicians to describe the locations where African-Americans continued to live, restrained to those places by socio-economic factors. Though decisions in federal courts were progressing toward ending *de jure* segregation, in fact segregation determined by residential living patterns was becoming more common. Black children increasingly went to schools within districts compatible with their neighborhoods. Hence, interaction with whites, and *vice versa*, was almost nonexistent. This situation is a dimension to *de facto* segregation, the reality of which persists to this day.

Another sociological term the media in the early 1960s began to use was "ethnic whites." It applied to those utilizing a hyphen when describing themselves, hence Irish-Americans, Italian-Americans, Polish-Americans, and so forth. Most ethnic whites living in northern cities, in the 1950s and '60s, had definite ideas about what their neighborhoods represented, what they were about and what they should be about. In certain instances it was easier for black professionals to move into white upper middle class WASP neighborhoods, than for blue collar African-Americans to move into working class Italian-American or Irish-American neighborhoods. Many times the ethnic whites' response to African-Americans moving into "their" neighborhood, was the question: "Why do you want to live where you're not wanted?" Begrudged tolerance or outright verbally expressed racist hostility sometimes accompanied by acts of petty vandalism often confronted many African-Americans trying to improve their living circumstances somewhat by moving to such neighborhoods.

In most northern cities better maintained public parks and recreation centers were located in white neighborhoods. Such places often had tennis courts, ball fields, and swimming pools. Though not segregated for use by law, *de facto* segregation was the rule in terms of who was most likely to use such public facilities. For three summers, 1960, '61, and '62, I was a life guard on the City of Philadelphia's payroll working for the Department of Parks & Recreation at my neighborhood recreation center's swimming pool. In those three summers, I can recall only two times when a small group of black folks, two adults and two or three pre teens, came to the pool to swim. In both instances I believe they had to take public transportation to come from their distant neighborhood which obviously didn't have a swimming pool. Their situation was, at heart, another dimension to the nature of *de facto* segregation.

Less than a year after the Supreme Court's *Brown v. Topeka Board of Education* decision, African-American voters in the North went to their polling places in November (1954) and gained more representation by elected black officials than they previously ever had. African-Americans had been elected to city councils, state legislatures, and two new black members of the U.S. House of Representatives joined Harlem's Adam Clayton Powell Jr. His new colleagues were: William Dawson of Illinois and Charles C. Diggs of Detroit, Michigan. When these three men took their oaths of office in January of 1955, it marked the first time in the 20th Century three persons of African ancestry served in the same session of Congress. In the summer of 1955, Congressman Diggs attended the Mississippi trial of two white men accused, and then acquitted, of murdering black teenager Emmett Till. Till lived in Chicago, but had been visiting relatives living in Mississippi at the time he was murdered. The trial of those accused of murdering young Till was covered more extensively in black news outlets than in white ones.

On the first day of the last month of the same year, Rosa Parks refused to give up her seat and sit in the back of the bus. Rosa Parks had been to college, but the job she held in the Fall of 1955 didn't require a college degree. Like many other black women in the South, she worked as a seamstress. (In the North at this time her occupation was mostly unionized, in the South it wasn't.) Basically, up to the time she was arrested her personal life was respectfully uneventful. She had no deep seated psychological need to attract attention to herself. But, attention came her way on December 1,

1955. That's when she dared to sit in the "white only" section of a Mont-gomery Alabama bus on her way home from work. Her action was rooted in her long held belief of the absurdity of the seating arrangement based on race. At the time of her arrest the media mostly overlooked her dedicated volunteerism supporting her local NAACP chapter. (One of my favorite Neville Brothers' songs is "Sister Rosa" on their *Yellow Moon* CD.)

Responding to the arrest of Rosa Parks, a group of black ministers including Martin Luther King, Jr., Rev. Joseph Lowery (Awarded the Presidential Medal of Freedom by President Obama in 2009), Rev. Fred Shuttlesworth, and the Rev. Ralph Abernathy laid plans to organize the Montgomery bus boycott. Implementation planning was undertaken by former NAACP community organizer Ella Baker. Within weeks this group took the name Montgomery Improvement Association. The ministers' call for Montgomery's African-American community to refrain from riding the buses was enthusiastically embraced. The boycott lasted for almost a year. Supporters of the boycott got to and from their jobs by car pooling or walking. Then too, some white women drove to the homes of black women in their employ as domestic workers to drive them to their homes. Noting the resolve of Montgomery's black community, African-Americans in other parts of the South began to take heart. It wasn't too long before Martin Luther King, Jr. and the African-American citizens of Montgomery became an inspiration to others across the South.

Earl Warren's Supreme Court came through again. On November 13, 1956, it ruled the Constitution was, indeed, transgressed by the bus com-pany's Jim Crow practice of segregated seating. Arna Bontemps quoted W.E.B. DuBois' reaction to the Court's favorable decision; "Can passive resistance win over race hate? I doubt it. But, if it does, then Mohandas Gandhi and the Black Folk of Montgomery have shown the world how to conquer war." A major consequence of the boycott's success was catapulting Martin Luther King, Jr. into national front page prominence.

The Montgomery Improvement Association served as the forerunner of the Southern Christian Leadership Conference (SCLC). Both organiza-tions had taken shape and become viable thanks to the energy expended by King and his associates. Dr. King established the SCLC's philosophical basis on the teachings of Jesus of Nazareth, Henry David Thoreau, and Mohandas Gandhi. The non-violent resistance practiced by SCLC adher-ents made them vulnerable to acts of violence themselves. Dr. King's home was bombed and members of his organization were frequently physically abused. His followers were often taunted and bullied in attempts to get them to physically react so their philosophy of non-violence would be sullied.

As the 1960s decade began some saw Dr. King's SCLC begin to eclipse the significance of the NAACP. Disappointed by the NAACP's seeming reluctance to launch initiatives of similar magnitude as those by the SCLC, black journalist Louis E. Lomax said, "the NAACP has consistently failed to take a positive and meaningful lead in initiating or giving concrete support to....mass action....and demonstrations." In response to that criticism some said it wasn't fair to compare the NAACP with the emerging more militant organizations, such as the SCLC or the Student Non-Violent Coordinating Committee (SNCC). It brings to mind the observation you can't compare apples to oranges.

The NAACP's traditional focus was to initiate actions in court rooms, state legislatures, and the halls of the United States Congress. From its inception the NAACP wasn't an organization inclined to take to the streets over every conceivable issue which could legitimately be raised. Taking issues to the streets wasn't the way the NAACP operated. Its executive board was always circumspect in selecting its battles. When selecting tactics for dealing with specific issues, it always carefully evaluated what could be gained versus what might be lost.

On the other hand, Dr. King was buoyed by the success of the Montgomery bus boycott, which brought him to believe in the efficacy of taking certain issues to the public by way of street demonstrations. The nature of King's tactics were in some respects similar to those used almost two decades earlier in New York City by Adam Clayton Powell, Jr. The difference, as King knew very well, was in the North politicians were beginning to concede to black demands in exchange for their votes, while in the South politicians didn't want to be known as the official who had something to do with allowing African-Americans to vote at all.

Southern police, in the early 1960s, didn't supervise street demonstrations with the understanding the demonstrators were exercising their constitutional rights. They based their actions on the premise they were upholding local laws, which, because of long standing local tradition, somehow took legal precedence over the constitutional rights of African-Americans. When southern police challenged and harassed civil rights demonstrators, it was from the perspective demonstrators were engaging in unwarranted disturbances disruptive of their communities' peace and tranquility. Totally out of sympathy with demonstrators regarding their reasons for demonstrating, the local authorities were not impressed by the fact demonstrators didn't respond with retaliatory violence in view of police provocations.

Once Reconstruction ended in 1877, the white power structure in the South had been willing to employ violence, and the threat of violence, to keep black people mindful of "their place." This was duly noted by the eminent Swedish sociologist, Gunnar Myrdal. In his extensive study, *An American Dilemma: The Negro Problem and Modern Democracy,* (1943) Myrdal observed the function of violence as a means for social control in the South. Myrdal's revelations brought certain issues to the attention of various receptive and well intentioned whites living outside the South, but he wasn't telling African-Americans living in the South the news.

Martin Luther King, Jr. knew his followers, demonstrating for their rights, would be recipients of various modes of violence at the hands of police supervised by the likes of Eugene "Bull" Connor. In the words of Theodore White, Connor was chief "of one of the most brutal racist police forces of the South." One dimension of King's strategy was to get southern police forces to reveal themselves for what they were – perpetrators of violence in the name of law and order. Blacks living across the South too frequently experienced that violence firsthand. But now, since events were being covered by the national media, southern blacks had to act in a manner revealing to the rest of the nation what they had always known about police tactics and the travesty of southern justice.

King's followers would become means for revealing the hypocrisy of the South. Politically pragmatic, Dr. King wanted the rest of America, folks living in Oregon and Wisconsin, to see the South for what it was as represented by Bull Connor. When the rest of the country became indignant at what was shown on televised news programs, King reasoned it would then be extremely difficult for southern leaders to maintain the fiction segregation was acceptable to African-Americans living there. When millions, myself included, viewed the televised scenes of hundreds of African-Americans being subjected to police water canon and dogs snapping at them, they came to understand circumstances in the South were totally unsatisfactory to African-Americans. The rest of the nation was beginning to see and understand why the chant "Jim Crow must go" had validity.

Participants unfamiliar with techniques of passive resistance might too readily engage in the violence of reactive self defense. Because of the highly charged dynamic of confrontation, Dr. King knew defensive behavior had the potential to be transformed instantaneously into retaliatory violence of which retribution played a prominent part. If police initiated violence first, there was always the possibility they would become victims in a quick turn of events whereby violated demonstrators responded to them with retaliatory violence. If the police themselves appeared to become victims, King believed the general public would immediately lose sight of the reasons why a demonstration was undertaken in the first place. Under no circumstances did he want that to happen! Dr. King knew bilateral violence would only result in debate on the justification each side would contend it had for resorting to violence.

Martin Luther King, Jr. lived long enough to see many militants of the mid 1960s belittle his philosophy of non-violence. For the most part his radical critics thought his belief was naïve. He responded to them by citing Gandhi's observation: "If cowardice is the only alternative to violence, it is better to fight." (I often wondered how many students were capable of grasping the subtle meaning of that Gandhi observation.) King's constant message to his followers was it required a special courage to take a stand for a morally righteous position in the face of those who couldn't comprehend it or those whose particular beliefs were challenged by the message the non-violent protestors presented. He urged his followers to become moral positivists. Staying positive (violence was a negative) called for one to draw upon inner strength bolstered by the conviction the cause engaged in was righteous.

Essentially the self discipline Dr. King hoped for in his supporters came down to individual will power. That's what enabled one to stand firm for what is right, positive if you prefer, in the face of negative or destructive behavior. Will power requires an inner core strength. Those who displayed it were very much in evidence when following the philosophy of Dr. King. Those sitting impassively at lunch counters while screaming people poured sugar in their hair or squirted mustard on their backs had it - no question. However, it seems there's always those unable to call on an inner strength to resist evil, but allow themselves to get carried away with negative group behavior such as lynching or, in a military action, shooting innocent civilians.

Up to the 1960s, African-Americans living in the South had not participated in anything of the magnitude which Martin Luther King, Jr.'s leadership called for. As such, with all the attendant news coverage, these non-violent demonstrations forced Americans by the millions to see the hypocrisy in race relations conveyed and perpetuated by certain governments which sanctioned discriminatory practices. His conviction, his dedication, his energy, finally began to move America away from institutionalized racism. King's momentous efforts helped set the American people more consciously on the course pursuing "liberty and justice for all."

On February 1, 1960, I was in the first week of second semester classes of my freshman year at Temple University. An event that day triggered events of greater magnitude to occur in its wake throughout the South regarding challenges to the racial status quo. (Exactly one decade later, in February of 1970, I was teaching my first African-American history course.) Anyway, that most significant date in 1960 saw four male African-American students from the Negro Agricultural and Technical College in Greensboro, North Carolina sit down in the "white only" section of a lunch counter in a variety store. Having been refused service, they remained seated until the store closed. Thus began the "sit-in" movement which dramatically got underway at various locations across the South that spring. Though black students initiated and carried out most of these actions, by mid summer a smattering of white students, mostly from progressive northern colleges, also joined in this protest activity.

At some places "sitting-in" resulted in being refused service and then ignored. At other locations it took special courage, a steadfast commitment to Martin Luther King Jr.'s philosophy of non-violence. It was required when white teenagers opposing them gathered about and taunted them. In the context of being harassed they often had beverages poured on them, mustard squirted at them, and were often pulled off their seats to be pommeled. Protestors knew in advance they would be abused and thus courageously remained unresponsive. By mid-summer of 1960 a half dozen major newspapers, including the *New York Times*, were running stories about the circumstances pertaining to sit-in demonstrations in the South. The magnitude of the sit-in phenomenon was something Americans in the South had never seen before.

In many respects the sit-ins set a tone for the 1960s. This was to be the decade of protest. Within a few years hundreds of thousands of white students, disillusioned with events associated with America's Vietnam policies, took to the streets and protested in ways frequently extrapolated from what they had seen African-Americans do at the beginning of the decade. The chant "Jim Crow must go!" was replaced with "Hell no, we won't go!" by those objecting to the Vietnam War. The protest tactics of the newly emerged black organization known as the Student Non-Violent Coordinating Committee (SNCC) were being mimicked by white kids protesting the draft and the war in Vietnam.

After the sit-ins of 1960, the next major civil rights initiative was the Freedom Rides in 1961. The national director of CORE, James Farmer, had advocated the 1947 Journey of Reconciliation, so it came as no surprise he favored a similar undertaking to again challenge segregation on buses engaged in interstate transportation. He and twelve others boarded a southern bound bus in Washington, D.C. on May 4, 1961. This was the first of what became known as the Freedom Rides. Rides in roughly the first two months were planned and financed by CORE. Its members on the first ride, James Farmer among them, were arrested and beaten. Soon the activity, originally conceived and initiated by CORE, was taken up by other major civil rights organizations. The Southern Christian Leadership Conference's Wyatt Walker, and his wife, joined a ride which resulted in their being jailed. But for Louis E. Lomax "without question, the glory and the victory of the freedom rides belongs to CORE and to James Farmer."

In his 1963 book, *The Negro Revolt*, African-American author Louis E. Lomax noted the impressive membership gains of CORE. Its budget for 1961 was $233,000 and had shot up to $750,000 the following year. He also said it was inevitable it would soon have its critics and James Farmer's leadership called into question. He referred to the January 12, 1962 issue of *Time* magazine quoting an unnamed NAACP official saying CORE's membership was made up of "looneybirds and crackpots." Essentially Lomax said timid types were attracted to the NAACP. He suggested they played it safe by belonging to the NAACP, which wouldn't call on members to protest in the streets the way CORE's members did. For Lomax the proof of the pudding, regarding dynamic actions and leadership, was the question which organization had more of its members arrested for challenging the injustices of Jim Crow laws?

CORE and the SCLC planned for a massive rally in Washington D.C. at summer's end in 1963. The NAACP then symbolically acknowledged the legitimacy of both organizations by its willingness to join in this undertaking. On August 28, 1963, approximately 250,000 people, about 80 percent black and 20 percent white, participated in The March on Washington For Jobs And Freedom. They gathered at the Lincoln Memorial to hear various speakers prod the conscience of America. Among those who spoke were: A. Philip Randolph, the man most responsible for inspiring the event, Roy Wilkins of the NAACP, Walter Reuther, president of the United Auto Workers Union, long time dedicated activist Bayard Rustin, and John Lewis of the Student Non-Violent Coordinating Committee. (In 1986, John Lewis was elected to the U.S. House of Representatives from a Georgia district.) However, the speaker who made the most indelible impression on the assembled multitude was Martin Luther King, Jr., of the Southern Christian Leadership Conference, who delivered his memorable *I Have A Dream* speech.

Unfortunately, James Farmer of CORE was unable to attend this historic gathering of August 28th, because he was serving a jail sentence in Louisiana for participating in a civil rights action. Also, some in attendance reflected on the death of Dr. W.E.B. DuBois who had passed away earlier in the year in Accra, Ghana. Those familiar with his protracted participation in the struggle for racial justice knew of the indelible legacy his life represented in the cause for which they now carried forward with a rejuvenated momentum he had not anticipated.

Back to presidential politics and John Kennedy's part in the dramatic civil rights upheavals occurring in the early 1960s during his presidency. Early in his administration Kennedy and many of his advisers were basically behind the curve, taken by surprise when headline making challenges to the racial status quo gained the broader public's attention. The Kennedy brothers, John as President and Robert as Attorney General, were initially cautious in taking a positive stand to lend their support to the cause of African-Americans demanding full civil rights. With regard to denial of rights to black Americans and other minorities, the Kennedy administration in its first two years was often evasive. The Reverend Theodore Hesburgh, former head of the Federal Civil Rights Commission and later president of Notre Dame University, said the Kennedy administration's attitude was "don't do anything until you absolutely have to."

Rather than pursue street demonstrations, likely to be disruptive and appear unwarranted to some, the Kennedy administration believed activist organizations should direct their energy toward voter registration. Congress, in 1960, with Democratic majorities in both houses, had passed a Civil Rights law which empowered the Attorney General to certify African-Americans as "qualified voters" in their districts of residency which had previously denied them the right to vote. The business of enrolling voters would be low key as compared with street demonstrations and, on the plus side, likely to result in the Democratic Party gaining more voters. So, in an attempt to pull abreast of civil rights activism, Attorney General Robert Kennedy instructed his office to more vigorously utilize the provisions of the 1960 Civil Rights law.

As John Kennedy began his third year in office, civil rights leaders had, to be sure, encouraged their supporters to organize voter registration activities, but they weren't ready to abandon street demonstrations in view of so many segregation practices yet to be challenged. Pressure was mounting on the president who lamented, "Surely, in 1963, one hundred years after emancipation, it should not be necessary for any American citizen to demonstrate in the streets for an opportunity to stop at a hotel, or eat at a lunch counter...on the same terms as any other American." Ironically, President Kennedy didn't learn of the plans for the March on Washington in August until a few weeks prior to it occurring.

A wave of demonstrations swept across the South in the Spring of 1963. The most publicized was the one begun on April 3rd in Birmingham, Alabama which the Southern Christian Leadership Council (SCLC) organized. Protestors made known their grievances which focused on lack of city employment opportunities, segregated public accommodations, denial of voting rights, and the failure of authorities to implement the Supreme Court's nine year old ruling prohibiting segregated schools. Previously I described the tactics employed by Police Chief Bull Connor. The nation and the world saw those tactics, i.e., the use of water canon and dogs turned on demonstrators. This was an embarrassment in foreign policy. With regard to staying ahead of the Soviet Union in terms of favorable world opinion, Secretary of State Dean Rusk said we were in a race "with one of our legs in a cast." because of domestic racial policies.

During ongoing demonstrations in Birmingham, participants indicated their awareness 1963 was a special year. It marked the 100th anniversary of the Emancipation Proclamation. With other organizations the NAACP was using the slogan "Free by '63." A Department of Justice survey revealed there were "forty-three major and minor demonstrations, ten of them in northern cities" during the week of May 18th. Additional demonstrations occurred the following month, the month in which Medgar Evers was shot and killed in the driveway of his Jackson, Mississippi home. As president of the state of Mississippi's NAACP organization, Evers had been a thorn in the side of his community's white power structure. By 1975 students were asking me who Medgar Evers was. I had to admit I'd never heard of him until five years after his death as I began to do extensive reading in recent events of African-American history.

By June of 1963, civil rights activities were creating a compelling national interest of great concern. Boycotts and various types of demonstrations were prompting die-hard segregationists to respond with bombings, burnings, and illegal incarcerations.(The latter happened to Chaney, Goodman, and Schwerner the following summer in Mississippi, shortly before they were murdered.) Knowing he had to respond as constructively as possible, in June President Kennedy presented a sweeping civil rights proposal to Congress. Public accommodations, voting rights, and equal employment opportunity were issues addressed in Kennedy's challenge to Congress to take action. Southern members of Congress responded with stalling tactics, thus it hadn't been passed at the time President Kennedy was assassinated that November. The language of the Kennedy civil rights proposal was more moderate then the bill finally passed and signed by Lyndon Johnson the following year.

In September of 1963, Congress came back into session. Southern members were not impressed by the March on Washington three weeks earlier. No matter how many people participated they were not going to be pressured. They clung more tenaciously to their respective committee rules allowing for stalling procedures regarding President Kennedy's civil rights proposal. I was oblivious to these negative measures occurring in the halls of Congress that September because I was in the first month of my first full time teaching position. In mid August I had decided I couldn't spare the time to go to the massive Washington rally because I was involved in preparing for teaching my classes. Damn, look what I missed - the largest protest gathering in Washington up to that time. To this day I regret not budgeting my time more wisely, so I could have gone to that historic event held in Washington D.C. on August 28, 1963.

As for Congress stalling on Kennedy's civil rights bill, let's consider how southern politicians worked the system. Their ability to effectively thwart its passage was rooted in the congressional committee system, which bestowed power based on seniority, i.e., longevity of continuous service. Since the South basically had a one party system at the time, incumbents were continuously reelected thus giving them seniority entitling them to become committee chairmen. When a bill they didn't care for came to their respective committees, they used their powers as chairmen to simply kill such bills. Unfavored civil rights bills were placed at the bottom of their committee's agenda or the chairman sponsored a vote of no action frequently after a superficial discussion of the bill's provisions took place. For two decades after WW II bills pertaining to civil rights or trimming fat out of Pentagon budgets were rarely voted upon to be reported out of committee – in effect they simply "died" in committee.

Later, in the Fall of 1963, before the year passed into history, two events caused great disappointment to African-Americans. First, in elections across the South more candidates sought election or re-election to become mayors or governors on pro segregation platforms and won. Secondly, of perhaps greater disappointment, President John F. Kennedy was assassinated on November 22, in Dallas, Texas. His death came as a numbing blow to most Americans, black and white alike. Because of his civil rights bill, African-Americans had recently come to believe President Kennedy was on their side. His unexpected death seemed to devastate their hopes, which his bill had dramatically raised even though it was languishing in Congress.

I was teaching a class in New Jersey's City of Burlington junior high in the early afternoon that Friday when the office called with instructions to curtail my class and send the students to their respective home rooms. Some students coming back to my homeroom had somehow learned of the tragedy in Dallas. Excited, they were just beginning to settle down when the principal's somber voice came over the public address system to announce the President's death. He concluded by announcing classes for the remainder of the day were canceled.

After the announcement a few students lingered. They wanted to talk to me about the significance of Kennedy's death. These were ninth graders who didn't know the name of the Vice President. Within a week most

Americans had learned a few things about Lyndon B. Johnson. Significant was the fact Johnson was from Texas, the first president in U.S. History to come from the Lone Star state. Of course they didn't know the circumstances of how Lyndon Johnson got to be Vice President. There's irony to that story. Later it became common knowledge John Kennedy had offered Johnson the vice-presidency, on the party's national presidential ticket, with the expectation he would decline the offer. Politics has been known to make strange bedfellows. Remember the 1864 ticket of Abraham Lincoln and Andrew Johnson?

At the beginning of 1964, many African-Americans wondered if they were back to square one respecting the national government's commitment to securing their civil rights. How would the new President, Lyndon Johnson, a Texan, respond to the various issues and mass demonstrations regarding the push for equal rights under the law? For some things seemed gloomy. Should they stay hopeful? What was on the horizon beyond the clouds of political uncertainty? But most African-Americans, nonetheless, stayed true to the tradition of searching for rays of hope.

So much had happened throughout the South in the decade's first three years. However, in most respects those events had acted to promote a new confidence by 1963, a confidence capable of sustaining the continuation of the struggle for equality and justice regardless of who occupied the White House. The year 1963 marked the one hundredth anniversary of the Emancipation Proclamation and that anniversary had inspired so many to believe there would be no turning back. This was understood by the new president Lyndon B. Johnson. He quickly indicated he was committed to keeping things moving forward toward the long held desired goals of true political equality and justice for all.

Chapter 14

O
n November 27, 1963, less than a week after assuming the presidency, Lyndon Baines Johnson addressed a joint session of Congress. And, as the *New York Times* reported the next day, he cast aside all doubts regarding where he stood on the civil rights bill (House Resolution 7152) languishing in Congress since before the death of John F. Kennedy. President Johnson urged Congress to pass a law which would enable the nation to "eliminate…every trace of discrimination and oppression…based upon race or color." His request was finally acted upon, seven months later, in June of 1964, when Congress passed what has become known as the Civil Rights Act of 1964.

In January of 1964, a significant measure enhancing political rights for African-Americans was achieved after a long political implementation process. The required number of states had been tallied for ratification of the Twenty-fourth Amendment to the Constitution. This addition to the highest law of the land prohibited the United States, or any state, from establishing "any poll tax or other tax" as an eligibility requirement to vote. Up to that time southern states had notorious reputations for utilizing poll taxes as a means for keeping vast numbers of African-Americans from voting.

Two years earlier the Supreme Court, in *Baker v. Carr*, had struck down unequal representation practices sanctioned by various state legislatures, especially those in the southern states. The Court ruled one person should be as proportionately represented as any other one person. Basically this meant representation districts for state legislature seats, or U.S. House of Representatives seats, etc., had to be comprised of the same population numbers for all. Hence, a state legislature district having 70,000 people would not get one representative if other districts with twice that population only had one as well. Prior to this decision cows in some rural districts of northern states had better representation than people living in cities – especially in minority neighborhoods of those cities.

The Civil Rights Act of 1964 was more comprehensive than any other passed in the 20th Century. In unprecedented fashion this legislation confronted both *de facto* and *de jure* segregation. Its provisions abolished discrimination in places of public accommodation, i.e., hotels, motels, restaurants, etc. Public facilities, such as parks, swimming pools, tennis courts, golf courses, and stadiums, were desegregated. Title VII of this law also forbade places of business, as well as unions, from discriminatory practice policies.

Under the 1964 law, the U.S. Attorney General's staff was empowered to initiate desegregation suits. The Department of Justice was also authorized to initiate law suits on behalf of persons alleging their Fourteenth Amendment rights (equal protection under the law) had been denied. This law also facilitated the distribution of federal funds to school districts which implemented desegregation, and allowed federal dispensing agencies to withhold funds when federal agencies determined the new civil rights law was being violated by given school districts. Pro segregation educators and politicians saw this new legal formula as a type of federal government blackmail.

As a consequence of the enactment of the Civil Rights Act of 1964, significant political repercussions occurred. Claiming it was personal conviction regarding the legitimacy of the scope of the new law and not antipathy toward African-Americans per se, arch conservative Barry Goldwater voted against it. Subsequently he was nominated for the presidency by the Republican Party. Voting against the Civil Rights Act ensured support for Goldwater from a majority of white voters in the deep South.

Goldwater won presidential electoral votes in his home state of Arizona plus those from Alabama, Georgia, Louisiana, Mississippi, and South Carolina. It was the first time in almost ninety years a Republican presidential candidate carried those states. Of course the irony in this is almost ninety years earlier carpetbag Republicans had been supporting civil rights for African-Americans, not voting to deny them as Goldwater had done. Winning five deep south states plus his home state was of no consequence for Goldwater. The Democratic candidates, Lyndon Johnson for president and Hubert Humphrey for vice president, received a landslide victory. At this time a journalists raised the question, "What black American in their right mind would vote for Barry Goldwater for president?" Political pundits were soon to comment on the fact a seismic shift in the political alignment of the South had begun.

The very credible journalist of six 20th Century presidential races, Theodore White, said Goldwater had gone "on record ... where the decisive morality of America was against him." Voting for the Civil Rights Act, in the House, was Michigan's more moderate Republican Gerald Ford. (Keep in mind in Ford's Congressional district alone there were probably more African-Americans than in Goldwater's entire state of Arizona.) Voting for the Civil Rights Act, Ford wasn't defeated for reelection because of it. As White noted, "no Congressman who voted for the Civil Rights Bill in 1964 was defeated ... eleven of the twenty-two northern Congressmen who voted against it did suffer defeat."

In 1964, the Democratic Party held its presidential nominating convention in Atlantic City, New Jersey. A few weeks prior to delegates assembling there, an event with dire implications for volunteers in the Freedom Summer projects in Mississippi occurred. The bodies of three young men, Freedom Summer volunteers, were found after an extensive search subsequent to their being reported missing. During the search for James Chaney of Mississippi, Andrew Goodman and Michael Schwerner, both of New York, two other bodies of murdered black men were also found. This episode drew national attention.

In many places some African-Americans claimed the widespread publicity given to the search for Chaney, Goodman, and Schwerner was due to the fact James Chaney had died with two white students. A pertinent question was raised by many: would as much attention be given to the disappearance of three black students? I asked students if there was an element of truth to that assertion. A majority of students, down through the years, agreed with the implied answer to the question by saying cynicism was justifiable. Roy Wilkins, of the NAACP, described Mississippi at that time as a society where its many dimensions to lawlessness, perpetrated against black folks, had daily occurrences somewhere in the state.

Eruptions of racial violence in Mississippi in the summer of 1964 seemed incessant. That year the Civil Rights Commission counted 186 incidents, which included arson at black churches, beatings, tires of black owned vehicles slashed, and telephone threats - caller identification wasn't available at that time. Such criminal activities rarely resulted in arrests. Also, on a near routine basis, false arrests and detentions were employed as tactics to intimidate civil rights volunteer activists. And, not to be overlooked, too frequently persons charged with assaulting civil rights activists were acquitted for lack of witnesses. Across the country African-Americans weren't surprised when the all white jury rendered a not guilty verdict for those charged with murdering Chaney, Goodman, and Schwerner. (The film I recommended to students for a somewhat realistic take on how things were in Mississippi in 1964 was *Mississippi Burning* released in 1988.)

Approximately 700 white college students with a dozen or so older white adults, mostly from California and northern states, went to Mississippi in the summer of 1964 to participate in what became known as Freedom Summer. Idealistic and motivated to bring positive change to Mississippi, they joined with members of SNCC and CORE to achieve realization of the projects' designated goals. One of their undertakings at the top of the list was voter registration. But, there were other projects volunteers were involved in as well. In addition to teaching algebra to teens, black activist Robert Moses played a prominent role in coordinating various other activities such as: rehabilitating and improving community centers, literacy programs, and providing transportation assistance. Again, white authorities subjected volunteers to many incidents of harassment intended to intimidate them and disrupt their activities.

A good portion of Freedom Summer activity was devoted to assisting the newly formed Mississippi Freedom Democratic Party, known as the MFDP. Eighty thousand of Mississippi's African-Americans had cast ballots in a 1963 mock election sponsored by the MFDP. It was conducted to show the nation that fear, not apathy, was responsible for keeping blacks in Mississippi from voting. In 1964, the MFDP stepped up its activity. They complied with all the legally required procedures, in most of the precincts and districts in Mississippi's eighty-two counties, to be placed on primary election ballots. However, election results favoring them were discarded by the regular Democrats, who chose only their own to be delegates to Atlantic City for the Democratic Party's national nominating convention. To protest the manipulated procedures by the regular Democrats, the MFDP decided to send sixty-eight delegates of their selection, including four whites, to Atlantic City for the Democrats' Convention at summer's end.

In late August of 1964, the eyes of the nation were focused on the Democrats assembled in Atlantic City, New Jersey. That Lyndon Johnson would obtain his party's nomination was a foregone conclusion. This seemed to indicate the convention might not be as news worthy as conventions in the past had been. The most pressing issue for the media was the question who would Lyndon Johnson choose to run with him as vice president?

Most component agencies of the media had not expected the appearance of the MFDP delegation arriving in chartered buses to participate in the convention. The MFDP and its various supporters, which included college students from nearby New York and Philadelphia, immediately set up an informational picket line on the boardwalk by Atlantic City's municipal convention center. The issue that immediately came front and center was would the convention's credentials committee officially recognize the MFDP delegates and allow them voting rights?

Consequential to the MFDP's sudden appearance in Atlantic City, television audiences across the country became acquainted with MFDP organizer Fannie Lou Hamer of Ruleville, Mississippi. Now the media had another story at its heart about discrimination and segregation to present to average Americans living outside the South. During a preliminary session, prior to major Democratic figures giving their speeches, Fannie Lou Hamer of the MFDP was permitted to address those in attendance. Sensing something significant was about to transpire, television news networks presented her story to hundreds of thousands of Americans watching the convention's proceedings. She gave an account of her despicable treatment at the hands of local authorities in her Mississippi community. When she began to speak, my attention became riveted to my television screen.

In a sad, yet almost melodious voice, interspersed by attempts to stifle sobbing, Fannie Lou Hamer testified to convention delegates, as well as to the nation, about how she had been incarcerated and beaten under the supervision of a Mississippi state trooper as a consequence of attempting to register to vote. It was a story not likely ever heard before by white middle class Democratic delegates representing small towns in the upper mid West as well as the Pacific Northwest - places having only a sprinkling of black folks. Her attempt to register to vote also resulted in her losing a job she held for eighteen years. Within the context of her relating the humiliations she and other Mississippi blacks experienced down through the years, she frequently paused and said, "I question America." To this day I can still hear that phrase and her tone of voice in which she expressed it. Ms. Hamer's testimony was an embarrassment to the National Democratic Party assembled in convention and claiming the lion's share of credit for the Civil Rights Act passed just two months earlier.

The Convention's Credentials Committee offered the MFDP a compromise. By its terms, they would seat two MFDP members as delegates at large. The compromise also included a provision all Democratic conventions thereafter would refuse recognition to any delegation discriminating against blacks in their convention delegate selection procedures. Hubert Humphrey, Walter Reuther of the United Auto Workers, and many black delegates urged the MFDP to accept the compromise resolution. However, it was rejected.

In writing about the MFDP rejecting the offered compromise, Martin Luther King, Jr. said, "…there was no compromise for these persons who had risked their lives to get this far. But life in Mississippi had involved too many compromises already…for them to take [this] seriously; so their skepticism must be viewed sympathetically." One MFDP delegate voting against the compromise said, it "wasn't enough for all the work, all the fear, and all the lives that had been lost." Assessing what had happened, Black Power advocate, Stokely Carmichael said, "Many labor, liberal, and civil rights leaders deserted the MFDP because of closer ties to the national Democratic Party. To seat the MFDP over the 'regulars' would have meant a displacement of power."

Ah yes, the election of 1964, I remember it well. Two blocks from where the Democrats were meeting there was a huge billboard sign above the famous Steel Pier featuring Barry Goldwater's picture and the words, "In Your Heart You Know He's Right." Temple students I was with laughed about it. We agreed Barry was right – far right! The Democrats portrayed Lyndon Johnson as responsible, not one who would impulsively press the red button to commence nuclear holocaust. On the other hand, in the nationally televised nuclear mushroom cloud image looming behind a little girl sitting and picking daisies, the Democrats implied Goldwater's election would put the little girl and all Americans at great risk because Goldwater was a simplistic impulsive person eager to have a nuclear showdown with the Soviet Union.

In the presidential election of 1964, Lyndon Johnson was portrayed as the clear choice peace candidate. In view of his soon to be initiated policy of escalated military action in Vietnam, that representation of Johnson as the peace candidate was ironic. Temple students I interacted with often referred to Goldwater as a political Neanderthal. But at the same time, we admitted to being ignorant regarding Johnson. Where did he stand regarding the Military Industrial Complex Eisenhower had warned us about just four years earlier?

Within two years we had formed a definite opinion about Johnson who had decided to greatly expand the U.S. Military's presence in Vietnam as part of the U.S. policy of taking sides in the Vietnamese civil war. Opposition to Lyndon Johnson's Vietnam policy, initiated with bombing strikes, was expressed early on by the chant "Hey, hey, LBJ, how many kids did you kill today?" This, of course, was a reference to the American bombing on Vietnamese villages whereby innocent children consequently died. The first time I heard the chant just mentioned was by protesters on the steps outside Philadelphia's Convention Hall where inside Temple University was holding its June of 1966 commencement ceremony. The protesters knew Johnson's Vice President, Hubert Humphrey, was the keynote speaker. I participated in the ceremony inside to receive my master's degree, but was frequently thinking of the message of the protestors outside.

In the election of 1964, African-American voters heard Lyndon Johnson and the Democratic Party say most of the things they wanted to be said. Barry Goldwater, on the other hand, carped on the issue of turbulence in the streets which to black Americans came through as a veiled condemnation of civil rights demonstrations in various cities. In contrast, Lyndon Johnson's persistent support of the recent Civil Rights Act and his vice presidential choice of Hubert H. Humphrey, an NAACP's agenda advocate, made him worthy of African-American support. Lyndon Johnson was clearly the better choice for African-Americans in 1964.

Black leaders chose not to bring to light Lyndon Johnson's late 1930s and '40s voting record, as a southern Congressman, which was dubious on civil rights issues. However, by the 1950s, Lyndon Johnson was serving in the U.S. Senate and likely sensed a new era was in the offing. Thus, in

1958, he worked hard to get the Civil Rights Act of that year passed. Given more than a pass, Johnson was wholeheartedly embraced in view of Barry Goldwater's vote against the 1964 Civil Rights Act. As the election returns of 1964 indicate, African-American voters, on a percentage basis, went "all the way with LBJ."

A case can be made it was African-American voters who kept Barry Goldwater from winning more southern states than he did. According to Bayard Rustin's analysis, Goldwater took only those states "where fewer than 45 percent of eligible Negroes were registered." In southern states with more than half of the black population registered to vote, nine Congressmen who had voted for the Civil Rights Act of 1964 were returned to Congress.

Goldwater's candidacy, as a Republican, indicated a shift in southern voting patterns was underway. The Republican Party's 1964 foothold in the South wouldn't be temporary. Sorting things out in early 1965, Bayard Rustin's observation seemed prophetic, "It may be premature to predict a southern Democratic Party of Negroes and white moderates, and a Republican Party of refugee racists and economic conservatives, but there certainly is a strong tendency toward such a realignment...."

Lyndon Johnson's last year in the White House saw black unemployment at almost double that of whites. That didn't change over the course of the following five years while Richard Nixon was president. Without economic gains there would be little upgrades in quality of life circumstances for a majority of African-Americans. White flight to the suburbs added to further social isolation for African-Americans living in run down inner city locations. Johnson's civil rights legislation (Civil Rights Act 1964 & Voting Rights Act 1965) didn't impact, per se, the economic status quo. As Professor Manning Marable observed, whites "didn't object to Negroes gaining the right to vote or eating in restaurants" or sitting next to them on a bus, "so long as they didn't move [in] next door." Those laws didn't alter major economic distinctions evidenced in racial categorization.

One can't do justice to reviewing events of the 1960s without addressing the phenomenon of Malcolm X. While in prison, Malcolm Little had become an avid reader of the Black Muslim newspaper *Muhammad Speaks* - frequently smuggled into prisons. Upon his release, he affiliated with Elijah Muhammad's organization, The Nation of Islam, and took the name Malcolm X. His impressive oratorical skills readily facilitated his ability to effectively function as a valued proselytizer and he quickly became one of Muhammad's key lieutenants. His persuasiveness was attested to by the actor Ossie Davis. He said, "Once Malcolm fastened on you, you could not escape. It was impossible to remain defensive and apologetic about being a Negro in his presence. And you always left his presence with the sneaky suspicion that maybe, after all, you were a man!"

A frequent theme in the compelling oratory of Malcolm X's message was the idea black males had been deprived of their manhood by the white dominated society. They were victims of a societal psychological emasculation which resulted in obsequious behavior patterns. In the course of many years whites had come to expect this behavior from black men. It had become a requirement, so to speak, in the course of interactions between blacks and whites in society at large. The only words racist whites wanted to hear from black men were "Yas Suh." Malcolm X vehemently refuted the behavioral responses of predictable passivity. African-Americans had to stop giving their consent to the negative treatment to which they were constantly subjected. He called for an end to what he saw as predictable willing participation in the social dynamic which held black people down.

Malcolm X was dubious regarding the philosophy of non-violence espoused by Martin Luther King, Jr. He wondered if that philosophy was cut from the same cloth of predictable passivity. If it was, then King was allowing white racists more options than those available to blacks for resisting racist transgressions. As for blacks practicing non-violence, Malcolm said, "as long as I see them teaching non-violence only in the black community, we can't go along with that. ... it's not fair." He wanted to know why the burden of being defenseless always fell on the black community? Within three years the Black Panthers would echo the same question Malcolm asked.

Elijah Muhammad saw the meteoric rise in the popularity of his lieutenant Malcolm X. To what extent he became threatened by this has prompted considerable speculation. Outsiders began to hear rumors of their differences. The Black Muslim policy of withdrawal and separatism from the larger society and their non-participation with other African-American organizations working on broader civil rights issues eventually seemed ill advised to Malcolm X. Toward the end of 1963, he had come to believe the Muslims should put forth an effort in the struggle for black dignity by participating with other African-American activist groups engaged in forming coalition strategies. However, Elijah Muhammad stood fast on original doctrine correctness banning secular involvement. It wasn't long before some of Malcolm's ideas were labeled heresy. Some said the final break between them was caused by Malcolm's publicized comment, "the chickens are coming home to roost," regarding President Kennedy's assassination.

Shortly after his break with Elijah Muhammad, Malcolm X made a trip to Mecca. On this trip he learned orthodox Islam regards all men, regardless of race, as brothers in the sight of God. This journey to Mecca changed Malcolm X. He stopped referring to persons with blue eyes, such as myself, as devils. Noting the change in Malcolm, Ossie Davis said, "No one who knew him before and after his trip to Mecca could doubt that he had completely abandoned racism, separatism, and hatred."

However, Malcolm had not abandoned his commitment to work for racial equality and social justice. At the time of his assassination (Feb. 21, 1965) it was said in some quarters he had begun to appreciate what certain other organizations, also engaged in the quest for racial justice, were committed to achieving. If this observation has merit, in some respects Malcolm was moving toward positions CORE and later SNCC advocated. But how far he might have been willing to go with his new followers toward engaging in secular political coalition activities is not really known. As for his relationship with Dr. King a point of contention between them was rooted in their disagreement as to when the use of force might be justifiable. As Malcolm saw it force for the purpose of self defense shouldn't be ruled out. With regard to the last point, Malcolm was an oracle to the Black Panthers.

Desiring to establish a support base, Malcolm X initiated the founding of the Muslim Mosque, Inc. and the Organization of Afro-American Unity. Undoubtedly he viewed these organizations as vehicles for gaining acknowledgment of his standing in the African-American community at large. They enabled him to rapidly become a force in Harlem's political mix just before his murder. As Louis E. Lomax observed, "No sane man, black or white, dares plan a mass program in Harlem without including Malcolm X. For if it comes down to a showdown, Malcolm can muster more people than Adam Powell, A. Philip Randolph, Martin Luther King, and Roy Wilkins all put together."

For racial equality to become a reality, Malcolm X believed blacks had to behave as though they believed they were equal to whites and, thus, stand as tall as whites. If oppression of African-Americans involved violence against them, then they had to challenge it by defending themselves. The Christian precept of turn the other cheek, espoused by Dr. King, wasn't acceptable to Malcolm X. His inclination was more Old Testament - "an eye for an eye." About to emerge Black Panther founders Huey Newton and Bobby Seale revered Malcolm X. They with others, such as Stokely Carmichael, summed up many of Malcolm's views in their espoused ideology of Black Power. Compared with rhetoric articulated by the NAACP and the Urban League, that of the Black Power movement seemed provocatively inflammatory to government authorities.

Malcolm's independence from the Nation of Islam was short lived. Just as he was beginning to come into his own as a molder of significant opinion in the nation's black community, he was gunned down. His assassination, on February 21, 1965, was front page copy in newspapers across the nation. When considering what Malcolm X stood for, the first thing that comes to my mind is his message to challenge what white America had foisted on African-Americans. He wanted a cessation of behaving and thinking like second class citizens. Malcolm despised those he would consider Uncle Toms, those who constantly deferred to white notions of how things should be.

The death of Malcolm X was shortly before Muhammad Ali stood up for himself regarding not fighting in Vietnam. I have no doubt had Malcolm X lived, he would have applauded Ali's decision. That being said, my line of reasoning would also see Malcolm echoing Martin Luther King's sentiments expressed at New York City's Riverside Church where the Nobel Prize winner was critical of America making war on Vietnam. Yes, the media's tone was to always portray Malcolm as an angry black man. As for me, he had good reason to be angry about many things he saw as an African-American living in the 1940s, '50s, and '60s.

Malcolm's explanation of how and why African-Americans historically made some gains in times of national crisis has merit for many. For more conservative African-Americans his assessment would probably be considered counter productive cynicism. Essentially he said African-Americans were put into the production system during World War II and began to receive living wages for the first time ever, only because it served the government's interest as well as the interests of civilian wartime contractors realizing unprecedented profits.

As World War II progressed, white males in the labor force were called into active military service. At that point, Malcolm said, the government turned to African-American workers to keep production requirements functioning at optimum. He said, the white power brokers "just put us into their system and let us advance a little bit farther because it served their interests." It wasn't "because they were interested in us as human beings."

Students sometimes asked if I agreed with Malcolm's view about involvement of blacks in World War II. My reply, "Malcolm's view has some validity." Then I would proceed to mentioned how the situation for blacks in many ways paralleled that of women. In WW II, women, as well as blacks, were allowed to hold jobs never open to them in peacetime. At war's end, Rosie the riveter was expected to go back to her traditional housewife role. As for black workers, those who had acquired skills were expected to relinquish the jobs utilizing those skills to returning white veterans and then be satisfied to resume working in the unskilled jobs they had prior to the war.

After Hitler's Germany and Tojo's Japan had been defeated, the Soviet Union was seen as a new threat. This caused the United States to again rely on African-Americans to help bolster the national defense posture. Malcolm's contention was if the communist threat wasn't perceived little progress for black Americans would have ever been realized. He told black teenagers visiting New York City from Mississippi, in December of 1964, that dignity and progress for African-Americans was "never" based solely "upon the internal good will of this country."

Elijah Muhammad's Nation of Islam movement was reminiscent of Marcus Garvey's movement. Both placed an emphasis on instilling racial pride and promoted a philosophy that encouraged independence from white society. But, by no means were all African-Americans willing to withdraw from white majority society. As for the idea of being the majority, regarding those of solely European ancestry, present population data projections indicates they won't be the majority in American society by 2050. And, presently, Caucasians are no longer the majority in California.

In the mid 1960s, it was apparent changes had occurred which hadn't as yet come to pass in Garvey's time of the early 1920s. Also, by then most African-Americans were uncomfortable with the requirements of Elijah Muhammad's movement which were reminiscent of Garvey's earlier message calling for racial separatism. Their separatist agendas implied entertainers

Duke Ellington and Ella Fitzgerald shouldn't perform for white or mixed audiences. At bottom neither would approve of Teddy Wilson playing piano for Benny Goodman's band and singer Sammy Davis Jr. would be chastised for associating with white singers Dean Martin and Frank Sinatra. Then too, talented black students only option would be to attend black institutions of higher education despite the fact Michigan, Penn, Rutgers, and others were encouraging them to apply for admission. Also, not appealing to aspiring black ball players would be an obligation to forsake the recently integrated major leagues and play only in revived Negro Leagues.

Black spokespersons A. Philip Randolph and Bayard Rustin objected to the Nation of Islam's assertion all white people were the devil incarnate. As far as they were concerned any black withdrawal from the larger society meant abandoning valuable options including coalition building and political muscle flexing to achieve both short and long term objectives. The NAACP and Urban League also believed Randolph and Rustin's strategy of pressing on in the larger context, to end second class citizenship, was the correct course of action. Both organizations had long held the dissenting opinion of Supreme Court Justice Harlan, in *Plessy v. Ferguson*, would eventually facilitate black participation in the larger society on an equitable basis. They remembered Justice John Harlan's words the Constitution was "color blind."

In March of 1965, while Congress was deliberating the contents of a proposed voting rights bill, various civil rights organizations were formulating plans to stage a march of fifty-four miles from Selma to Montgomery, Alabama, the state capitol. These activists had formed a coalition which drew up a petition of redress to be presented to Alabama's governor. At its core was the charge against various counties where blacks were being denied the right to vote. For example, in Lowndes and Wilcox counties not a single black was registered to vote, though they constituted a larger percentage of the whole population of neighboring Dallas County. As a result of the Freedom Summer project the year before in neighboring Mississippi, Alabama, in comparison, now seemed more intransigent regarding African-American voter registration.

Representatives of diverse religious faiths came together to support the coalition's stated goals eloquently articulated by Dr. Martin Luther King, Jr., the recent recipient of the Nobel Peace Prize. The groundswell of support for the Selma to Montgomery march was comprised of various people.

They were the "people of good will," so frequently acknowledged by Dr. King. Among the fifty thousand people ready to march were Jewish rabbis, Catholic priests, Protestant ministers, and, predictably, a dozen or so Unitarian-Universalist ministers. Participating also were theology students of various religious denominations.

A few weeks prior to the March on Montgomery, intense local demonstrations had occurred in Selma. The sheriff, James G. Clark, Jr., dealt with the demonstrators in much the same way Bull Connor had done in Birmingham two years earlier. He arrested and detained 3,400 demonstrators in the course of two weeks. Clark received notorious national recognition when, on March 7, 1965, Black Sunday, he ordered his men and state police to attack some 600 marchers with billy clubs and tear gas as they attempted to cross the Edmund Pettus Bridge. The horror of this spectacle was viewed nationally on the evening news. As for its impact, one of Dr. King's lieutenants observed, "Bull Connor gave us the civil rights bill…and Jim Clark is going to give us the voting rights bill."

Because of the Edmund Pettus Bridge debacle, the nation's attention was focused on Selma. The coalition sponsoring the march to Montgomery was acutely aware of the national media's attention and wished to capitalize on it. Martin Luther King, Jr. and Ralph Bunche, both Nobel Prize winners, were in the front rank when the marchers moved out of Selma, on March 21, 1965. This time the participants of the march were protected by units of the Alabama National Guard, recently federalized for that purpose by President Lyndon Johnson.

By court order, the number of actual marchers had to be reduced to three hundred after the first seven miles. After four days, this contingent reached Montgomery where they joined with 25,000 demonstrators already assembled in the vicinity of the state capitol. A delegation, including Dr. King, attempted to present the coalition's petition of redress to Governor George C. Wallace. Rather than acknowledge the demonstration by receiving the petition, Governor Wallace had a subordinate announce that his office had closed for the day.

The content of the refused petition became, in part, the basis for Dr. King's stirring Montgomery Address. In this oration, he reminded his assembled black and white supporters of the purpose for their presence. "We must appeal to the seat of government with the only…non-violent resources at our command; our physical presence and the moral power of our souls," because "we are deliberately denied the right to vote...." That evening millions saw and heard his impassioned oratory on national network television. In some respects it was reminiscent of his Washington "I Have a Dream" speech made in August of 1963.

Not one to miss a special moment, President Lyndon Johnson shortly went on national television to comment on the Selma to Montgomery March. He praised the participants by saying they called upon America to make good the promise of America. They could depend on his support to fight for their cause "in the courts, in the Congress, and in the hearts of men." President Johnson dramatically acknowledged the dreams and hopes of those supporting the civil rights movement when he invoked the compelling title of the song which had become the anthem of the civil rights movement. In a forceful tone of voice, indicative of his commitment, he concluded his address by simply saying, "We shall overcome!" (This was a flash of genius on the part of Lyndon Johnson's speech writer.)

Acting with unusual haste, Congress took action on a Voting Rights bill within a week of the President's televised address. With President Johnson's signature on August 7th, it became the Voting Rights Act of 1965. Eighteen months earlier the poll tax had been prohibited when the 24th Amendment to the Constitution was ratified in January of 1964. So, two critical barriers to full citizenship rights had indeed been overcome during the presidency of Lyndon Baines Johnson.

The preceding events meant African-Americans could participate without hindrances in the election process long denied them since the end of the Reconstruction Era. Their experience had differed markedly from that of European immigrants during the four decades prior to World War I. European immigrants of that era didn't face the restrictions imposed on African-Americans. For example after a five year wait, as part of the citizenship naturalization process, my paternal grandfather was then eligible to vote in 1894. Though he hadn't mastered the English language, he didn't have to take a literacy exam or pay a poll tax to register to vote. He was never confronted with the same obstacles to voting his fellow Americans of African ancestry faced under the Jim Crow system in the South.

The Voting Rights Act of 1965 rendered literacy exams and other discriminatory subterfuges illegal. It permitted registrars, working under authority of the U.S. Attorney General's office, to supervise the registration of voters in areas where less than fifty percent of the otherwise eligible voters

had voted in the 1964 election. The Attorney General's office was also authorized to initiate investigations, when requested to do so by interested
parties, when it was believed the spirit of the law was being repressed by
delay tactics. African-American organizations kept a pressure on Attorney
General Nicholas Katzenbach's office - initially thought not moving quickly
enough to enforce the law.

Less than four months after passage of the 1965 Voting Rights Act,
Julian Bond was elected to the Georgia state legislature. However, as one
of the first African-American public figures to speak out in opposition to
Lyndon Johnson's Vietnam War policy, the Georgia state legislature refused
to swear him in and allow his participation as a recognized member of that
body. Thirty-two years later, in 1998, Julian Bond was elected national
Chairman of the NAACP and served in that capacity until 2010.

Before the 1960s decade ended, noticeable numbers of African-Americans had been elected to southern state legislatures, municipal offices, and
in a few counties even elected sheriff. Blacks in the South easily recognized
it was the doing of the Democratic Party which had paved the way for these
positive political results. No surprise, they had come to overwhelmingly
identify with that party. This was not lost on hundreds of thousands of
southern whites who now saw the Republican Party as most likely to express and attempt to uphold their values. Bayard Rustin's prediction about
political party realignment was underway.

Passage of the Voting Rights Act of 1965 was a giant step forward to be
sure, but the question of how to make use of its potential was the question
those engaged in politics knew was crucial. The African-American community would immediately have to learn what white ethnics had quickly
learned. Achieving desired results hinged upon not voting for what wasn't
in the best interest of the group – for example not voting for a racially big-
oted candidate.

Writing in 1968, regarding voting against one's best interest, C. Sumner Stone reported an episode in 1964 where Chicago African-American
voters did just that in the April Democratic primary of Illinois' Sixth Congressional District. In this race an elderly fourteen term white Congressman had been challenged by a black woman "who had been active in civic
and civil rights programs." She campaigned vigorously in the "dominantly
black district of Chicago's west side," where the incumbent, because of failing health, was barely active. The white incumbent died on the day of the

election, "but that did not matter to the black voters in his district. They went out ... and voted for a dead white man" in preference to a woman of their own race!

In relating the story of that Chicago primary election, I couldn't pass up the opportunity for a bit of sarcasm. I asked my class if they thought one of those black voters, who voted for the dead white man, "would be able to teach a worthwhile course in African-American history?" The class took the jab in stride, laughed because they understood my motive for the question, and resoundingly said, "No way!" Then a student said, "Hey, Professor Reiss, you like to put us on sometimes, don't you?" My response was, "Hasn't this course always been a two way street?" We had another good laugh.

Another significant point Stone made was in reference to the treatment the Mississippi Freedom Democratic Party's delegate received at the Democratic Party's convention in 1964 at Atlantic City. You'll recall the convention wasn't going to seat the black MFDP party delegates. That was disappointing, but of greater disappointment was learning the black delegates from other states wouldn't support them. (Many states from the far west, the Great Lakes region, and the northeast had black delegates.) Stone said the MFDP delegates were denied support from other African-Americans because "racial loyalties were overcome by political chains."

Stone offered conjecture if a similar scenario presented itself with respect to Jewish-American interests. Had certain Jewish delegates been barred for one political reason or another implying bigotry, he claimed all Jewish delegates would have quickly assembled to reach a consensus for taking responsive action. And, they wouldn't show concern that whatever action they took might be considered disruptive of the party's convention proceedings by the non Jewish delegates. Until African-Americans acted in similar fashion, facilitated by group cohesion, he said they lacked the political sophistication discernible in other voting blocs. Other interest groups all knew political cohesion was the prerequisite necessary to implement effective political tactics.

Black elected officials knew obtaining the right to vote was like winning the first battle of a protracted broader struggle. The struggle would see many obstacles designed to dishearten and hamper getting a large voter turnout. Among the obstacles were apathy and ignorance of the issues – both undermined the desired goal of sustaining political muscle.

The previously mentioned are serious considerations, but are particulars of the larger question: How long would it take for the African-American community to acquire the same level of political sophistication as other hyphenated Americans?

Beyond Lyndon Johnson's support for the Civil Rights Act (1964) and the Voting Rights Act (1965), he favorably impressed millions, black and white alike, by appointing African-Americans to positions previously held only by white Americans. Though Johnson gave more prestigious federal appointments to African-Americans than any of his predecessors, however, none were part of the inner circle where major policy decisions were made such as defining the scope of American military involvement in Vietnam. His savvy press secretary, Bill Moyers, ensured much publicity went to LBJ's black appointees. They were heralded because of their being "the first" to hold certain posts formerly held only by white persons.

Lyndon Johnson's appointment of Thurgood Marshall to the U.S. Supreme Court was his most important appointment in terms of long term consequential impact. He served on the Court for twenty-four years before retiring in 1991. Other African-Americans he appointed were: Robert C. Weaver as Secretary of Housing and Urban Development, Andrew F. Brimmer to the Federal Reserve Board, Patricia Harris, the first black woman to be named as an ambassador (to Luxembourg), and syndicated newspaper columnist Carl T. Rowan was appointed ambassador to Finland.

Regarding the circumstances of the preceding appointments and other less significant ones, the positions they held rarely allowed them to hire other African-Americans. Johnson's black appointees, except for Justice Marshall, would be revolving door positions. Richard Nixon, Johnson's successor, was under no legal obligation to reappoint them. Under President Johnson, Thurgood Marshall had gone from Solicitor General to Supreme Court Justice. But, Richard Nixon did not fill the Solicitor General position with another qualified African-American. Contrary to what some believed blacks didn't continue to gain positions in unprecedented numbers. During the Nixon administration (he was sworn in on January 20, 1969), there was no net gain for African-Americans in the executive branch of the government.

As for the eruptions of inner city violence during the mid 1960s, while Lyndon Johnson was president, I found the assessment offered by historian Eugene Genovese has merit. This scholar of the antebellum South said

the behavioral response of violence by certain African-Americans was un-
derstandably born of profound frustration and resentment. However, he
characterized the behavior as "essentially nihilistic thrashing about." He
noted most instances of violence were initiated by a few and generally ex-
acerbated, not ameliorated, the circumstances for most blacks within the
social context of the violence's location. Genovese pondered what was to
be gained when either antebellum slaves or ghetto residents resorted to
violence? He concluded, "...a few slaves might do enough damage to ruin
a planter," forcing him "to sell out and...break up slave families and friend-
ships." However, advocates of "'burn baby - burn,' whether on a Mississippi
plantation in the 1850s or in a northern ghetto in the 1960s" should realize
"that of necessity it is primarily the blacks who get burned."

One outcome of the various urban riots in the mid 1960s was the
creation of a National Advisory Commission on Civil Disorders. President
Johnson named Otto Kerner, then governor of Illinois, to be its chairperson. Regarding recent ghetto riots the *Kerner Commission*, as it came to be
known, reported they had "minimal support from Negroes themselves" Of
greater significance was the commission's conclusion - "White society is
deeply implicated in the ghetto. White institutions created it, white institutions maintain it, and white society condones it."

Less then a week before his death, Martin L. King Jr. issued a pre-
liminary assessment of the *Kerner Commission Report*. Most telling, he said,
"Not a single basic cause of the...riots has been corrected." President Johnson called it a "good report by men of good will." But then, he buried it.
His so doing some said was a factor in prompting New York Senator Robert Kennedy to announce his candidacy for the presidency. After Lyndon
Johnson announced he wouldn't seek reelection in March of 1968, African-
Americans realized the best place to turn was to Kennedy's candidacy. They
quickly became the core constituency for Robert Kennedy's 1968 bid for
the White House.

Chapter 15

fter passage of the Voting Rights Act of 1965, many activists of the civil rights movement changed their emphasis. The issue of poverty became of great concern. Attention to this issue came into focus in conjunction with President Johnson's War On Poverty - at the core of his Great Society agenda. Did white Americans living in suburban communities fully understand the pervasiveness of poverty among African-Americans or poor whites living in Appalachia? To this Jesse Jackson might respond, "If aware, did they care?" During the Nixon years, black students would respond to these questions with an emphatic "Hell No!"

Many years before Kennedy and Johnson acknowledged poverty as an issue African-American intellectual Bayard Rustin had addressed its impact on black America. Then John Kennedy saw poverty close up while campaigning for the presidency in West Virginia in 1960. Also, within Kennedy's intellectual circle were those familiar with Michael Harrington's recent book *The Other America* which exposed poverty. President Kennedy was on the verge of addressing the issue of poverty at the time of his death. So, his successor, Lyndon Johnson, moved the issue forward within the context of his Great Society agenda.

Upon President Johnson giving special attention to poverty more activists and intellectuals did likewise. Even corporate interests didn't immediately dismiss the issue of poverty. Thanks to Johnson's orientation poverty was briefly in political vogue. It was featured in various magazines and Sunday morning news programs and accorded a degree of objective analysis. (This wouldn't be possible by Fox News in the first decade of the 21st Century where blame the victim would be the topic's focal point.) Even the *Wall Street Journal* danced around the issue in a circumspect way – but less than five years later it would remind readers of no such thing as a free lunch. Looking back on the years 1965 – '66, the media gave more attention to poverty in those two years than the total coverage given to it during the Republican administrations of Ronald Reagan and George H.W. Bush – 1981 to 1993.

In the mid 1960s, many taking up the poverty issue began to echo Bayard Rustin's persistent concern, namely, who gets what and why? In the wake of the 1960s civil rights movement's success, Rustin added an insightful observation: "We must recognize that in desegregating public accommodations, we affected institutions that are relatively peripheral both to the American socio-economic order and to...fundamental conditions of life of...black people." Bayard Rustin's thoughts would certainly elicit negative responses from supporters of the economic status quo. And, predictably, he would be accused of being a Marxist ideologue. However, who gets what and why was recently at the core of the Occupy Wall Street Movement. Though not given attention by the corporate media the question was of great concern to Wall Street occupiers aware the top 1% of the public annually accrues a greater and greater percentage of the nation's wealth.

Various studies in the 1960s reported data indicating where African-Americans stood compared with others in the socio-economic scheme of things as predicated on salaries and wages. Economist Herman P. Miller of the Census Bureau learned black workers, in 1964, were paid only 55 percent of what white workers were paid. The study also indicated black workers were twice as likely to be unemployed. Additional information revealed a white worker, having just eight years of education, was going to earn more in a lifetime than a black college graduate will earn in his or her lifetime. Certainly the *Wall Street Journal* today wouldn't focus on such information for socio-economic analysis since now, more than ever before, it avoids addressing economic disparities endemic to the American version of capitalism.

Another theme in President Lyndon B. Johnson's Great Society was the idea of equal opportunity – especially for post secondary education.

Seemingly implicit was an understanding young people disadvantaged by
parents' economic circumstances would receive financial aid, grants not
loans, necessary to attend college. Time after time African-Americans heard
white society claim to endorse the principle of equality of opportunity.
However, as the emerging Black Caucus in the House of Representatives
soon realized, there would always be predictable equivocation when it came
to supporting the means (read funding) to achieve meaningful equality of
opportunity in higher education. To be opposed to institutional manifestations of racism on the surface of the social dynamic was one thing, but
to go below the surface and acknowledge monetary resources had to play
a part as a means, i.e., a social tool, to redress prior injustices was another
matter.

When assessing Johnson's War On Poverty programs it's abundantly
clear they hadn't facilitating droves of African-Americans moving to suburbia. This wasn't going to happen considering the national economy's
distribution of wealth. Bayard Rustin in the past and Cornel West of this
time have observed economics still play the paramount role in determining the nature of change for better or worse. At bottom regarding economic factors is that usually avoided question regarding the distribution
of wealth. This question was one Martin Luther King Jr.'s Poor People's
Campaign intended to address that summer of 1968. Most white folks
involved successfully in corporate America's business, back in the 1960s
and to this day, do their best to ignore that troublesome question: Who
gets what and why?

As for the various inner city riots in the mid 1960s, when President
Johnson was trying to implement his War On Poverty programs, most students in the 1990s were ignorant about them. They were surprised to learn
army jeeps with mounted machine guns patrolled the streets of inner cities such as Newark, Detroit, Rochester, and others. They had no idea the
1965 Watts riot in Los Angeles resulted in 35 deaths and over 100 injured,
some to have disabilities for the rest of their lives. During comments on
the riots a student, who I believed was a veteran, said, "A nervous national
guardsman, poorly trained, puts innocent people at risk." He immediately
agreed with my observation the behavior of arsonists probably puts even
more innocent people at great risk. Upon Dr. King's assassination, on April
4th, 1968 in Memphis, spontaneous rioting broke out in various American
cities from coast to coast.

Actually few white Americans ever contemplate what course of action would necessarily have to be taken if society really wanted to eradicate negative racial attitudes attributable to economic circumstances. One initiative not costly to implement and seen in a positive light by liberals was Affirmative Action. Overall it was a small step in the right direction intended to facilitate a degree of economic parity when it came to educational and employment opportunities. Unfortunately, it soon became a hot button topic and was frequently challenged on the grounds it sanctioned reverse discrimination by various conservative media pundits. Shortly after Nixon's first year in the presidency, Affirmative Action was coming increasingly under fire and he wasn't inclined to blunt criticism of it. It loomed as a significant reason, among others, which strained the long standing advantageous relationship between African and Jewish Americans. By the time Ronald Reagan was campaigning for the presidency in 1980, conservatives weren't holding back on their vehement opposition to Affirmative Action.

Much has been written about the politically tumultuous year 1968. In retrospect I'm compelled to see it as one of the most fascinating years in the 20th Century – certainly in my lifetime! This year saw a level of political activism not seen since the 1930s. But did these young activists quickly dubbed "radical" by the corporate media really deserve that description? Were they radical simply because they believed in the idealistic New Frontier rhetoric of John Kennedy and then in Lyndon Johnson's Great Society goals?

Students saw career type politicians benefit when Johnson, at their urging, began shifting resources away from his original commitment to a War on Poverty. More money began to flow toward the Pentagon which in turn sent it to certain congressional districts having businesses that received Pentagon contracts. This process didn't expand the food stamp program but secured dividend checks for those holding stock in the companies getting the Pentagon contracts. Money circulating that way, which it still does, benefits the rich and powerful in those districts, not constituents living there in poverty. The war in Vietnam accelerated this process which is at the heart of how the Military-Industrial Complex functions within the Corporatocracy.

The escalation of U.S. military activity in Vietnam was clearly seen by young college age activists as gross hypocrisy. They couldn't understand why most Americans didn't see the bait and switch policy of Lyndon Johnson. He had promised a Great Society and his campaign had convincingly

advanced the idea he was more committed to peace than his opponent
Goldwater in the election of 1964. But as 1968 began, his credibility was
at rock bottom (pundits referred to his "credibility gap") since he was failing at what he had earlier presented himself to stand for. With regard to
the lesser of two evils, pertaining to an inclination to go to war, black sati-
rist turned political activist Dick Gregory said, "You show people the wolf
[Goldwater] and they'll run to the fox [Johnson]." This implied Lyndon
Johnson had fooled the people or as Gregory might say the "sheeple."

Lyndon Johnson was extremely angered by Martin Luther King, Jr.'s
Riverside Church Address on April 4th, 1967 in which he questioned the
President's Vietnam policy. Head of the FBI, J. Edgar Hoover lost no time
informing the President of the content of King's address. For over a decade
Hoover had King under surveillance believing him to be a communist sympathizer. After King's death it became better known Hoover had authorized
bugging King's motel rooms and had intended to expose his alleged extra-
marital sexual activities to discredit him. In a message to Dr. King, Hoover
even went so far as to suggest Dr. King take his own life as an appropriate
response to the accusations he wanted to make against him.

Generally, the corporate sponsored media responded negatively to Dr.
King's Riverside Church Address. However, of interest, most negative pieces
on King did avoid blatant racist references as had been used in some quarters two decades earlier toward Paul Robeson for his statements on what
he saw as misguided Cold War foreign policy. King said his motivation for
offering criticism of policy was because of his concern for his country. He
explained concern is primarily expressed because something or someone is
loved and revered. To King's way of thinking concern and love for country
went hand in hand. Down through the years I was always pleased students
understood Dr. King's explanation - basically if you don't love something
then you have no concern for it.

After Dr. King's Riverside Church Address many conservative pundits
were sly with their insinuations he was unpatriotic or, worse, held views too
similar to those expressed by communists. At this time a few African-Americans were gaining footholds in the corporate sponsored power structure,
like those appointed to positions by President Johnson. Some felt obligated
to condemn Dr. King's anti Vietnam war statements. African-American
Carl Rowan, a prominent syndicated media journalist, blasted Dr. King's
Riverside Church Address. (Presently the *New York Times* has Charles Blow

offering thoughts that reveal an intellectual capacity superior to that evidenced back in the day by Carl Rowan.)

When he spoke out against the Vietnam War, Dr. King rightly understood the economic implications of spending for the war and the consequential loss of funding for improving quality of life circumstances on the home front. He knew of the exploitative nature the war held for black communities. It was doubly burdensome. First, there would be neglect of community improvement projects and, secondly, black families lost loved ones as casualties in greater proportional numbers than did families in white communities. Also, Vietnam veteran acquaintances have told me of their observations indicating African-American troops seemed over represented in combat units and under represented in rear echelon support units out of range of enemy fire.

Hundreds of thousands of middle class young white men would simply evade the military draft by attending college and getting the 2-S student deferment. Within this category, immediately coming to mind, are two former presidents: William Jefferson Clinton and George W. Bush. Most young black men at this time were unable to afford college, thus were likely to be drafted because they lacked the 2-S deferment. So, they were drafted to serve involuntarily in the white man's war against a non white population which their government had denied the opportunity to have an election in 1956.

From 1967 to 1972, I gave male students the option to do extra credit to secure a grade useful for keeping their 2-S student draft deferments, thus possibly enabling them to avoid having to go to Vietnam. Some colleagues, aware of my policy, disapproved. Twenty-five years later, in the 1990s, they were telling classes they actively protested the Vietnam War during its time.

As I see it, based on his Riverside Church Address, Dr. Martin Luther King Jr. would probably agree with a particular, but not well publicized, Mark Twain observation. Twain said at play in American politics were three political parties - not two! There were Democrats and Republicans, but also the under reported insidious "war party." Twain, and we can surmise Dr. King as well, would view the latter as always ultimately influencing national agenda priorities. All one has to do today, to verify Twain's observation, is look at the national budget. Presently the United States spends more for defense (read war) ahead of the total allocations for military purposes of the next twelve economically developed countries of the world combined.

Dr. King saw governmental policy calling for half of the Congressional budget spending proposals inspired by the influence of the Military Industrial Complex. Congress had become predictably responsive to its needs based on the Pentagon's self serving projections that war was unavoidably looming at all times somewhere in the world with American national interests (read Wall Street corporate interests) eminently threatened.

As the Nobel Peace Prize winner (Dec. 10, 1964), Dr. King most certainly approved of President Dwight Eisenhower's last official message to Congress and the people. The President warned of the growing influence of the Military Industrial Complex. To an appreciable extent Dr. King's Riverside Church Address reiterates Eisenhower's warning. Eisenhower said something is amiss when we spend more for the military than for food and shelter for the nation's needy. Dr. King said, "A nation that continues to spend more money on military defense than on programs of social uplift is approaching spiritual death."

Many opposed to the Vietnam War, such as myself, took heart when the winner of the Nobel Peace Prize made public his opposition to it, thus indicating he was deserving of the Peace Prize. Basically Dr. King said the U.S. had drifted away from following policies inspired by acknowledging the wisdom of the Golden Rule. He begged the question had America lost its moral compass? This question causes me to pose another question: will his non violence and anti-war statements be taught in our schools and be recalled during future January ceremonies celebrating his birth?

Dr. Martin Luther King, Jr. held fast to his belief "people of good will" would ultimately prevail in bringing the rest of America to see the humanity common to all people. This, he knew, would not happen spontaneously. It would require a commitment to action based on non violent means to achieve the desired end of social justice. One obstacle he was aware of was the difficulty for some to comprehend participation in an activity where violence was eschewed required as much bravery as those taking a path featuring violence in the name of patriotism. He urged people to get beyond mundane justifications for violence and to then comprehend the often illusive but compelling righteous moral message of non violence.

Americans were asked by Dr. King to oppose injustice on the home front and oppose it within the context of American foreign policy as well. For him the notion of bombing a Vietnamese village to "save it" was a moral obscenity! The media doesn't emphasize the mayhem resulting from bombing villages. I've often wondered how much thought John McCain, navy pilot and Republican presidential candidate in 2008, has given to the consequences of missions he flew over Vietnam? If he's had regrets I'm un-aware. They haven't prompted him to join Veterans For Peace.

Early in any United States military action, the media quickly con-structs a theme U.S. aggression is justifiable and our troops the good guys. So, those pictures of American soldiers giving kids candy are predictable. A child may have a candy bar but later no house to sleep in. Dr. King knew very well how American culture emphasized the glory and self proclaimed righteousness of wars engaged in by the United States. He also knew early educational experiences of American youths placed a special emphasis on heroes engaging in violent activity of some sort, but slighted non violent social reformers like Sojourner Truth, Gloria Steinem, Caesar Chavez, or black feminist Florynce Kennedy, associated with Steinem in the early days of the National Organization of Women (NOW).

At the beginning of the 1960s, the media covered sit-ins, pray-ins, swim-ins, and peaceful assemblies with a somewhat balanced view. These events were newsworthy, but not as sensational as events occurring later in the decade with the rise of the Black Power movement. After passage of the Voting Rights Act (1965), those earlier events seemed part of a hazy dimly remembered past. They were ho hum when compared to more recent news of certain inner cities going up in flames and alarming stories about Black Panthers openly carrying firearms in public. I think we can assume stories about Black Panthers were expected to sell more newspapers.

As the summer of 1967 approached the media began reporting more sensational news pertaining to certain black activists, hence to be desig-nated as militants and deemed unreasonable extremists. The media seemed eager to establish a new orientation for news coverage. A lead in for some-thing new was the following question: Has the philosophy of Martin Lu-ther King, Jr. become passe in various quarters of black activism? The media now chose to focus on those who rebuked his philosophy of non-violence. Black Power militancy gave the media more exciting copy.

The black militants understanding of history was, essentially, that blacks had historically gained nothing by turning the other cheek. The media, in turn, frequently overlooked the responses Dr. King made in reply to charges laid at his feet by black radicals such as H. Rap Brown and Stokely Carmichael. However, regarding the media's new emphasis on

Black Power militants, African-American psychologist Kenneth B. Clark
faulted it for focusing "with disproportionate time and attention" on the
demands by these militants "viewed as extremists by the general public,"
and of whom the Kerner Commission reported had "minimal support from
Negroes themselves."

Various recently emerged Black Power advocates seemed willing to
go beyond the bounds of non-violence which, as a tactic, they considered
demeaning and restrictive. Black Panther Eldridge Cleaver said whites
wouldn't hesitate to use violence, because they were "on top in America"
and they wanted "to stay up there." Their use of violence wasn't a recent
thing he asserted. Whites had been utilizing violence on blacks all along
to prevent "the erosion of their privileged position." Stokely Carmichael,
said to have coined the term Black Power, called for white violence to be
met head on. He claimed the white power structure had long depended
on violence and had either rationalized or concealed its use. (Recently, I
imagine many Occupy Wall Street Movement folks might share some of
Carmichael's views regarding the power structure's use of violence.)

Also, black nationalists were cynical toward those favoring social and
political equality facilitated through racial integration. Dr. King of the
SCLC and Roy Wilkins of the NAACP saw the desirability of participating
within the framework of the given political system. For them progress was
achievable within the system. They would condemn the current injustices
without falling into the trap of condemning the entire system without having something better to offer – the trap black nationalists put themselves
in. King and Wilkins understood the old maxim about not throwing the
baby out with the bath water. Black Power militants, however, constantly
laced their rhetoric with condemnations of the system without offering
something better in its place. Most African-Americans had difficulty believing black separatism would somehow promote economic advances to
facilitate things improving overall. Generally, Black Power advocates and
especially Black Panthers, because of negative treatment they received
from the media, were an embarrassment to those groups believing progress
would come through more acceptable political activities.

In the last few years of the 1960s, Black Power militancy had become
the media's special news emphasis. However, not much in depth analysis
was given to what spokespersons, such as Stokely Carmichael or Eldridge
Cleaver, tried to bring to the public's attention. Carmichael was embraced

by the media as the symbolic figure epitomizing Black Power extremism. He, like Malcolm X, was often quoted out of context. Many white folks I knew at the time tended to be alarmed by statements both were reputed to have made. I guess I'm atypical. I never felt threatened or took offense, except when the term "blue eyed devil" was invoked, by the statements reportedly made by them. As I saw it Malcolm's speech titled "The ballot or the bullet" was simply a truth to power statement. Years ago, persons such as myself who saw African-Americans burdened by gross injustice and were sympathetic would frequently be dismissed as "N" lovers by white racists.

Issues raised by Black Panthers were usually obscured by their being depicted, by alarming photos, as gun toting loonies. Recently Tea Party types have engaged in carrying guns openly to public hearings held by elected officials. Oh, but that's O K. That's about white folks and the term radical militants wasn't used to describe them as it was when black folks with grievances showed up at such meetings. But racist thinking lingers because the public would judge black folks with side arms to be more dangerous.

Black Panthers saw the use of violence falling into two basic categories. It had potential as a means to repress and subjugate or be used as a means to challenge repression and subjugation. They pointed to the fact they had never repressed or subjugated others and noted they were victims, with most other black Americans, of the larger society's subjugation by economic, political, and social means. As for subjugation beyond the ghetto, the Panthers didn't overlook the police cracking heads of white anti-war protestors with the same zeal used on black protestors.

Ultimately the Panthers' perspective went beyond race issues per se. By mid 1969 they had taken a closer look at the American economic system. They now reasoned economic factors were of utmost significance in the totality of phenomena generating racism. The original gulf between their views and that of the deceased Martin Luther King Jr. seemed to be narrowing on economic issues as they too now addressed the question - who gets what and why? That question, as Occupy Wall Street folks would also learn, creates a great uneasiness in the corporate capitalist power structure which John Perkins referred to as the Corporatocracy.

On the significance of an emerging coalition between Panthers and certain white activists, Eldridge Cleaver wrote: "This prospect of an alliance between the Negro revolution, the new left, and the peace movement, fills the power structure with apprehension...." (Cleaver saw his book, *Soul On Ice,* slip onto the best seller list.) This statement and others similar in nature made by Black Panthers were anathema to the racist J. Edgar Hoover, Director of the Federal Bureau of Investigation. Cleaver and others had come to see racism in a broader context. This context revealed itself by way of their coming to understand how political power functions to maintain the economic and racial status quo, since the two were so intrinsically linked.

Police harassment of Black Panthers went on and on. Bobby Seale said 300 arrests were made from July to December of 1969, Nixon's first year in office. Approximately fifty key leadership figures were special police targets for constant surveillance and frequent arrests. Though ninety-nine percent of the charges on those arrested were dropped, the criminal justice system was a burden on the Panthers even as it seemed to be working for them. Arranging for bails siphoned off energy and funds they would have liked to use for social uplift needs in black communities. Seale said the bails the courts set were "exorbitant ransoms ... used to deplete our funds."

One aspect of Black Power was the associated "black is beautiful" theme. This idea first broadly elaborated upon by Marcus Garvey forty years earlier was resuscitated in the mid 1960s. Suppose you were of lighter complexion and proud of your African ancestry, but sensed you might be judged negatively because of not looking as black as a stereotype depiction. What then? Apparently the darker one's skin color the likelihood of fitting in with the black is beautiful crowd seemed more certain. From observations by myself and others, as well as lively classroom discussions, I think some African-Americans of lighter complexions had to cope with identity insecurities in some circumstances at this time. Thus, some then went the compensatory route which could mean wearing an elaborate Afro hairdo, a dashiki, or something understood to be authentically African in origin, plus using politically correct jargon as well.

Projecting a black is beautiful image, a correct image for acceptance, went a long way toward removing doubts others might have that one wasn't proud to be black because of a lighter skin color. The blacker one's skin the better became a prevalent attitude in many black militant nationalists' quarters. But, then too, one having very dark features wouldn't want to be called an Oreo. Sort of humorous to me was the fact in one class in the 1990s, no one knew the significance of Oreo except Lenny Blake, my World War II friend. He told the class it applied to those who looked black on the outside, but on the inside thought like a white person – someone who ruled out black values in favor of white values and then thought of themselves superior to other black folks. There it is, like an Oreo cookie, black on the outside but white on the inside. However, what is really meant and commonly understood by notions of black values or white values? This question always resulted in a lively discussion and agreement acknowledging ultimate understanding was predictably illusive.

As for black is beautiful fashion statements in clothing, World War II veteran Lenny said, "You go for a job interview in that Afro outfit, they're not going to hire you. You self handicap when you think you're laying your cool on the man. It will only put you one down not one up in his game." Another of his observations was "being cool with jive nonsense doesn't pay the rent or get you a quarterly dividend check." One thing cool to me was having this older black gentleman in my class. He helped keep things interesting. Also, I was pleased the class always respected him. He was certainly deserving of that.

Regarding the term "the Man," used to identify authority or a specific authority figure, well, it was unknown to me until I enlisted in the Air Force in 1955. I first heard it used by fellow black enlisted men making reference to our squadron's commanding officer. Overall anyone with authority, like a boss, a bank loan officer, a judge, a college administrator, or a Veterans' Administration official can in specific circumstances be "the Man." I gleaned more of what seemed black idioms while serving in the Air Force. My first week stationed at Goose Air Base in Labrador (1957), I became acquainted with Al Fleming from Elizabeth, New Jersey. He, as did other black airmen, used the term "the hawk is talking." (Classes had no clue what this meant.) At that time in Labrador and Thule Greenland it meant a vicious wind creating a dangerous wind chill condition capable of quickly resulting in frostbite to the unthinking.

Legend has it Fats Waller's next to last statement was a reference to "the Hawk" made to his traveling companion just before he fell asleep in their first class compartment aboard the Santa Fe Chief struggling to keep moving East, on tracks quickly becoming covered with snow, through a raging Kansas blizzard. On the morning of December 15, 1943, his traveling companion discovered Fats had died in his sleep from bronchial pneumonia according to a Kansas City coroner's report. Because the train was snowed in at Kansas City's Union Station for two days, there was the unfortunate delay in getting a train bearing his body back to New York City which wasn't reached until the night of December 19th.

Adam Clayton Powell, Jr. spoke last at Fats Waller's memorial service. Waller's son Maurice recalled Rev. Powell saying the following of the man he knew since childhood: "Fats Waller always played to a packed house. We are gathered here this morning to mourn the passing of a simple soul, a soul touched with the genius of music which brought relief from our cares and woes." Yes, I'm a big fan of Fats Waller's piano playing and singing. Beyond doubt, he was always having great fun while performing. What's not to like about this musical genius and his spontaneous rollicking style? He was a master of droll comedic musical put on.

Yes, I digressed from the initiated topic of Black Power. Getting back to that, let's now consider the 1967 essay "Postscript on Black Power," by black intellectual Harold Cruse. He viewed black skin chauvinism as pure folly. It would prove politically divisive, consequently detrimental to promoting a maximization of numbers for political strategies implementation. Placing a priority on degrees of blackness, he observed, unwittingly extended an invitation to the power structure itself to divide and conquer based on skin color differences. His point is well taken when one remembers how South Africa's apartheid system worked.

Harold Cruse noted the American experience for people having African ancestry was often multifaceted. In his time of the black is beautiful era, he knew many believed their ancestry was solely African, yet others, acknowledging their physical appearance, knew better. Recent DNA evidence indicates the American experience has generated an expanded diversified genetic spectrum for more Americans than was ever previously socially acknowledged. Case in point, my brother has a granddaughter and grandson whose genetic inheritance is one quarter African, one quarter Korean, and half European. Upon showing their pictures to classes, because of appearances their white ancestry, their father's, was never acknowledged.

Compared with twenty years ago, more people today are aware of the varying degrees of both African and European ancestry that's possible as part of a genetic inheritance. At present the postulation made by Cruse, almost five decades ago, has been validated by research with DNA testing. Prominent in advancing the knowledge revealed by such testing is African-American scholar Henry Louis Gates Jr. of Harvard University. Because of his understanding of DNA evidence, Gates knows his own ancestry is not exclusively African.

Because of miscegenation, intentionally occurring more noticeably after the 1960s, or as a consequence of untold numbers of white on black rape over the course of three prior centuries, there's only slight justification for a sole supposed authentic African appearance for African-Americans to identify with. Taking the black is beautiful idea to the extreme was for Cruse both unrealistic and not politically useful either. For Cruse coalition politics was something minorities had to master, if their voices were to be heard within the framework of a national discourse on a given topic. Two decades later, in the 1980s, Jesse Jackson's Rainbow Coalition was in many respects compatible with the thinking of Harold Cruse.

Spin-offs from black is beautiful had little significant impact for determining which way things would go for individual African-Americans. Having an Afro hair style was no substitute qualification for admission to law school. As for artistic manifestations of black is beautiful, Cruse questioned their practical impact. Were they of significant consequence for the hard pressed majority of blacks not getting proper health care, necessary nourishment, quality education, and decent housing?

Sporadically, after the early 1970s, mainstream corporate media publicized some black artistic achievements by such persons as playwright August Wilson, opera star Leontyne Price, and ballet dance master Alvin Ailey. Also, the long term trend of a plethora of televised sporting events with impressive numbers of black athletes served to make African-Americans less invisible. But, taken overall, did public presentations of such fortunate persons change popular thinking mindsets about the circumstances of the overwhelming numbers of other African-Americans? When white police officers see a black male driving an expensive Lexus, what's the first thing that comes to their minds? Is the driver thought to be a car thief, a drug dealer, an NBA player, or a successful businessman? Entrance into the middle class by the small numbers of fortunate black folks hasn't changed stereotype perceptions of blacks by most blue collar whites.

Also, I don't believe socio-economic circumstances, like educational or employment opportunities, for the vast majority of African-Americans has kept pace with gains others have made in the last forty years. Of course worthy achievements by some are well publicized to lend credence to the notion there is equal opportunity. Governmental agencies compiling statistical information indicate equal opportunity in this early 21st Century is a chimera which most politicians don't want to acknowledge.

In late June of 1967, the *New York Times* reported the Black Power Conference taking place in Newark, New Jersey. Many attending called for black separatism. The *Times* then solicited NAACP head Roy Wilkins for his response. He regarded black separatism as the antithesis of what his organization had strove to achieve for almost sixty years – namely meaningful integration. Conference militants remembered what Wilkins said at the NAACP national convention the previous year. "No matter how endlessly they try to explain it, the term 'black power' means anti-white power. We of the NAACP will have none of this. It is the ranging of race against race on the irrelevant basis of skin color." Delegates at the Newark Conference regarded Wilkins words as those of an Uncle Tom.

As for the integration Wilkins favored, black power separatists claimed it would merely result in tokenism. They acknowledged the white power structure would pragmatically accept a few extraordinarily talented blacks. The following appointments, a few years later, would probably serve as examples to illustrate their point about window dressing tokenism. Andrew Young was selected by Jimmy Carter to be Ambassador to the U.N., General Colin Powell was promoted to Chairman of the Joint Chiefs of Staff by George H.W. Bush, and Ron Brown chosen by Bill Clinton as a special adviser. However, Young and Brown were on the periphery of the power structure.

An early example of window dressing had to do with Paul Robeson. (In the 1980s and 1990s barely two or three students in all my classes per year had ever heard of him.) Fresh out of Columbia Law School in 1923, it didn't take long for Robeson to realize the law partners hired him only to talk about college football to prospective clients, since he had earned All American honors playing at Rutgers University. He wasn't given cases to take on and practice law. So, he quit the law firm.

Paul Robeson then pursued an acting and singing career and received much acclaim. Acknowledged Broadway critics essentially said Robeson was superb in capturing the spiritual essence of the song "Ol' Man River." in the hit musical *Showboat* back on Broadway for a second time May 20, 1932. According to biographer, Martin B. Duberman, Edna Ferber, author of the book upon which the show was based, said of Robeson's performance "the ovation given Robeson on opening night exceeded any," she had ever heard "accorded to a 'figure of the stage, the concert hall, or the opera.'"

Popular culture would have you believe white comedian Bob Hope was the first American entertainer to do an overseas show for Americans engaged in war. Not true! As Duberman revealed, Paul Robeson went to Spain during their Civil War to sing for Americans in the Lincoln Brigade fighting against the forces of, soon to be dictator, Francisco Franco. The Lincoln Brigade was comprised of black and white Americans fighting side by side against fascism.

Most of the Black Power delegates at the Newark Conference believed bringing some talented persons into the corporate and governmental power structure conveniently served to deflect charges of widespread racial discrimination. Various delegates said the white power structure was being realistic by favoring token integration. And, most students understood the corporate world saw policies emanating from black separatism as fraught with instability, thus jeopardizing the profitable status quo. For corporate America the idea of selective integration, determined by powerful whites, was less threatening, more acceptable, than separatism defined by militant blacks.

Hiring a calculated number of African-American employees was a way for corporations to avoid being part of the solution when it came to the problems associated with inner cities. Resolving persistent problems associated with urban decay might entail taking money, in the form of taxes, away from a given corporation's bottom line of profit. Instead of paying slightly higher taxes to promote social uplift, corporations preferred to make political campaign contributions to conservative politicians who rejected proposals to fund programs to benefit ghetto dwellers. So, on the surface, for public relations purposes, corporations might look liberal for hiring a few black employees. However, in terms of bigger social problems and a commitment to solving them, corporations just aren't part of the solution. Most often they are a big part of the problem.

Have major corporations ever given big campaign contributions to progressive candidates favoring raising the minimum wage or extending the length of time and increasing the amount to be paid in unemployment benefits? When have they supported candidates favoring larger food stamp allocations or called for raising the amount for Aid For Dependent Children living in single parent households?

Journalist Robert S. Browne said corporate America's plan was to get talented African-Americans to identify less with the ghetto, its 'hood values. Of course corporate employers wouldn't want people to think their employees "sold out," but rather as having "bought in" to the American dream. For upwardly mobile blacks corporate America's implied message for advancement was: Do for yourself and let others do for themselves. If you succeed and others don't, that's not your problem. Why should failures of others diminish your success? Don't let dubious ghetto values hold you back. Overall the black power delegates at the 1967 Newark Conference were suspicious of those who made it out of the ghetto.

Those exiting the 'hood knew in some circles they would be seen as acting white. Students told me accusations of acting white were evident as early as junior high school. Students who didn't do homework assignments often accused those who did with "acting white." It's a shame when those so accused stop being responsible to gain on the street peer approval - talk about self handicapping!

As for some of the supposedly seminal ideas offered by those attending the Black Power Newark Conference, Harold Cruse heard nothing new. In their theoretical expository, he concluded they had not advanced "one whit in their thinking beyond the 1919 writers of A. Philip Randolph's *Messenger* magazine." His criticism verged on ridicule. Their way of thinking, he observed, had actually retrogressed. As for the 1960s Black Power publications (there weren't many), Cruse dismissed them by saying none compared with the intellectual substance found in articles featured by editors W.E.B. DuBois and A. Philip Randolph in their earlier publications. According to Cruse those writers more realistically acknowledged economic and political factors as determinants affecting the experiences of African-Americans.

Going beyond the acting white insult, from the 1950s into the 1970s, a most egregious insult an African-American male could make was to call another man an Uncle Tom. By the late 1990s, it had become a vague reference which few seemed completely familiar with. Singing the lyrics of the power structure's song, for an anticipated reward, is a dimension of the Uncle Tom syndrome. In other contexts, where race doesn't enter the equation, the term suck-up or yes man is used to describe obsequious behavior which often includes calculated flattery toward "the Man."

The role of shill is a nuanced dimension to the yes man or Uncle Tom syndrome. In politics the shill is usually a person having public credibility useful to the power structure when it seeks public approval to initiate a dubious undertaking. The prestige of the shill is calculated to sway acceptance of a goal the powers that be desire. Political shills know their complicit behavior is a quid pro quo bargain with the politically powerful. The shill receives a hidden reward for doing the establishment's bidding and understands silence is expected about how favorable public opinion was hustled for the political establishment's purpose. When this happens the media rarely examines the shill's behavior in the light a quid pro quo bargain has occurred.

There's many opinions associated with the question did General Colin Powell play the shill role so President Bush gained a semblance of credibility, thanks to Powell's then credibility, to attack Iraq? As for me, I know I don't have the blood of hundreds of thousands of innocent Iraqis on my hands. Pertinent here is Howard Zinn's observation, "There's no flag large enough to cover the shame of killing innocent people."

As for a definitive Tom in this era, one has to look no further than Supreme Court Justice Clarence Thomas. He was appointed by Republican President George H. W. Bush to fill the vacancy created when liberal Justice Thurgood Marshall retired in July of 1991. His selling out almost makes Booker T. Washington's behavior seem innocuous in comparison. Justice Thomas is one with four other conservative justices who are super shills for corporate interests. Consider this Justice Thomas: Slavery was the legal fiction a person was property, corporate personhood is the legal fiction property is a person. Maybe someday you'll understand how wrong your decision in the *Citizens United* case was Justice Thomas. You and your four conservative colleagues have bowed down at the altar of mammon.

Regarding the pejorative term Uncle Tom, its origin is rooted in the behavior of Harriet Beecher Stowe's fictional slave character of the same name used in her book's title. His behavior became synonymous with obsequiousness intended to constantly please "the Man." White folks don't have a race related term for the behavior in question, so, substitute flunky, suck-up, or toady. Many English believe their former Prime Minister Tony Blair was President Bush's toady, his lapdog, on the issue of war against Iraq.

Actually, we all know there's a universality to the behavior. It's not exhibited solely by one race or another. Focusing specifically on the behavior per se, there's been hundreds of thousands of white Uncle Toms down through the centuries. In present day corporate culture there's always someone who purposely loses a round of golf or a tennis match to their boss. That's sucking up! As for the terms, Uncle Tom, etc., describing the behavior, I'm reminded of the saying "a rose is a rose by any other name is still a rose."

When considering the Uncle Tom syndrome the name Muhammad Ali would never come to mind. His announcement of his refusal to be drafted and go to Vietnam came a few weeks after Dr. King's Riverside Church Address of April 4, 1967. Uncle Toms are anti-heroes, Ali became a hero to many young white anti-Vietnam War activists. Ali had publicly stated, "No Vietnamese ever called me nigger," adding he had "no quarrel with them" either. The anti-war chant, "Hell no, we won't go," had become synonymous with his belief.

I recall older white males coming to the realization Ali, who had rejected his birth name of Cassius Clay, wasn't going to seek their approval with behavior reminiscent of Joe Louis. Louis was quiet, humble, and had served in the military. Louis never spoke about issues of his day – not so Ali! If asked for his opinion he would give it, without concern it might rankle some. Compared with Louis, Ali was seen by many, many, whites (I was acquainted with some) as a boastful loudmouth. They wanted to see him defeated. Prior to his fights, and just after a victory, Ali's proclamation "I am the greatest" was regarded as obnoxiously arrogant by his detractors. Ali just rubbed many whites still having Uncle Tom expectations the wrong way.

I'd say it's doubtful persons now under forty can sufficiently comprehend what Ali represented, in terms of boxing's popularity, when he was fighting. He was his own man – following the beat of a different drummer! Refusing to be drafted resulted in his title being taken away. During the five years he wasn't allowed in the ring, the popularity of boxing took a nose dive. Minus Muhammad Ali the sport didn't seem the same. What other pugilist would come up with responses to sportswriters' inquiries with comments like, "I'll float like a butterfly, but sting like a bee" or, regarding an opponent, "he can run, but he can't hide." Was that obnoxious arrogance or supreme confidence? Whatever, his fans loved it!

In a February 12, 1997, issue of *USA Today*, Ali's daughter, Khaliah, said this about her father's change of heart regarding former beliefs based on the teachings of the Nation of Islam. "Whatever my father's views on race relations in 1974, his vision for the approaching millennium…is one of tolerance, racial healing, and the universal brotherhood of people of all colors, consistent with his conversion to mainstream Islam." She looked back to some of his statements in the early 1970s, when he subscribed to black separatism, as "a period of confusion." She requested her father "be spared any misguided attempt to use his pervasive influence to promote… racism in America and the world." Her statement came approximately sixteen months after the Nation of Islam sponsored the Million Man March in Washington on October 16, 1995.

Early in 1968, Dr. King and his close associate the Reverend Ralph Abernathy were planning for a massive summer rally in Washington to be known as the Poor People's Campaign. After Dr. King's death on April 4th, the Southern Christian Leadership Conference made the Poor People's Campaign its 1968 agenda priority. Measures for this prodigious undertaking included lobbying members of Congress and holding a massive rally and encampment in Washington in early August. Unfortunately Reverend Abernathy's undertaking would require a greater sustained effort than was seemingly possible without the inspirational leadership of Martin Luther King, Jr. Overall there seemed a void at the heart of the Poor People's Campaign.

Meetings with certain members of Congress didn't result in gaining renewed commitments regarding remedies to challenge poverty. In view of the eminent national elections the Congressmen were cautious, likely wanting to discern the mood of the country after the pending election results. Then too, the media didn't give as much attention to the Poor People's Campaign as was expected. It seemed minimal to Rev. Abernathy and was a source of great frustration. However, news coverage focused abundantly on the upcoming Democratic convention in Chicago, which promised to be a knock down drag out affair. Hence, the Poor People's Campaign seemed inconsequential in comparison. Even before the Poor People's Campaign tried to put things in motion, I sensed interest in the issue of poverty had noticeably slumped in the Spring shortly after Lyndon Johnson announced he wouldn't seek another term as president. So, given the inconsequential impact of the Poor People's Campaign, one could make a case that by August (1968) it appeared poverty, as a major national issue, had had its day.

As stated earlier, in the lifetime of a person such as myself, the year 1968 is not one easily forgotten. Overshadowing the failure of the Poor People's Campaign, and lingering as a bigger disappointment was the April 4th assassination of Martin Luther King, Jr. in Memphis, Tennessee. Dr.

King was there to support the city's sanitation workers striking for a live-able wage and recognition of their union. Before a large gathering the night before his murder, he seemed clairvoyant when he said, "Like anybody, I would like to live a long life.... But I'm not concerned about that now. And I've seen the promised land. I may not get there with you. But I want you to know tonight, that we as a people will get to the Promised Land." Down through the years most of the students I taught, black and white alike, were unaware of this last public statement he made and of its seeming prophetic content.

In the immediate wake of Dr. King's assassination spontaneous rioting occurred in the ghettos of nearly two dozen cities. A Chicago social worker reported, "furious burning and pillaging that devastated a four mike stretch of West Madison Street...." President Johnson ordered all flags at federal buildings be displayed at half mast on April 7th as tribute to Dr. King. That measure didn't spare Washington D. C. from violence. Also, reported by William L. O'Neill, in *Coming Apart* (1971), arrangements for Dr. King's funeral proceeded "while the cities burned." However, for most African-Americans the overriding emotion wasn't one prompting destructive retaliation. Shock and then dismay gave way to various widespread expressions of grief.

African-American scholar Manning Marable recalled his 1968 trip to Atlanta to attend the funeral of Dr. King in his book *The Great Wells of Democracy* (2002). He was seventeen when he left his home in Dayton, Ohio to arrive at Ebenezer Church in Atlanta. Standing in the crowd waiting to enter the church, he recalled hearing people objecting to the presence of Republican Richard Nixon, at the time seeking his party's endorsement for the presidency. Manning observed Nixon, "trying his best to push through the crowd." Obviously Nixon wanted equal recognition with the Democratic presidential hopeful Hubert Humphrey, who was also present. The young Marable also observed black celebrities Harry Belafonte, Lena Horne, Mahalia Jackson, and comedian turned activist Dick Gregory in attendance.

Barely ten weeks after Dr. King's murder came the assassination of New York Senator Bobby Kennedy in June. Press coverage was equal to that given to Dr. King's death but in two weeks time media attention slid back to greater coverage of the war in Vietnam and the upcoming presidential nominating conventions to be held later in the summer at Chicago. The widely reported tumultuous Democratic convention nominated Hubert Humphrey, but the Republican candidate, Richard Nixon, defeated him that November in the second closest race of the 20th Century. Once the media acknowledged the election of Nixon, it again focused on the activities of the Black Panther Party.

The media chose to keep things simple for the public by reporting seemingly outrageous statements made by the Panthers and other Black Power militants. Minimal attention was given to the Panthers' recent assessments of how corporate capitalism thrived in part because issues of race and social class were essentially prohibited from being evaluated in the broadest possible public context. Biased media reporting presented alarming conjectures regarding the Panther's activities and intentions. Overall, it came down to allowing the public the excuse to permit law enforcement agencies to act as though it were open season on the Black Panthers.

Media exaggerations of what Black Panthers represented made it easier for many officials of the law to act unlawfully. Illegal measures initiated by various FBI regional authorities resulted in two Black Panthers being killed in their beds during early morning raids. Many other raids were undertaken across the country without court authorizations for search and seizure purposes. Unpredictable break-ins on Panther gatherings across the country served the purpose of intimidating members and others considering joining their ranks. By the time Nixon ran for a second term in 1972, the Panthers had essentially been purged from a public presence as similarly experienced by the International Workers of the World two generations earlier. The Panthers and the IWW had been slandered by the corporate sponsored media for daring to expose capitalism's exploitative nature.

There was little public outcry, hardly a peep, regarding implementation of excessive measures taken against Black Panthers. The various police authorities weren't held to much accountability. As for holding authorities or certain people accountable, let's consider the case of Lt. William Calley, Jr. brought to the public's attention at roughly the same time Black Panthers were in the news. He was initially convicted by a military court for murdering 109 unarmed Vietnamese civilians, including old women with babies in their arms, in their village of My Lai on March 16, of 1968. But, his 1969 conviction prompted a huge public outcry from Americans more sympathetic to him than to those 109 non white folks he murdered in Vietnam.

All across the country hundreds of rallies were held by indignant Americans carrying signs and chanting "Free Lt. Calley." Responding to pro Calley events, the ever calculating Richard Nixon essentially nullified Lt. Calley's life in prison sentence. He never saw the inside of a cell after Nixon's intervention on his behalf. Nixon allowed for a punishment of two years of house arrest. Calley's girlfriend was allowed to visit and he had phone service. She ran errands for him like buying groceries and beer. How's that for punishment for killing 109 innocent people?

On the question of just punishment one might wonder what kind of punishment a black teenager would get for stealing fifteen dollars worth of food from a convenience store? He or she certainly wouldn't have white privilege considerations working on their behalf as did Lt. Calley or the Wall Street wheelers and dealers responsible for the financial collapse of 2008, which imposed severe economic hardships on so many. In contrast to that we see appalling numbers of African-Americans incarcerated for non violent crimes, such as marijuana possession. Calley's two years of house arrest under cushy circumstances made a mockery of American justice. At the end of two years Calley was free as a bird. Within a year he easily got a bank loan, opened a jewelry store, and was driving a Mercedes-Benz. Talk about white privilege!

As for accountability, I'm past seventy-six now and I know I won't see the day when George W. Bush, Dick Cheney, Donald Rumsfeld, and their administration associates get indicted for war crimes. That cabal is ultimately responsible for incredibly more innocent civilian deaths than Lt. William Calley was. The crimes of Bush and his political inner circle amply illustrate one of my regular comments to classes: "The bigger the crime the less the time." How does our pledge to the flag end? Isn't it liberty and *justice for all*? That phrase rings rather hollow at times in the course of our nation's history. When taking our history into consideration hasn't white privilege, more than we care to admit, usually been a factor with respect to who gets arrested, charged with a crime, and ultimately punished?

Chapter 16

Campaigning for the presidency in the Fall of 1968, Richard Nixon became attuned to the grumblings of many whites who viewed Lyndon Johnson's War On Poverty negatively. He referred to this segment of the population as the "Silent Majority." From their perspective, influenced by conservative spin based on flawed analysis, measures initiated to promote social uplift were seen to negatively impact their economic circumstances. Of major concern was the question would their taxes go up to pay for social uplift programs? These folks weren't inclined to see the costs of the Vietnam War as a more likely cause for increased taxes.

At that time, some adults in my evening class voiced the revealing question: "Why should I pay to give someone else advantages over me?" Many white taxpayers had come to believe they were footing bills to facilitate certain programs hardly advantageous to themselves, but only beneficial to others. Those inclined to thinking this way preferred to disbelieve or ignore society's injustices based on otherwise verifiable economic and social factor data.

The outcome of the presidential election of 1968 indicated a significant turning point in American history. In many ways it compared to the election of 1920. In both instances American voters set their government's direction on a more conservative course. Nixon correctly perceived the public's growing indifference to the plight of people struggling in poverty. In his award winning *The Making of the President, 1968*, Theodore H. White wrote, "...the American people repudiated the administration of Lyndon Johnson in one of the greatest somersaults of their political history. The mood was undeniably a swing to the right, an expression of a vague sentiment for a government oriented to caution and restraint."

Nixon's policies slashed the budgets of agencies engaged in social uplift. Most associated with Johnson's Great Society soon became irrelevant - fading entities on dated organizational charts. For the most part abandonment of Johnson administration programs went under the corporate media's radar. The demise of the War On Poverty paralleled the public's growing indifference to poverty. Forsaking Johnson's poverty programs put Nixon at odds with the Congressional Black Caucus. This was evident when its members boycotted his 1971 State of the Union Address. Poverty had quickly became the elephant in the room elected officials chose to ignore and to this day still do.

As for Nixon and the unpopular war in Vietnam, he promised to make known his peace plan upon being elected to the presidency. But, during the campaign itself, to the consternation of his Democratic opponent Hubert Humphrey, Nixon refused to make known details of his plan. Supposedly this was for his concern not to jeopardize the ongoing peace talks then taking place in Paris which President Johnson had initiated.

In many quarters it's believed Nixon essentially could have gotten the same peace terms in his first three months in office, by May of 1969, that he later agreed to after his reelection in 1972. Nixon, always a political creature, didn't want it to appear he "cut and ran," so he dragged things out to give the impression he was a tough negotiator and could outlast the enemy. Nixon was totally dishonest in this matter with the American people. His dishonesty meant the United States suffered an additional 25,000 deaths while he postured as Mr. Tough Guy. Those who served in Vietnam while Nixon was president would prefer to think, though most know better, they were still engaged in a just cause, not being used as political pawns in Nixon's scheme to win reelection in 1972. Within the additional 25,000 deaths in Vietnam, after Nixon took office, were an approximate 5,000 African-American lives lost as well.

Elected in 1968, Shirley Chisholm was the first African-American woman elected to the U. S. House of Representatives. She represented her Brooklyn district from 1968 until 1982. After the election of 1972, Andrew

Young of Georgia and Barbara Jordan of Texas became the first elected in the South to also join the Black Caucus. By 1978, the Black Caucus numbered 27 persons. A decade earlier, at the time of the Newark Black Power meeting, critic Simon Lazarus correctly predicted both Stokely Carmichael and Martin Luther King Jr. would be superseded by "conventional politicians." Within four years of his prophesy such black politicians as Richard Hatcher, Carl Stokes, and Kenneth Gibson had been elected mayors (same order) of Gary, Indiana, Cleveland, Ohio, and Newark, New Jersey.

Sometimes overlooked, the first African-American to win election to the U.S. Senate in the 20th Century was a Republican. It was the party affiliation of Edward William Brooke III who was elected in 1966 by Massachusetts voters to represent their state in Congress. From 1972 to 1992, African-Americans were elected to govern the following cities: Chicago, Cleveland, Detroit, Los Angeles, New York, Philadelphia, and the District of Columbia. In 1990, Virginia elected L. Douglas Wilder, the first African-American to become governor of a state.

On the significance of cities having black mayors, Simon Lazarus said they would be under certain political constraints, hence to function in conventional modes to "reaffirm...ethnic control" where blacks were in the majority. But, he added this caveat, the overall impact black mayors would have wasn't likely to "produce dramatic material gain" for their constituencies. Instead they would function in a manner that would "soothe...status insecurities enough to assure tranquility." His observation seems to be the case. Since African-Americans have been elected mayors of big cities, such cities have enjoyed relative calm when compared with the turmoil they experienced in the 1960s. As for material gain it didn't happen. Though various cities had black mayors they were unable to reverse trends associated with deplorable inner city decay most evident in the 1980s – the Reagan years.

Most situations Great Society programs had not begun to remedy went from bad to worse under Nixon. People living in the south Bronx saw their circumstances deteriorate at an alarmingly quicker pace. Before Nixon resigned from office in 1974, one police station in the south Bronx had become known as "Fort Apache." It was surrounded by a rapidly deteriorating and hostile crime ridden environment which politicians ignored.

Concerned with society's inequities, the catch phrase for many 1960s activists had been: "If you're not part of the solution then you're part of the problem!" To be sure this was somewhat nebulous and simplistic. However, all the mid 1970s late baby boomers came up with was "have a nice day." Did that more profoundly resonate as a philosophical touchstone? "Have a nice day?" Do retail clerks working for a dollar or two above minimum wage and mouthing that trite saying have a nice day? It certainly won't be on payday at those stores where corporate ownership contributes huge sums of money to Republican candidates for their election campaigns.

The peace symbol, iconic to the 1960s, was replaced by a big round yellow smiling face to accompany the "Have a nice day" admonition. By 1974, faded bell bottomed blue jean and T-shirts with peace symbols and slogans had given way to leisure suits. Massive horsepower autos, despite the spike in gasoline prices resulting from the formation of OPEC, had become significantly more popular than the Volkswagen micro bus, a favorite vehicle of the previous decade's Age of Aquarius free spirited types.

Though Nixon's administration was characterized by indifference to the issues easily seventy percent of African-Americans cared about, significant African-American contributions to American culture, especially in sports, continued none the less. Many "firsts" took place while he was president. After Jackie Robinson broke the major league baseball color barrier in 1947, others accomplished firsts and set impressive records thus warranting their selection to baseball's Hall of Fame in the 1960s and 1970s. Prior to their selection, these black super stars had appeared in All Star games for six and seven consecutive seasons.

Such outstanding players who immediately come to mind are baseball's Henry "Hammering Hank" Aaron, Ernie Banks, Roy Campanella, Ferguson Jenkins, Don Newcombe, first black pitcher to win the Cy Young Award in 1956, and Frank Robinson, the first to win Most Valuable Player Awards in both the National and American Leagues. As for professional football, the most impressive running back I ever saw was Jim Brown who played for the Cleveland Browns near the end of the 1950s and into the 1960s. His career record of 126 touchdowns wasn't broken for thirty years until Jerry Rice, also African-American, did it in 1994. As for pro basketball, prior to the Michael Jordan era, I was impressed by Oscar Robertson – the "Big O." Also, the match-ups between Philadelphia's Wilt Chamberlain versus Boston's Bill Russell for recognition as best NBA center were memorable contests epitomizing a unique on court rivalry from 1960 until 1972.

Beyond sports, in other venues, black firsts expanded at an impressive rate. Ed Sullivan's weekly televised variety show in the 1960s featured black entertainers at an accelerating pace. But, it was Bill Cosby who broke a significant television racial barrier when he co-starred in a weekly show called *I Spy*. In 1966 and 1967, he received Emmy Award recognition for his work in television. He was the first black entertainer to receive this show business honor. Cosby was featured in many other popular long running television shows beyond an additional three decades. Every once in a while, to the amusement of a class, I'd mention I had four things in common with Bill Cosby. They are: (1) both born in 1937, (2) both grew up in Philadelphia, (3) both honorably discharged veterans, and (4) we hold degrees from Temple University.

Of note, appearing on the literary scene and achieving best seller status was Toni Morrison's *The Bluest Eyes*. Also in 1970, Maya Angelou's *I Know Why the Caged Bird Sings* was published. Angelou's book was the first non fiction by a black woman to attain best seller status. Then too, Black Panther Bobby Seale's revealing *Seize The Time* was soon on book store shelves.

As for music, the first Earth Day occurred on April 22, 1970 and the next year concern for the environment was explicit in Marvin Gaye's hit song "What's Going On?" The same year (1971) the O'Jay's song "Love Train" went high on the hits charts, as did the 1973 song "Ghetto Child" by the Spinners. Released in 1971, never achieving hit status, but somewhat reflecting the era's Black Power political disillusionment, was Gil Scott-Heron's "The Revolution Will Not Be Televised." The Motown sound's popularity in the early 1970s gave way to the disco craze of the mid 1970s which then faded quickly after Gloria Gaynor's 1978 hit song "I Will Survive." Before the 1970s ended, Sister Sledge released "We Are Family" in 1979. This song's enduring popularity is indicated by the fact it's predictably played to this day at family reunions and wedding receptions.

Soon to bypass disco in popularity, especially with young adult male African- Americans, was rap music. The first time I heard it was on the last day of 1979 at a New Year's Eve party. I went to the party with Demosthenes 'Demos' Kontos, a faculty colleague. The party was at the home of mutual friend Lou Fernandez, then living in the Orange County (NY) village of Ridgebury. The song we danced to, "Rapper's Delight," by the Sugar Hill Gang helped kick off the popularity of that evolving music genre which lasted far too long as far as jazz critic Stanley Crouch and myself were concerned. However, at the party that night I did a white man's dance a few times to that song. Lou and I had a good laugh after he said, "Man, if only your students could see you now." No doubt they would have laughed, probably hysterically, if they saw me dancing.

While Nixon was president (1969-1974) the momentum toward implementing and achieving worthy goals beneficial to African-American communities went from the rapid pace Tommie C. Smith ran, in the 200 meters at the 1968 Olympic Games in Mexico City, down to the motions of a thirteen month old taking first steps. By the mid 1980s, when making the analogy, most students had no clue who Tommie C. Smith was. They were informed he and John Carlos had won Olympic medals in track events, but were then denied them because they gave Black Power raised fists salutes during the recognition ceremony. Photos of them making the gesture were prominently presented in newspapers across the country and around the world as well.

When news sources revealed President Nixon had an "enemies list," late night talk show hosts had quirky material for humorous banter. African-Americans on the list included Bill Cosby, Dick Gregory, Carl Rowan, Bayard Rustin, and vocalist Eartha Kitt who, a few years earlier, had the *chutzpah* to tell Lady Bird Johnson to her face her husband's Vietnam War policy was wrong. Also, Ron Dellums was on the list along with New York Jets quarterback Joe Namath. Humorous to some, but distasteful to others, was a publicized news photo showing Sammy Davis Jr. giving Richard Nixon a spontaneous hug. It seemed an awkward moment for Richard Nixon.

In terms of race relations the 1970s Governor of Georgia, Jimmy Carter, had taken steps to minimize divisive racial issues. A New South, where race played no part in politics, was the theme he presented in political campaigning. In the South race baiting had long been a tactic to divert people's attention from real issues. The course of action Carter stressed was to make the political process color blind, so his actions and message didn't feature playing the race card.

Jimmy Carter was the Democrats' front runner for president in 1976. When discussing his candidacy with students at the time, the question of his sincerity regarding his enlightened approach to politics, *sans* racism, came up. Cynical about Carter, one student said, "Like the others, he'll say whatever to get elected." I responded, "Are you saying he's insincere regarding racial political equality?" He hesitated slightly and then responded, "Oh come on professor, he's a white southerner. Can a leopard change its spots?" His last comment caused me to join the class in laughter.

In the dozen years since Fannie Lou Hamer appeared on national television at the Democratic convention in Atlantic City, the Democrats had come a long way in securing a strong, duly noted, commitment to their party by a significant majority of African-Americans. Their 1976 nominating convention was held in New York City's Madison Square Garden. The impressive articulate African-American Barbara Jordan, a member of the House of Representatives from Texas, delivered the Keynote Address. In the late 1980s an older black woman said to class, "Forget this black English stuff. It's nonsense! Learn how to speak as well as Barbara Jordan." (At this time can there be any doubt President Obama's command of the English language and speaking skills are vastly superior to those of his predecessor in the White House?)

The Democratic convention of 1976 placed Jimmy Carter at the top of the ticket with Walter Mondale its candidate for vice president. Before adjourning the civil rights struggles of the preceding decade were acknowledged when the delegates stood and sang the anthem of that time - "We Shall Overcome." The convention concluded when the Rev. Martin Luther King Sr. offered a benediction.

Early in the Fall semester of 1976, a student asked if Carter had a chance at defeating incumbent Gerald Ford. You'll recall Ford had been selected by Nixon to serve as vice president because Spiro Agnew had resigned in disgrace. Upon Nixon's resignation, to stay one step ahead of impeachment, Gerald Ford then became president. Compared to Nixon Ford appeared to have personal integrity, but that came into question when he pardoned Richard Nixon. As for the student's question, I responded with this: "So, O K, you know Jimmy Carter got the Democratic nomination, but what do you know about his party's platform?" The class fell silent. No surprise!

It's not unusual for most Americans to be clueless about party platforms three or four weeks after nominating conventions adjourn. And many times candidates fashion their own agendas which either partly contradict or obscure what convention delegates endorsed as the party's positions. Democrats said little about poverty in 1976, compared to 1972 when it was addressed and George McGovern nominated for president.

Essentially Republicans were silent on the issue of poverty in both 1972, when Nixon sought a second term, and in 1976 when Gerald Ford sought election in his own right.

Back to Carter and the question regarding his chances. Many times a new face, such as Carter, has special appeal to voters as compared with longtime politicians such as Gerald Ford or Tip O'Neill, later Speaker of the House while Reagan was president. Carter said he would "never lie" to the American people and their memory of Nixon caught in lies during Watergate hearings, just two years earlier, caused his promise to strike a responsive chord. So, I said newcomer Carter did have an advantage over Jerry Ford, who didn't effectively distance himself from Nixon's legacy. Carter, compared with Ford who pardoned Nixon, seemed cast from a refreshingly different mold. This was noted by Theodore H. White who wrote: "Ford is a nice man. So, too, is Jimmy Carter. But Jimmy Carter is running *against* Washington, while Ford, the appointed President, *is* Washington."

Jimmy Carter took a chance and stirred things up by his candor in a *Playboy* magazine interview - a first for a presidential candidate. Some said he was courageous and others thought it foolish for him to say what he did in the interview, considering the potential for negative political repercussions at that time. Carter's *Playboy* interview, in the words of Bob Dylan's song a dozen years earlier, indeed indicated "the times were a changing." A black college chorus from Atlanta sang the "Battle Hymn of the Republic" at Carter's inaugural celebration.

During the 1970s, the conservative drift in public opinion gathered momentum and was reflected in the nature of debates in state legislative bodies across the nation. Many states refused proposals to honor Martin Luther King's life in some way. However, a significant episode going counter to the conservative drift occurred when the Supreme Court issued its *Roe v. Wade* decision (1973) which came while Nixon was president. The Court's decision sustained a woman's right to choose regarding abortion. Thurgood Marshall, the first African-American to serve on the Supreme Court, stood tall for women by affirming their right to have final say when it came to unwanted pregnancies.

However, the conservative political climate in the country was evident by the end of the decade when Carter was president. Thirty-two year old Allan Bakke had been refused admission to a California medical school. So, he responded by charging it was because of "reverse racism." Political conservatives pounced on this idea. They loved it! It suited their purpose in their opposition to Affirmative Action. Essentially Bakke claimed he was passed over so the University of California at Davis Medical College could implement a special minority assistance program whereby African-American applicants, having lower admission test scores than he, were accepted on a preferential basis. This case passed through lower federal courts to ultimately come before the Supreme Court headed by Chief Justice Warren Burger, a Nixon appointee.

On June 28, 1978, the Supreme Court ruled, in a five to four decision, in Bakke's favor. The medical college was ordered to admit Bakke and required to negate the special admissions program for minorities. According to biographer Juan Williams, "The Bakke defeat left a deep scar on the seventy-year-old Marshall." Williams said Thurgood Marshall expressed the opinion recently held beliefs African-Americans were making significant socio-economic advances were "myth." Ronald Reagan, California's governor six years earlier, expressed approval of the Supreme Court's Bakke decision. Two years later he was the Republican Party's candidate for president.

After Nixon many were hopeful Jimmy Carter would revive the issue of poverty and restore funding for domestic programs deleted from Nixon's budgets. They were sorely disappointed. He turned his back on the issue because he became intent on balancing the federal budget, in part because those on the right were beginning to make noise about the deficit. However, liberal Democrats, such as Ted Kennedy in the Senate and Ron Dellums with other House Black Caucus members, opposed cutting the deficit at the expense of domestic programs seen as urgently needed. In addition to differences over budget allocations, some antagonism between President Carter and members of his own party was rooted in the fact he had never served in Congress and was seen by some as an outsider.

Senator Ted Kennedy, the progressive Democrat from Massachusetts, opposed President Carter for their party's presidential nomination in the Spring of 1980. While campaigning in Philadelphia, prior to Pennsylvania's primary election, Senator Kennedy said, "We aren't going to turn our backs on the poor, on the elderly...." The 1980 Democratic convention renominated President Carter, but he lost the November election to Ronald Reagan. The Reagan landslide saw some Democrats in Congress begin to express views similar to Republicans. They were soon referred to as Blue Dog Democrats. But, Senator Ted Kennedy stayed on in the U.S. Senate for another two decades as the voice for what social uplift Democrats had once advocated in the 1960s, that decade of the 20th Century's most momentous political and social changes.

In 1980, Ronald Reagan was challenged in early Republican party primaries by George H. W. Bush, who was a younger man. All things considered Bush was a more moderate Republican than Reagan. Not a devotee of Milton Friedman's economic tenets, as was Reagan, Bush labeled those beliefs "voodoo economics." Republicans didn't want protracted public disagreements. So, an understanding was reached for the sake of party harmony and unity. Bush agreed to go on the ticket as candidate for vice president, bide his time during Reagan's terms, and then get party leaders to endorse him in a 1988 presidential run.

While holding office as Governor of California, the record indicates Ronald Reagan never approved of any significant civil rights measures. Classes were amused upon being informed how alarmed Governor Reagan became at one time when Black Panthers showed up with shotguns on the steps of the state legislature in Sacramento. As for the rights of black South Africans while he was president, Reagan showed no concern. His administration steadfastly supported the racist apartheid system the minority white government of South Africa imposed on the black majority masses.

As for the issue of poverty, frequently mentioned here, in the words of Cornel West, Reagan "... made it fashionable to be indifferent to the poor and gave permission to be greedy with little or no conscience." Yes, Reagan's years typified the "greed is good" mentality which had become rather pervasive during his tenure in office. Reagan's budgets reduced spending for domestic programs more severely than what Carter's administration had done. Reagan even skimped on the federal school lunch program by classifying ketchup a vegetable to meet the program's vegetable requirement.

The 1980s became known as the decade of greed - symbolically represented in a film titled *Wall Street*. The main character, Gordon Gekko, was played by Michael Douglass. He won an Academy Award for his performance depicting the contemptible ruthlessness of Gekko. A famous line from the film was Gekko saying, "Greed is Good." Also, during Reagan's second term a popular television show was titled "Lifestyles of the Rich and Famous." Television executives knew there wouldn't be an audience for a series featuring the down and outs of the Reagan years. Governments from the Reagan administration to Bill Clinton's chose to ignore the tens of thousands of homeless many of whom were African-American Vietnam War veterans.

Today students know little about the negative social impact of Reagan's policies in the 1980s. Just as back then, in the 1980s, most of my students knew little of the positive things associated with Lyndon Johnson's War On Poverty. Hence, one obstacle to overcoming a retrogressive political climate is the amnesia too many Americans suffer from when pressed to recall events just five years earlier. Also, I often wonder if H. L. Mencken's observation, "You can never overestimate the ignorance of the American public," is at the crux allowing for corporate interests to constantly pull the wool over the public's eyes?

Reagan readily chastised congressional Democrats when their defense appropriations projections didn't meet his expectations for higher levels of military spending. On his massive appropriations request for his proposed grandiose Star Wars project, Democrats finally stood firm and refused it. Much debated and opposed by public outcry, the Star Wars project finally became a dead issue. However, other costly projects were soon approved which kept Military-Industrial Complex interests satisfied for the time being.

Conservatives loved Reagan's speech in which he said the federal government "was the problem." But, of course, anti-war groups knew the federal government was never a problem for favored corporations getting predictable obscenely profitable Pentagon contracts. During his two terms the influence of the Military Industrial Complex was like the ominously growing snowball unable to be stopped as it rolled downhill. Spending for the military grew at a rate thrilling to the many corporations expecting and used to getting Pentagon contracts. The public, for the most part, was unaware Reagan had allowed the deficit, thanks to the borrowing for military spending, to go beyond threefold what it was when he first took office.

Though frequently ignored by the corporate media because of his predictable critical assessments of Pentagon budget requests, California's black Congressman Ron Dellums tenaciously tried to shed light on the Military Industrial Complex's influence during the Reagan years. Toward the end of the 1990s, students knew nothing about former member of Congress Ron Dellums or, for that matter, Brooklyn's Shirley Chisholm who also saw most Pentagon spending bringing no benefit to her constituents. Hopefully, biographies will soon be forthcoming about these two deserving former members of Congress who challenged Reagan's trickle down economic policies.

Alarming deficit spending in the Reagan years didn't go to addressing poverty issues. His ploy of creating welfare for poor families as a self serving political issue diverted public attention away from the more significant issue of corporate welfare. It was, of course, facilitated by the extensive influence Wall Street interests had on the United States Congress. The corporate sponsored media didn't look closely at this trend and barely brought the public's attention to the fact the United States had gone from being a creditor nation to a debtor nation in terms of balance of trade payments with other countries of the world, due in large part to Reagan's economic policies.

Because of unemployment and consequential poverty, inner city landlords had difficulty collecting their often exorbitant rents. So, many simply abandoned their buildings. Such buildings were subject to graffiti and vandalism. Block after block in the south Bronx and in areas surrounding Temple University in Philadelphia had run down abandoned buildings - testimony to poverty's continued prevalence in places designated as the ghetto. Urban blight spread like a cancer. In such locations hard drug use became more common. Who's more likely to become addicted to hard drugs, a person steadily employed or a chronically unemployed person? Did Reaganites want to realistically deal with that question? Not politicians, my students never shied away from answering that question.

At roughly the time Reagan was sworn in for his second term on Jan. 20, 1985, hundreds of thousands of white males came to realize their wives also had to earn a salary in order to make mortgage payments and pay other expenses associated with suburban living. Basically they were living the American Dream by hard work to be sure, but also because of white privilege. Did it ever occur to them to look around in their work places and ask why weren't some of their fellow employees African-Americans? Unlike white couples living in suburbia, most black couples weren't able to earn fifteen to twenty dollars an hour above minimum wage. It was of no concern to the Reagan administration. His policies didn't address issues inherent to lack of jobs and continuation of de facto segregation in living circumstances for most African-Americans. The corporate media rarely paid close attention to objections the Black Caucus raised to Reagan's policies.

Often it was black women having high school diplomas who got jobs whereas black men without diplomas didn't. In the 1970s and '80s a greater percentage of white males got diplomas than black males. Hence, a greater percentage of white males with high school diplomas got jobs before black males without diplomas. So, in effect, jobs requiring high school diplomas gave white workers an advantage over black workers. However, sociologists had learned many job performance requirements were learned in the first three to four weeks on the job and high school diplomas meant little in the learning process necessary to performing such jobs satisfactorily. Hence, the high school diploma came to have a selective utilization for purposes of racial discrimination. Strictly speaking the bias was not based on race per se, but, none the less, served to sort out employment opportunities along racial lines. It seems rather ironic black males were under employed while many suburban whites were getting "moonlighting" second jobs in the 1980s.

Overall college educated whites in the 1970s and '80s were able to do such things as buy suburban homes, go on cruises, join country clubs, and send their kids away to college – all things most African-Americans were unable to do. And the corporate media spared the white middle class from having to look too closely at how circumstances were for inner city folks. But, some middle class whites, not on corporate payrolls, such as inner city school teachers, social workers, police officers, and nurses working in certain hospitals, were aware of the extent of socio-economic deprivation associated with life in the ghetto. However, most American politicians, from the time Nixon sought reelection until Al Gore opposed George W. Bush for president in 2000, correctly assumed most Americans didn't want to address the issue of poverty. Hence, poverty as an issue was something astute politicians avoided – to them it was the equivalent of a subway's third rail.

During the Reagan years, the 1980s, when discussing poverty students and I agreed it wasn't the compelling issue it had been in the 1960s. We acknowledged it wasn't at the top of either party's agenda. Reagan never discussed root causation of poverty. The Black Caucus did try to focus on poverty, but other Democrats, once supportive of Lyndon Johnson's War On Poverty, weren't inclined to do so. The Democratic presidential candidate in 1988 was Michael Dukakis and he definitely shied away from the issue of poverty. But one Democrat willing to address the issue was African-American Jesse Jackson, who ran in Democratic presidential primaries in

1984 and again in 1988. Jackson was willing to discuss root causation factors of poverty.

President Reagan used the stereotype image of, in his words, "welfare queens" to curry favor with blue collar whites, who political pundits had begun referring to as Reagan Democrats. These white folks tended to be indignantly self righteous when presented with carefully selected images of African-American women with many children but no apparent supportive husbands. Reagan and candidates for Congress who supported him were appealing to white blue collar workers likely to respond to code words which were understood to mean giving black Americans undeserved advantages. Such programs as Affirmative Action, Head Start, busing for diversity, and scatter site housing came under fire in the Reagan years.

Welfare, as a code word, came to mean African-Americans by Reagan and his supporters. There were other code words employed by Republican party strategists after the Democrat Lyndon Johnson was no longer in the White House. African-American historian Clarence Lusane quoted Republican adviser Lee Atwater's acknowledgment of such words. The South Carolinian Atwater said, "You start out in 1954 by saying, Nigger, nigger, nigger.' By 1968 you can't say 'nigger.' ...So you say stuff like forced busing, states rights." Add affirmative action and welfare queen to the list of code words used during the Reagan years, by Republicans seeking office, to sway anxious working class whites to feel superior to *those* people. And more recently, it's not a stretch to conclude Mitt Romney's supporters viewed African-Americans and Hispanics as large components of the 47% Romney viewed as parasitical.

When Democrats nominated the lack luster Michael Dukakis, in 1988, the first Bush was assured a victory. As in the previous dozen years, Democrats didn't address the issue of poverty in their party's platform. And, neither party called for reducing the Pentagon's budget even though it's been said intelligence agencies knew the Soviet military threat had been exaggerated for almost a decade. Leaders in both parties wouldn't want their opposing counterparts to charge them with being soft on communism should they call for reducing the military budget.

Then a dozen years after the collapse of the Soviet Union, because of 9/11/2001, a similar political scenario reemerged as both parties strove to prove they weren't soft on terrorism. Both Democrats and Republicans have jointly, year in and out, sponsored bigger defense budgets than approved the previous year. Exaggerations of possible threats allows the war party to hold the trump cards of fear and ignorance, both necessary to keep the American public compliant while Congress meets the demands made by the Military Industrial Complex.

Federal funding for urban renewal, including adding more public housing, was never a priority during the administration of Republican Ronald Reagan and that orientation continued when George H.W. Bush succeeded him. The Bush administration looked favorably upon privately funded urban gentrification projects. Poor older black folks were displaced from certain neighborhoods where they had lived all their lives. Banks then provided loans to promising college educated younger white folks who went about rehabilitating houses in those neighborhoods. Likely to receive loans with desirable terms were those who came to be known as "Yuppies." They expected their newly revitalized neighborhoods to become "where it's at" places to live.

In his inaugural address on January 20th, 1989, George H.W. Bush spoke of a "thousand points of light" to be facilitated by individuals doing good deeds for others. At the time there were tens of thousands of homeless persons, many Vietnam veterans. His idea of "compassionate conservatism" seemed an oxymoron to hundreds of thousands who were disadvantaged in the "greed is good" time of his predecessor. After he initiated the first war in Iraq, Papa Bush told Americans not to let it interfere with going about everyday activities such as shopping at malls.

In his 1996 endeavor to be reelected to a second term, Democrat Bill Clinton believed many whites were still agitated about perceived welfare abuse. Of course Republican candidates thrived on addressing exaggerated examples of abuse and Clinton wanted to blunt advantages they might gain regarding that issue. He believed political points might possibly be gained if he dealt with it, but in some fashion seeming less negative than how Republicans responded. He didn't belabor abuses in the system and moved to address the issue with what seemed palatable by calling for the end of "welfare as we know it."

Clinton's statements were calculated to bring Reagan Democrats back into the Democratic Party's base. Simply put, his welfare proposal was a pitch to those vocal in their self righteous indignation about the welfare system of which, in reality, they knew little about. Addressing the issue Clinton was both nuanced and vague. He avoided specifying extreme implementation measures, thus he gained many liberals support. To be sure, enough voters thought his explanations were sufficient and he denied his 1996 Republican opponent, Bob Dole, much leeway to make welfare an issue advantageous to himself.

At the welfare reform law's signing ceremony there was a middle aged black woman present surrounded by white politicos. Was she a staged prop implying her presence symbolically represented all African-Americans supposedly giving the new law their approval? Her name was Lillie Harden. She was forty-two and had three children. The *Washington Post* reported she had met Clinton ten years earlier in Little Rock. Now she was present reportedly because she approved of the new law, officially known as the Personal Responsibility and Work Opportunity Act, signed into law on August 22, 1996.

The corporate media generally overlooked the fact various black and white liberals were disappointed with Clinton's handling of the welfare issue. Many saw Clinton's sly pandering on the issue in a light giving them pause to think maybe the nickname "Slick Willie," Republican pundits gave him, might be deserved. At present I am curious about what's become of Lillie Harden and her children? What have her socio-economic circumstances been like since she approved of the welfare reform law and posed with Bill Clinton? I also wonder how grateful Bill was for her political support?Did he set up a college trust fund for Lillie Harden's three children?

Signing the welfare reform bill "deeply flawed," in Professor Randall Kennedy's opinion, moved the topic away from being a front page issue. But, of note is the fact on the next day, August 23, 1996, the *Washington Post* did report "Labor unions, religious groups and organizations representing women, minorities and immigrants....have expressed outrage over Clinton's decision to support the bill." For the most part other major media venues didn't echo the *Post's* reported criticism, but covered the bill's passage with commentary implying Clinton did the right thing.

On economic issues Clinton was as pro business as Republican Calvin Coolidge. He may not have used Coolidge's famous phrase, "the business of America is business," but his mantra of *globalization* served corporate interests as well as had Coolidge's commitment to *laissez faire* principles in the 1920s. As for the philosophy of the New Deal, i.e., concern for the "forgotten man," we saw policies associated with Democrat Jimmy Carter and especially his successor Ronald Reagan significantly move away from assisting the less fortunate. Then, under Democrat Bill Clinton the less fortunate, a large percentage of whom were African-Americans, were basically told "get a job," which would most likely pay minimum wage with no fringe benefits. (A few years later the "get a job" remark was hurled at people, such as myself, protesting George W. Bush's war on Iraq.)

In the 1990s, before my retirement, I always referred to Clinton as "Republican lite" as did others disappointed by his big business orientation. During his presidency big bank presidents never had to worry about becoming forgotten men. His Secretary of the Treasury Robert Rubin assiduously looked after their interests with Clinton's approval.

Clinton's globalization policy accelerated the trend of outsourcing jobs to overseas production facilities owned by American corporate interests. Clinton's Secretary of Labor Robert Reich knew outsourcing had negative implications for creating and retaining jobs in the United States. Reich was more of a New Deal Democrat than his boss Bill Clinton. Some called Bill Clinton a supreme pragmatist, others saw him as the quintessential political opportunist. I wonder which term Bob Reich would, in confidence, use?

Secretary of the Treasury Robert Rubin, in agreement with Federal Reserve Chairman Alan Greenspan's basic philosophy, initiated policies subsequently elaborated upon which laid the groundwork ultimately leading to Wall Street's financial meltdown of 2008. Like his Republican predecessors, Clinton listened to corporate banking and investing interests more often than labor's concerns presented by Robert Reich. Clinton condoned policies giving corporate interests special advantages incompatible with true *laissez faire* theory. Thus, Secretary Reich viewed those policies as corporate welfare. Robert Rubin objected to the term being used in cabinet meetings. Secretary of Labor Robert Reich declined to serve in Clinton's second term.

During Clinton's administration the greed of the 1980's was still evident on Wall Street. Clinton supporters would be reluctant to admit the "greed is good" culture hadn't changed during his administration. Clinton Democrats, with corporate media assistance, crafted a smoke screen message implying his policies were incompatible with the "greed is good" culture associated with the Reagan era. The public was hustled into believing the Clinton administration was committed to changing that culture. It didn't happen! Behind closed doors Clinton took advice from Wall Street wolves who then posed as lambs in public. The wolves had no qualms about accelerating the number of jobs to be outsourced to American corporate owned overseas facilities and they were able to get the Glass-Steagall Banking Reform Act of the New Deal overturned!

Upon returning to Wall Street Robert Rubin and others of his opportunistic orientation initiated and put in play more dubious practices, such as buying and selling mortgage derivative bundles, which ultimately led to the crash and economic melt down begun in late 2008. An irony here is that when Ralph Nader contemplated running for president again in 2004, he warned that government oversight of Wall Street's activities had become slipshod and things could unexpectedly take a dramatic turn for the worse. At the time scrutiny of Wall Street practices was not something the Bush administration zealously engaged in and little action was taken to reign in practices sliding under the radar of federal regulatory laws.

In the last three decades of the 20th Century most proposals to promote black social uplift were frequently seen by whites as negatively impacting their schools, their job opportunities, their political influence, and, significant to most, their tax bills. Again, what they didn't grasp was such proposals weren't intended to give advantages, but merely to level the playing field so no one had an advantage based on race and, to some degree, extremely disproportionate economic advantages. Can we honestly say race plays no part in the fact African-Americans are minimally represented in occupations essentially calling for college degrees? Why aren't there more black dentists, doctors, lawyers, pharmacists, psychologists, certified public accountants, and college professors teaching chemistry, math, physics, and various engineering specialties?

Shortly before retiring, I asked a class in which occupation African-Americans were over represented? A male student immediately exclaimed "the N.B.A." (I had to explain to some women the N.B.A. was a reference to professional basketball.) The class had a good laugh about the N.B.A. answer, but that wasn't what I had in mind. I was thinking of big city sanitation workers who collected trash. Whites are very much a minority and blacks the majority in such low status jobs. Fortunately most working at that job in big cities are unionized and have a living wage. Most municipal service jobs in the economy, like trash removal, can't be outsourced to overseas locations.

However, service jobs on municipal payrolls are presently being threatened not by outsourcing but by being privatized. When cities and towns look to have private corporations perform trash removal, among other services, those private corporations getting the contracts employ non unionized workers. Such employees make half the pay unionized municipal employees earn. The privatization of services undermines the wages employees in service unions can reasonably bargain for so they won't fall back into the working poor category. The reason Dr. King was in Memphis, Tennessee in April of 1968 was to support that city's trash collectors (now usually referred to as sanitation workers) gain recognition for their union and obtain a contract paying enough to make them ineligible for food stamps.

Tavis Smiley and Cornel West, among others, have observed economic factors are still, at bottom, determinants regarding the nature of change for better or worse. White folks, thanks in part to white privilege, have jobs enabling them to live in the suburbs. Black folks without jobs can't do that. Inherent in the issue of social justice is that persistent economic question who gets what and why? Those benefiting from their involvement in corporate America's business, living in the suburbs, want to avoid the previous question - as did Richard Nixon and all presidents who followed him.

When Bill Clinton took office the Black Caucus hoped he would address issues associated with the decay of inner cities - urban blight, etc. After all, just before Clinton took office the Berlin Wall came down and the Soviet Union collapsed. Wasn't this supposed to mean the Pentagon budget could finally be reduced and then, logically, funds in turn allocated for domestic quality of life upgrades? Wasn't the public at large, not special interest recipients of Pentagon contracts, supposed to reap the broader benefits of an anticipated peace dividend? Social uplift advances beyond anything New Deal visionaries could imagine would now be possible – right? Dream On!

Corporate America, including all facets of the Military Industrial Complex, got immediate attention from the new Democratic president who once believed the war in Vietnam was wrong. Bill Clinton quickly learned how to dance to the tune played by his Secretary of the Treasury, former Wall Street mogul Robert Rubin. Ending "welfare as we know it," sponsored by Clinton, meant elimination of welfare benefits to hundreds of thousands who truly needed them. This Clinton measure was a boon to corporations, especially to those where near seventy percent of their employees were paid minimum wages.

Without needed welfare benefits desperate persons became compelled to join the ranks of the working poor struggling to survive at jobs paying the minimum wage or perhaps a dollar or two above it. Such low paying jobs, especially in retail sales, were rarely designated full time. Workers' schedules kept them three or four hours a week from being full time, so if laid off no unemployment benefits were forthcoming. Also, their schedules usually changed from week to week and they seldom got two consecutive days off. (An overnight trip to visit a friend – forget it!) Fast food and national retailing corporations appreciated Bill Clinton's welfare reform.

The corporate media assisted Clinton's NAFTA (North American Free Trade Agreement) proposal to achieve public acceptance. The concerns of organized labor were downplayed by Clinton and the media as well, neither responded forthrightly to questions labor raised. However, union spokespersons, such as African-American Bill Fletcher Jr., saw the pervasive influence corporate America would have in determining what the agreement entailed. He was concerned it didn't bode well for working Americans or those looking for jobs. Union leaders saw NAFTA and subsequent Clinton sponsored "globalization" policies as slick ploys for outsourcing union jobs to other countries with non union workforces.

Labor leaders realized Clinton's forthcoming international trade agreements would benefit working Americans minimally but American corporations mightily. Now we know Fletcher and other union leaders' assessments were correct with regard to Clinton's economic policies. Overall they caused an erosion of former higher wages. Corporations were able to tell American workers their wages had to be reduced or their jobs would be outsourced to their overseas facilities.

As for Clinton and the Military Industrial Complex, since the Cold War was over progressives hoped he would put the brakes on and curtail the dominating influence it persistently had on his two Republican predecessors. But no, Clinton cranked up an activist mode of foreign policy. It included intervention in Balkan affairs and was evident also by constant flights over Iraq with more bombings than the public was ever informed about. His military initiatives in the Middle East weren't widely made public, but probably spurred more Muslims of the region to excuse acts of terror aimed at the United States and its client Arab states.

Clinton also approved of continued funding for Egypt's dictatorship. So, in many respects the present instability in Egypt is a consequence of Reagan, Clinton, Bush, and Obama policies. When the seeming unexpected happens it is often caused by factors rooted in American policy that seemed appropriate for circumstances at a given time. Delayed negative reactions to American policies, as a consequence of those policies, is generally known as "blowback." Present instability in Egypt is one example of political "blowback." Late in Carter's administration, he was faced with "blowback" when radical Iranian students, objecting to long standing U.S. support of the dictatorial Shah, took control of the United States embassy and held 52 Americans hostage for 444 days.

During the Clinton years the needs of corporations depending on Pentagon contracts took precedence over the needs of the unemployed poor as well as the new category of folks known as the working poor. I agree with courageous African-Americans who have observed it's a sad comment on our society when African-Americans and Hispanics view the military as their best employment option.

During the years I taught, from a year and a half before Nixon became president to near the end of Clinton's second term, I saw American society overcome considerable endemic racism. In that regard our country has come a long way. During my first year of teaching African-American history, I was once asked if we would ever have a black president. At that time, in 1970, Nixon was president and given the fact he played a race card in the guise of "law and order" I didn't think it would happen in my lifetime. I'm pleased to be wrong.

However, as for endemic racism it's not dying a quick death, but rather a slow death. I say this with AM radio talk show criticisms aimed at President Obama in mind. Many aspersions cast his way are motivated by a latent racism, just beneath the political surface - let's not kid ourselves about that. During the 2012 election season my son Andy said he saw signs on residential properties in Berks County (PA) saying "Get the black out of the White House." Five years earlier, on September 22, 2007, one J. J. McLaughlin of Lower Macungie Township had this to say in a letter to the *Allentown Morning Call*: "It time we whites join together and bring this country back to the way when our forefathers had established it. This is a WHITE CHRISTIAN COUNTRY." No point in asking Mr. McLaughlin what he thinks of multiculturalism. The preceding reflects why areas of Pennsylvania beyond the suburbs of Philadelphia and Pittsburgh are frequently referred to as "Pennsyltucky."

Yes, certainly one aspect of social injustice is racism, but what about the other dimensions of social injustice - particularly the ones inherent in economic disparities? Republican Party spokespersons still carp about high taxes implying tax revenues go to the undeserving – as Mitt Romney's reference to 47% of Americans indicated. Does it occur to such self righteous people laid off workers never have a say, no input, when it comes to corporate decisions resulting in loss of jobs? And hourly rate workers are certainly not in the loop regarding flimflam decisions made by Wall Street manipulators.

A majority of Americans are ignorant, intentionally kept that way by the Corporatocracy. One thing lingering in American culture is the impulse to blame the victim and AM radio talk shows rarely challenge that simplistic response, too often given in lieu of thoughtful assessments realistically addressing economic issues. The notion the media is liberal has been embraced by too many of the unthinking. Repeated often enough, the idea has become believable to them as a fact. This is laughable! How many air time hours does Cornel West or Bill Fletcher Jr. get compared with Sean Hannity or Rush Limbaugh? Of course when the corporate media reenforces the idea, its so doing then serves as a major hurdle preventing the media from actually becoming liberal. And that's the desired goal of the Corporatocracy.

Why is it Tea Party folks never talk about who's getting dramatically richer thanks to corporate sponsored governmental policies? Would they acknowledge we spend more on the military than the next dozen industrialized countries of the world, including China, combined? Of course they wouldn't, mainly because they're ignorant about such information. Fox News doesn't present such information. Would the Koch brothers who have funded planned sham rallies, supposedly grassroots in origin, educate participants to realize spending for the military is intrinsically related to sustaining the U.S. Corporatocracy's economic exploitation in the rest of the world? Tea Party folks go on and on about welfare, but are silent about the tax code structure which essentially creates a welfare system for the super rich of corporate America.

Why were Wall Street executives deserving of bonuses after 2008, when the government's huge financial bailout was put in place to ameliorate the economic disaster their greed inspired policies foisted on the American public? Their reprehensible decisions caused so many to need unemployment benefits, of which certain politicians beholden to corporate interests would try to curtail. Tea Party types either wont acknowledge or can't comprehend the super rich own the political system, not the folks needing food stamps. When will high schools teach the political reality inherent in the meaning of the word plutocracy?

At present politicians making their pitch to folks living in segregated suburban communities, where political contributions are larger than what's coming to them from inner cities, will not likely raise the following questions to their constituents: What happened to equal opportunity? Why should new born children be severely socially handicapped because of the economic circumstances of their parents? Why isn't there an African-American family living in your neighborhood, on your street? The last question was addressed by Sheryll Cashin in her book *The Failures of Integration*. She observed the Clinton administration didn't counter "the tide…that encouraged and even subsidized greater suburbanization and separation," because of its concern "to appeal to suburban voters."

Most whites living in the suburbs don't want to acknowledge the idea of white privilege. Addressing it and comprehending its implications poses a threat to their comfortable existence within the context of the present status quo. Given the political climate at this time, with its economic and social implications, I think if Fannie Lou Hamer were alive today she would still say "I question America."

Presently, super rich white folks are still getting more than a fair share and most African-Americans, many whites also, are still on the periphery regarding the distribution of wealth created by their labor and the tasks they conscientiously perform enabling businesses to thrive. Fair and just compensation for those who toil and upon whose backs others have gained impressively has always been a sub context issue in our history, but is too frequently glossed over or ignored. The paradigm of early American society's allowance for slavery amply illustrates my point.

It would please me if more folks, black and white alike, became acquainted with commentary offered by various present activists appearing on Bill Moyers' and Tavis Smiley's television programs. They and their guests know there's a great need to challenge *dumbing down,* which otherwise allows dubious corporate interests to escape scrutiny needed to protect the public from their detrimental practices coming at high costs to the tax paying public. For sure Fox News, and other similar venues, won't readily present, honestly and spin free, what Bill Fletcher Jr, Chris Hedges, Michael Parenti, or Cornel West have to say anytime soon. It should be obvious all critics of the Corporatocracy are dutifully marginalized by the corporate controlled major media. Thank goodness for *Al Jazeera, Google,* and other independent news outlets.

Presently our society has overcome much endemic racism, now it's time to challenge endemic corporatism with its extensive influence and power to determine what policies the government puts in place. My vehicle bumper sticker says: "We don't have a democracy, we have an auction." Yes, at this time corporations are the highest bidders and that ensures they get what serves their interests. If things are going to improve for the other 99% of us, corporate domination of government will have to be severely curtailed. We can be sure corporate interests will resist any proposals for change appearing to constrict their bottom line profit potential.

It may take a while before the needs of the overwhelming majority become a national priority again, just as it took the abolitionists seven decades to finally nullify the power of the *slavocracy.* Hopefully the time is coming when the heavy hand of corporate power, based on almost incomprehensible wealth, won't determine governmental policies now ostensibly claiming to serve all Americans. A new economic paradigm addressing deprivation issues present day capitalism chooses to ignore will be required, especially if racism is to truly become a thing of the past.

In conclusion, as for attributing credibility to this reemerged popular notion of *American Exceptionalism,* a new definition is needed. It should acknowledge *all* Americans must have true equal opportunity to reach their full potential, but include an understanding some not measuring up to cultural notions of success are still deserving of dignity predicated upon having a decent place to live and not going to bed hungry at night. When that truly comes to pass then we may boast of *American Exceptionalism.*

Appendix

The sources from which I've occasionally utilized pertinent quotations are listed in the bibliography which follows this appendix. The indicated titles constitute a portion of those in my American history collection, many representing original research by various African-American and European-American scholars. Hopefully readers will go beyond this general narrative as I've only scratched the surface of the African-American dimension to America's history. I haven't implied or suggested this is a presentation of original research on my part. The intention of this work is to present what I, and others, would consider basic for an introductory course in African-American history - a subject I taught for over a quarter of a century.

No doubt criticism is likely to come my way because I've neglected certain historical figures whose stories are, I readily admit, as compelling as the ones I've presented. One can only do so much and, consequently, encourage others to address what they perceive as shortcomings in one's work. I ask critics to keep in mind the scope and substance of this undertaking was formatted, compressed to be sure, as a one semester course. I wish my academic superiors realized, as I had right at the outset, that to do justice to so much historical information a two semester format was actually needed.

In the mix of historical information are some personal experiences I shared with students. They are based upon growing up in an all white Philadelphia neighborhood in the 1940s and 1950s and when I served an enlistment in the United States Air Force from 1955 to 1959. Included also are some accounts of interactions I had with students in and out of class. Then too, I readily admit to presenting my opinions on certain issues, such as the socio-economic implications of the Military Industrial Complex. I always hoped philosophical considerations would surface for contemplation when I did that. My so doing will likely result in conservatives being critical of my overall orientation.

My hat is off to African-American scholars for their impressive research during the past half century. Their endeavors notably served to broaden the American historical narrative to include what had once been excluded. The American story, if it's to be authentic, must necessarily include contributions made by all of its people so an understanding of its uniqueness may be appreciated and esteemed. Indeed, we are now fortunate to have a more complete version of our history. However, early in my lifetime the American experience was narrowly defined by racism predicated upon unexamined and unchallenged racist beliefs. Hopefully the positive direction in which our country now seems to be moving, taking us away from racism, will continue and all Americans will come to realize we are a better nation because of that.

Selected General Sources

Appiah, Kwami A. & Gates, Henry L (editors)
Africana Arts and Letters, (2004)

Aptheker, Herbert (ed.)
The Correspondence of W.E.B. DuBois, (1973)

Badger, Reid
A Life in Ragtime: A Biography of James Reese Europe, (1995)

Blassingame, John W.
*The Slave Community: Plantation Life
in the Antebellum South*, (1979)

Davis, Daniel S.
Mr Black Labor: The Story of A. Philip Randolph... (1972)

Carson, Clayborne, editor
*The Autobiography of Martin Luther
King, Jr.* (1998)

Cashin, Sheryll
The Failure of Integration, (2004)

Cowan, Tom & Maguire, Jack
Timelines of African-American History
500 Years of Black Achievement (1994)

Cripps, Thomas
Slow Fade to Black: the Negro in
American Films, 1900-1942 (1977)

Cruse, Harold
The Crisis of the Negro Intellectual, (1969)

Cunliffe, Marcus
The American Heritage History of the Presidency, (1968)

Duberman, Martin B.
Paul Robeson: A Biography, (1989)

Dyson, Michael E.
Race Rules: Navigating The Color Line (1996)

Dyson, Michael E.
APRIL 4, 1968- Martin Luther King Jr.'s Death
And How It Changed America, (2008)

Foner, Philip S.
Frederick Douglass, (1964)

Franklin, John Hope & Moss, Alfred A. *Jr.*
From Slavery To Freedom: A History of
Negro Americans, (1974)

Genovese, Eugene D.
Roll Jordan Roll: The World the Slaves Made, (1974)

Gordon-Reed, Annette
The Hemingses of Monticello: An American Family, (2008)

Johnson, Haynes
The Best Of Times, (2002)

Lusane, Clarence
The Black History of the White House, (2011)

Marable, Manning
The Great Wells of Democracy, (2002)

McPherson, James M.
*Ordeal By Fire: The Civil War
and Reconstruction*, (1992)

Osofsky, Gilbert
Harlem: The Making of a Ghetto:
Negro New York 1890-1930, (1971)

Russell, Francis
*American Heritage History of the Making
of the Nation, 1783-1860*, (1969)

Shirer, William L.
The Nightmare Years (1984)

Smith, Jessie Carney
*Black firsts: 4,000 Ground Breaking and
Pioneering Historical Events*, (2003)

Thompson, Vincent Bakpetu
*The Making of the African Diaspora
in the Americas 1441 - 1900*, (1987)

Waller, Maurice & Calabrese, Anthony
Fats Waller, (1977)

Weigley, Russell F.
A Great Civil War, (2000)

West, Cornel
Democracy Matters: Winning the Fight Against Imperialism, (2004)

West, Cornel
Brother West: Living And Loving Out Loud, (2009)

White, Theodore H.
America In Search Of Itself: The Making Of The President 1956 - 1980 (1982)

Wilkerson, Isabel
The Warmth Of Other Suns, (2010)

Williams, Juan
Thurgood Marshall: American Revolutionary, (1998)

Zinn, Howard
A People's History of the United States, (2003)

Zinn, Howard
SNCC: The New Abolitionists (1964)

Acknowledgments

This work is dedicated to the memory of Erastus Carleton Anderson, my mother's maternal grandfather. He endured many hardships as a sixteen year old serving with Company K of Maine's 20th Infantry Regiment during the Civil War. I wouldn't likely be here had he decided to go back to Maine as a bachelor after his 1876 visit to Philadelphia for the Centennial celebration. Also, I'm grateful to my wife Ellen M. Bell for her assistance and understanding while I spent countless hours working on this undertaking. Ellen, your steadfast support was vital. Thank you!

About The Author

Philip (J.) Reiss taught history at Orange County Community College (S.U.N.Y. campus located in Middletown, NY) from 1967 to 1999. He has two degrees from Temple University. For 1975-1976, he was awarded a graduate Urban Studies Fellowship at the University of Miami. In 2001, he published an historical romance novel *Time Echo*. At present he lives in the Lehigh Valley region of Pennsylvania.